How to File FOR Divorce IN Maryland, Virginia and the District of Columbia

James J. Gross

Michael F. Callahan

Attorneys at Law

SPHINX® PUBLISHING
AN IMPRINT OF SOURCEBOOKS, INC.®
NAPERVILLE, ILLINOIS
www.SphinxLegal.com

First Edition, 2003

Published by: **Sphinx® Publishing, a division of Sourcebooks, Inc.®**

Naperville Office
P.O. Box 4410
Naperville, Illinois 60567-4410
630-961-3900
Fax: 630-961-2168
www.sourcebooks.com
www.SphinxLegal.com

This publication is designed to provide accurate and authoritative information in regard to the subject matter covered. It is sold with the understanding that the publisher is not engaged in rendering legal, accounting, or other professional service. If legal advice or other expert assistance is required, the services of a competent professional person should be sought.

From a Declaration of Principles Jointly Adopted by a Committee of the American Bar Association and a Committee of Publishers and Associations

This product is not a substitute for legal advice.

Disclaimer required by Texas statutes.

Library of Congress Cataloging-in-Publication Data
Gross, James J.
  How to file for divorce in Maryland, Virginia, and the District of Columbia by / James J. Gross and Michael F. Callahan.
    p. cm.
  ISBN 1-57248-240-0 (pbk.)
  1. Divorce suits--Maryland--Popular works. 2. Divorce suits--Virginia--Popular works. 3. Divorce suits--District of Columbia--Popular works. I. Callahan, Michael. II. Title.
KF505.5.Z95 G76 2003
346.75201'66--dc21
                          2002153840

Printed and bound in the United States of America.

VHG Paperback — 10 9 8 7 6 5 4 3 2 1

CONTENTS

DEDICATION

To our wives,
Holly Gross and Madelyn Callahan,
who make it easy to stay married.

Using Self-Help Law Books

Before using a self-help law book, you should realize the advantages and disadvantages of doing your own legal work and understand the challenges and diligence that this requires.

THE GROWING TREND

Rest assured that you won't be the first or only person handling your own legal matter. For example, in some states, more than seventy-five percent of divorces and other cases have at least one party representing him or herself. Because of the high cost of legal services, this is a major trend and many courts are struggling to make it easier for people to represent themselves. However, some courts are not happy with people who do not use attorneys and refuse to help them in any way. For some, the attitude is, "Go to the law library and figure it out for yourself."

We at Sphinx write and publish self-help law books to give people an alternative to the often complicated and confusing legal books found in most law libraries. We have made the explanations of the law as simple and easy to understand as possible. Of course, unlike an attorney advising an individual client, we cannot cover every conceivable possibility.

COST/VALUE ANALYSIS

Whenever you shop for a product or service, you are faced with various levels of quality and price. In deciding what product or service to buy, you make a cost/value analysis on the basis of your willingness to pay and the quality you desire.

When buying a car, you decide whether you want transportation, comfort, status, or sex appeal. Accordingly, you decide among such choices as a Neon, a Lincoln, a Rolls Royce, or a Porsche. Before making a decision, you usually weigh the merits of each option against the cost.

When you get a headache, you can take a pain reliever (such as aspirin) or visit a medical specialist for a neurological examination. Given this choice, most people, of course, take a pain reliever, since it costs only pennies; whereas a medical examination costs hundreds of dollars and takes a lot of time. This is usually a logical choice because it is rare to need anything more than a pain reliever for a headache. But in some cases, a headache may indicate a brain tumor and failing to see a specialist right away can result in complications. Should everyone with a headache go to a specialist? Of course not, but people treating their own illnesses must realize that they are betting on the basis of their cost/value analysis of the situation. They are taking the most logical option.

The same cost/value analysis must be made when deciding to do one's own legal work. Many legal situations are very straight forward, requiring a simple form and no complicated analysis. Anyone with a little intelligence and a book of instructions can handle the matter without outside help.

But there is always the chance that complications are involved that only an attorney would notice. To simplify the law into a book like this, several legal cases often must be condensed into a single sentence or paragraph. Otherwise, the book would be several hundred pages long and too complicated for most people. However, this simplification necessarily leaves out many details and nuances that would apply to special or unusual situations. Also, there are many ways to interpret most legal questions. Your case may come before a judge who disagrees with the analysis of our authors.

Therefore, in deciding to use a self-help law book and to do your own legal work, you must realize that you are making a cost/value analysis. You have decided that the money you will save in doing it yourself outweighs the chance that your case will not turn out to your satisfaction. Most people handling their own simple legal matters never have a problem, but occasionally people find that it ended up costing them more to have an attorney straighten out the situation than it would have if they had hired an attorney in the beginning. Keep this in mind if you decide to handle your own case, and be sure to consult an attorney if you feel you might need further guidance.

LOCAL RULES   The next thing to remember is that a book that covers the law for the entire nation, or even for an entire state, cannot possibly include every procedural difference of every county court. Whenever possible, we provide the exact form needed; however, in some areas, each county, or even each judge, may require unique forms and procedures. In our *state* books, our forms usually cover the majority of counties in the state, or provide examples of the type of form that will be required. In our *national* books, our forms are sometimes even more general in nature but are designed to give a good idea of the type of form that will be needed in most locations. Nonetheless, keep in mind that your *state*, county, or judge may have a requirement, or use a form, that is not included in this book.

You should not necessarily expect to be able to get all of the information and resources you need solely from within the pages of this book. This book will serve as your guide, giving you specific information whenever possible and helping you to find out what else you will need to know. This is just like if you decided to build your own backyard deck. You might purchase a book on how to build decks. However, such a book would not include the building codes and permit requirements of every city, town, county, and township in the nation; nor would it include the lumber, nails, saws, hammers, and other materials and tools you would need to actually build the deck. You would use the book as your guide, and then do some work and research involving such matters as whether you need a permit of some kind, what type and grade of wood are available in your area, whether to use hand tools or power tools, and how to use those tools.

Before using the forms in a book like this, you should check with your court clerk to see if there are any local rules of which you should be aware, or local forms you will need to use. Often, such forms will require the same information as the forms in the book but are merely laid out differently, use slightly different language, or use different color paper so the clerks can easily find them. They will sometimes require additional information.

CHANGES IN THE LAW   Besides being subject to state and local rules and practices, the law is subject to change at any time. The courts and the legislatures of all fifty states are constantly revising the laws. It is possible that while you are reading this book, some aspect of the law is being changed or a court is interpreting a law in a different way. You should always check the most recent statutes, rules and regulations to see what, if any changes have been made.

In most cases, the change will be of minimal significance. A form will be redesigned, additional information will be required, or a waiting period will be extended. As a result, you might need to revise a form, file an extra form, or wait out a longer time period; these types of changes will not usually affect the outcome of your case. On the other hand, sometimes a major part of the law is changed, the entire law in a particular area is rewritten, or a case that was the basis of a central legal point is overruled. In such instances, your entire ability to pursue your case may be impaired.

Again, you should weigh the value of your case against the cost of an attorney and make a decision as to what you believe is in your best interest.

INTRODUCTION

Divorce is a confusing and complicated business. Nothing about it is easy, whether you are the one that is leaving or the one that is being left. We wrote this book to make divorce less difficult.

This is not a legal treatise and it cannot substitute for three years of law school, the bar exam, and expertise that comes from years of trying cases. But we will explain the law and process of divorce in plain English in the jurisdictions where we currently practice law—Maryland, Virginia, and the District of Columbia.

New laws are being passed by the legislatures; new cases are being decided by the courts; and therefore the law is constantly changing. Also, every case is different. We do not know the specific facts of your particular case, so we cannot give you legal advice. We can only give you information about the law that will make you more knowledgeable as you go through the process.

We were inspired to talk and write about divorce, and what we do for a living, by Larry Rice, another divorce lawyer. We have adapted some of his ideas to Virginia, Maryland and D.C. from *About Divorce in Tennessee*. These ideas are reprinted with the permission of his copyright holder, the American Bar Association.

This book is set up in sections. The first section describes what you need to know and do before you start the process of divorce. The second section explains how to settle out of court. (You should know that most cases settle out of court.) The third, fourth, and fifth sections describe the litigation process for uncontested and contested divorces. The sixth and seventh sections discuss children and financial issues and procedures you will encounter after or while you are obtaining a divorce.

Each chapter in the book describes a different topic and they are more or less in the order that you might encounter these topics in your divorce. Several chapters contain general information that is common to all jurisdictions. There are significant differences in the laws of each jurisdiction. Therefore, in the chapters where there are differences, we give you the specific details for each jurisdiction. In Chapters 16 (Maryland), 17 (Virginia), and 18 (District of Columbia) covering Uncontested Divorces, the procedures are so different, that we devoted a whole chapter to each jurisdiction.

There is a separate section for each jurisdiction. Within each section, we provide separate appendices of forms, legal research, and legal resources.

You can use the forms in this book for your divorce, but we recommend you also make copies. A few of the forms you will have to get from the court because they are a certain color or tri-part, and those are indicated. Usually the court will require that you fill them out with a typewriter, but some just have boxes to check and you can do those by hand.

Each county will have different and unique forms, but they will be similar to the ones in this book. There will always be a particular clerk or judge who will not accept the forms in this book for one reason or another. Just be patient; do not get frustrated; and, ask the court clerk for current forms specific to your county.

We have summarized the most important laws that govern divorce in each jurisdiction in the appendixes.

Finally, If you want to do additional research on your own, or are in need of additional help, the appendixes also contain resources, including reading materials, websites, agency and courthouse information.

SECTION 1:
WHAT YOU NEED TO KNOW

MARRIAGE AND DIVORCE 1

We all get married till death do us part and for better or worse. We have hopes and dreams of a long future together. No one expects to get divorced when they get married. As it turns out, the odds of your getting divorced are about one in two. This chapter will introduce you to general legal concepts about marriage, separation, annulments, and divorce.

MARRIAGE—A STEALTH CONTRACT

Unless you had a *prenuptial agreement* when you got married, you entered into a *stealth contract* that you probably did not even know existed. The contract consists of hundreds of pages of law and cases for the jurisdiction where you live. It is a major undertaking involving children, support, and property. And you are presumed to know all of the terms of this contract, because you will be held to them.

The contract is not very intuitive. It is different from any other contract you may have signed. For example, your paycheck is no longer *your* paycheck, but becomes *marital property*, which is distributable by the court upon divorce. If you start a business during your marriage, and it becomes successful solely through your efforts, you will probably have to buy your spouse's marital interest upon divorce. If your spouse breaks the contract and wants a divorce, he or she may still get half, and you may have to pay your own attorney fees and your spouse's as well.

This "stealth contract" may never affect you, as long as you stay married. But it will govern if you ever get divorced.

COMMON LAW MARRIAGE

In Maryland and Virginia, you can get married in a religious or civil ceremony, but first you have to obtain a license from the government. The District of Columbia recognizes *common law marriages*, which are legal marriages without a ceremony or license.

The requirements for a common law marriage in D.C. are that both parties:

- must be free to marry;

- intended to be married;

- told other people they were married; and,

- had sexual relations and lived together in a state that recognizes common law marriages.

There is no time limit for a common law marriage in D.C.

MARRIAGE COUNSELING

Even though we are divorce lawyers, we are still in favor of marriage. When a client shows up at our offices seeking a divorce, we ask first if they have tried reconciliation. We encourage them to talk to their spouses, and confront the problems in their marriage head on. If that does not work, we refer them to marriage counselors. Marriage counselors are social workers, psychologists, psychiatrists, and other therapists who deal with relationship issues. You can find a good counselor by word of mouth, searching the Internet, or looking in the telephone directory.

LEGAL SEPARATION

There is also a procedure in each jurisdiction for obtaining support and other relief when you do not have grounds for a final divorce. This is called a *limited divorce* in Maryland, a *legal separation* in D.C., and a *divorce a mensa et thoro* (meaning divorce from bed and board or limited divorce) in Virginia. The grounds for a legal separation are easier to meet than those for a final divorce. For example, any separation, even for one day, qualifies as grounds for a limited divorce (or legal separation) in all three jurisdictions.

A limited divorce or legal separation permits you to establish custody, visitation and support until you qualify for a final or absolute divorce. If you do not need to establish those matters, then you may not need to incur the additional costs of this extra proceeding. You do not have to file for a limited divorce or legal separation first in order to get a final or absolute divorce.

ANNULMENTS

Annulments are granted by the court only in certain rare cases. The legal effect is to void a marriage from the very beginning—as if the parties had never married.

A divorce says this marriage is ended. An annulment says this marriage never existed. Annulments are rarely granted and usually there has to be some kind of serious fraud involved.

For example, grounds for annulment in the District of Columbia are:

- you marry someone who is already married;

- you marry someone who is insane, except you cannot obtain an annulment if you live together after you discover the insanity;

- the marriage was obtained by fraud or force;

- you marry someone under 16, or someone who is otherwise matrimonially incapacitated without your knowledge; or,

- the marriage of certain relatives.

Religious annulments are easier to obtain, and you may request one even after you have a legal divorce from the court. You may want to get your spouse's agreement to cooperate in a religious annulment or divorce, but it is possible to obtain one even over your spouse's objection.

PENDENT LITE RELIEF

The court can also award *pendente lite* support. *Pendente lite* is Latin for "pending the litigation," so it means temporary support until the divorce trial. There are things you may need for the court to do pending the final trial. The court, upon request, can set a hearing to determine the needs and the abilities of the parties and children, and the ability of a party to pay, and order support accordingly. This award is subject to rehearing at the final trial. The court can also order custody or specific visitation pending the final trial.

DIVORCE

Even if you are the best husband or wife in the world, you may still end up in a divorce. Although it takes two people to get married, it takes only one to get a divorce. It may take longer to get a divorce if only one person wants it, but it is inevitable.

Sometimes you just have no choice but to get a divorce. You may need to get out of your marriage to have a better life. You may have chosen the wrong person to marry—or your spouse may demand a divorce.

Divorce is a way of ending a marriage. You have to go to court to get a divorce. In Maryland and D.C. you can have an *absolute divorce*, which means a final and permanent divorce. In Virginia, you can have a *divorce a vinculo matrimonii*, which means a divorce from the bonds of matrimony or final divorce.

A final divorce allows you to get remarried again, resolves all issues of custody, support, and property, and may allow the court to award use and possession orders for family property. It also allows the court to enter an award to adjust equity, permits the sale or retitling of property (depending on the jurisdiction), and permits a wife to resume a former name. We will explain these issues in detail in later chapters.

THE EMOTIONAL DIVORCE

Divorce is like a train wreck. It is just as traumatic to the parties and the children involved. There are enormous currents of emotions at play during a divorce as well as major legal and financial issues.

We know what you are feeling right now, because we have had many clients who felt the same way. Those that followed our advice have found that they feel better today.

There is a difference between the legal divorce and the *emotional divorce*. The emotional divorce may not coincide in timing with the legal divorce. It may take years to get over your divorce and move on with your life. We recommend discussing your emotional divorce with a good therapist.

ANXIETY

Anxiety is a common human emotion. People will find something to worry about even when times are good. When going through a divorce, you will find many things to worry about, and you will have good reason to worry. Even if we tell you not to worry, you will worry. Instead of letting your mind be consumed with worrying about how bad the situation is, you should concern yourself with what you can do to solve the problems. Outline your problems in writing. It helps you to focus clearly. (Then destroy these notes.)

DEPRESSION

Depression is another fairly common experience in divorce. If you are going through a divorce and you feel uncertain, insecure, or depressed, then you have a normal problem. You may want to obtain some counseling.

SUPPORT

There are support groups for separated and divorcing parties. You can find support on the Internet where there are virtual communities of separated and divorced people. We have included a list of resources in Sections 8, 9, and 10 for Maryland, Virginia, and the District of Columbia, respectively.

The support of friends and family is invaluable during divorce, but we offer one word of caution. Your family and friends may offer you advice about your case. They will tell you about someone who got life-time alimony or someone who did not have to pay any alimony. The facts and circumstances of your marriage, divorce, children, and property are unique and are different from any other case. Often such advice is not correct, and you need to take it with a grain of salt. This is not your neighbor's divorce or your Aunt May's divorce. It is *your* divorce and it is different from anyone else's.

We tell our clients that during a divorce:

- your ears do not work;

- your eyes do not work;

- your mouth does not work; and,

- your head does not work.

By this we mean you may not hear or understand everything we say; you do not always say what you mean; you may not perceive things correctly; and, you may exercise poor judgment.

Your spouse will probably say things that will upset you. Keep in mind that it is only what the judge says that counts, not what your spouse says. So when your spouse is upsetting you, we recommend using the "Old McDonald" method. No matter what your spouse is saying, all you hear is

"EEE III EEE III OOO."

If you are feeling depressed right now, or anxious, or crazy, you are not alone. In fact, you may be joining the majority. And while this is not a particularly pleasant life lesson, you will survive it, and become much stronger and wiser in the process.

LAWYERS 2

If you are reading this book because you want a divorce, your spouse wants a divorce, or you are thinking about getting a divorce, then you may be asking whether you can do it yourself. This chapter will help you decide whether it is in your best interest to obtain a lawyer.

PRO SE (DOING IT YOURSELF)

A number of divorce cases are granted by the courts each year with no lawyers involved. If you have an uncontested divorce, with a little patience and persistence, you should be able to complete your own divorce by following the forms and instructions in this book. If you represent yourself, you will be a *pro se* litigant. *Pro se* is Latin meaning by yourself or on your own behalf.

The chief advantage to representing yourself is that you save the expense of a lawyer. The main disadvantage is that you do not know the law. A judge may be sympathetic to a *pro se litigant*. On the other hand, you will be held to the same rules and procedures that a lawyer would have to follow, and it is easy to make a serious mistake.

NEEDING A LAWYER

You have no automatic right to a lawyer in divorce cases, and there is no law that requires you to hire a lawyer. Divorce, however, is a complicated business and most people want a lawyer. You should at least think about getting a lawyer when the case is *contested* and the stakes (such as custody, support or property) are high. You have a contested case when you and your spouse disagree about any issue regarding your divorce.

You should also hire a lawyer if your spouse has a lawyer. That lawyer can only represent your spouse and is required to do it in a manner that is in your spouse's favor and not necessarily fair to you. And you should hire a lawyer if you do not have the time, interest, or tolerance for the frustration sometimes encountered in the legal system.

A good lawyer will guide you through the process, help you avoid mistakes, save you time, and protect your interests. If you have a lot at stake, like alimony, children, or property, then you will probably want to hire an attorney. It is customary for divorce lawyers to have an initial conference with a client to discuss the facts of your case and fees.

There are benefits and costs to hiring a lawyer, and you will have to weigh those, and make a decision.

BENEFITS   If you have a lawyer, you can let the lawyer do all the worrying about your case. You can sleep at night. Lawyers have the training, skills, and experience for this job. Lawyers are used to dealing with the courts and know the rules, the laws, and the cases where the courts have interpreted the laws. When you represent yourself, the judge will not give you much leeway. You are expected to know the rules, the laws, and the cases.

Two good lawyers can efficiently and effectively negotiate and draft a *Separation Agreement* and guide you through the divorce process. Lawyers and judges share a common language that contains lots of terms that are shortcuts for a body of law they understand.

The judge and your spouse's attorney may give more consideration to you if you have an attorney. Your spouse's attorney is not permitted to give you advice or help you.

Lawyers know what to do when there are complications in your case like not being able to serve your spouse, or difficult issues like pension plans, alimony, custody and so forth.

COSTS   The main downside to a lawyer is expense. Do not be penny-wise and pound-foolish though. If a lawyer costs $5,000 and you and your spouse are arguing over $100,000, it makes sense to hire a lawyer. However, some people argue over $5,000 and the lawyer costs them $10,000.

There are different types of costs in divorce cases. The largest cost is usually attorney's fees, which is what is charged for the work lawyers do on your case. Court costs are the fees that are charged by the court for the filing of the divorce papers and various other papers.

In contested cases, attorneys fees and court costs are higher and there may be other costs for things such as depositions, private investigators, photographs, psychological evaluations, and tax consultants. You must pay these costs, as lawyers are ethically prohibited from lending clients money.

Any discussion about what the costs or attorneys fees will be is the roughest of estimates. There are many variables in any divorce case, including some over which your lawyer has no control. Who your spouse will hire as an attorney, how complex the financial records are, or what mood the judge is in on the day of trial will affect how your case is handled and, therefore, what it will cost you.

The emotional cost of a divorce can be greater than the dollar cost. The damage of having a broken marriage examined in court is something only those who have lived through it can understand.

Sometimes one party ends up paying not only their own legal fees but also some portion of the other party's. If there is a trial, the economically dominant party can be ordered to pay some of the economically dependent party's attorney's fees. The order will rarely pay the full amount. For example, if you are the wife, you are responsible for paying the agreed fee to your lawyer who will give you credit for any payments made by your husband.

Divorce lawyers require a *retainer* to accept your case and to begin drawing up the necessary papers. A retainer is a set amount of money that is placed in the lawyer's trust account. The lawyer draws against it at his or her hourly rate as the work is completed. If you decide not to retain them, you may be charged for the initial office conference. If you retain them, you will sign a contract setting out the terms of representation in writing. The retainer is refundable to the extent not used. If the hourly fees earned exceed the retainer, the lawyer will probably ask you for more money.

FINDING A LAWYER

Same as everything else, there are good lawyers and bad lawyers. There are lawyers who care and lawyers who are burned out. There are new lawyers and experienced lawyers.

If you decide to hire a lawyer, try to find an experienced family lawyer who will settle or try your case in a professional manner, with a minimum of histrionics and hostility. We believe a constructive approach toward your spouse, opposing counsel, and the court is the best way to navigate the divorce process. That way you can end your marriage without destroying the relationships you have built with children, other family members, and friends.

Some lawyers are not good at returning telephone calls. This is important to you in the middle of a divorce. Ask about this in your initial interview. If your lawyer does not return your calls, get another lawyer.

You will save yourself a lot of frustration if you know that real time is not the same as lawyer time. Lawyers are used to the hurry up and wait scheduling of the court's crowded docket, and so a three or four month wait to get before a judge is fast for a lawyer.

If you decide to hire a lawyer, do your research. Here are a few ways to find a lawyer:

- check the Internet (see the appendices at the end of this book for specific recommendations);

- ask your friends who have been divorced about their experience with their lawyer;

- get recommendations from the county bar association or the chair of the family law section of the county, state, or American bar associations;

- go to seminars on divorce; or,

- ask your therapist.

We think you ought to find a lawyer with some passion for divorce law. You can find this out by looking at their credentials. For example, lawyers who publish books or articles, or teach other lawyers, would seem to have a passion for their work. Martindale-Hubbel maintains a website that has ratings of lawyers by their peers. An "a-v" rating is the highest rating.

You and your spouse cannot be represented by the same lawyer. It is against the law in Maryland, Virginia, and D.C. If there ever was a conflict of interest, it has to be two people getting a divorce. It is not legal for an attorney to represent both parties in a divorce. If you and your spouse have agreed on everything, it may be possible for one lawyer to do all the legal work, but he or she can represent only one of you. Your spouse should see a separate lawyer for advice. If you and your spouse disagree later, each lawyer can still only represent the person with whom they started.

Red Flags 3

At our first conference, we advise our clients to put "red flags" next to the following items on their list of action items. These are the first things you should think about at the beginning of your divorce.

Bank Account

At the bank you may want to divide joint accounts or put them in your name. This sometimes will make the judge angry with you, but it is often easier to give money back than to get it back. If you are the breadwinner, do not put your dependent spouse out in the cold without some money to get by on. This will aggravate the judge who will make you pay anyway. Let your spouse know as soon as possible, but not before you do it or you may wake up and find nothing in the accounts. It has happened to our clients.

Credit

Close all joint accounts and notify the banks, charge cards, and others by a certified, return receipt letter that you are no longer responsible for your spouse's expenses. You may want the company to reopen an account in your own name. This is a good time to request it. Let your spouse know so he or she is not caught by surprise at the gas pump when the credit card does not work.

INSURANCE

If you cover your spouse or children on your insurance, do not drop them from the policy at least until the divorce is final. You are probably responsible for their medical bills until then anyway. Even after the divorce, the employed spouse may want to keep the spouse and children covered.

If you are paying child support, a large unexpected medical expense for the child could be assessed against the noncustodial parent as additional child support. The same could happen with alimony and an ex-spouse. Federal law allows most employees to cover their spouses for up to thirty-six months for a small additional premium. However, the employer must be notified prior to the FINAL DECREE.

UTILITIES

Do not cut off the utilities on your spouse or your spouse and children without giving them plenty of notice. Make sure you can prove this notice to the court because leaving your spouse and children home without heat or light in December seldom sits well with the judge.

DATING

Do not date until you have a *Separation Agreement* or a divorce. You are married. Your spouse can use it against you. If you are divorced, moving in with your lover could cause problems with custody, visitation, or alimony. If you do date, be prepared to face the problems that may arise.

WILLS

You probably need a new will now. Even though you are separated, if you were to die, your spouse would still inherit unless you have executed a new will providing otherwise. If you have given your spouse a power of attorney, cancel it as soon as possible. Until you do, your spouse has control over your property and can sell it or give it away.

DOMESTIC VIOLENCE

If you must leave your home because of domestic violence and have no place to stay, we have listed some places in the appendices that will provide you with shelter and assistance. If you are afraid that your spouse will physically harm you, take your money out of the bank, or run off with your children, then the court can enjoin or prohibit these things by issuing an injunction. *Injunctions*, or protective orders, are orders of the court that are issued to prevent harm pending further hearings.

In some cases the court will issue an injunction when the case is filed; in other cases, the court may require a hearing before deciding on issuing the injunction. If you disobey an injunction, the court can put you in jail. Even if the judge does not put you in jail, you can be fined and the judge will have a hard time trusting you later when you testify. Also, the court can refuse to hear anything you have to say if you are in contempt. The police will normally not get involved in problems between spouses, but if you show them an injunction, they will often remove the other party, and they have to act if you have a protective order.

In addition to filing criminal charges for abuse, you can petition the court for a civil protective order if you are harmed or threatened by an abusive spouse. File as soon as possible after the abuse occurs. The clerk's office will have the forms for you to fill out. Then you will speak with a judge and tell him or her what happened.

The judge can grant an *Ex Parte* Order (meaning the judge has only heard one side so far), which the sheriff will serve on your spouse. The abuser will have to leave the home temporarily. The order can also prevent your spouse from contacting you at home or work, give you temporary custody of the children, and set a hearing date when you, your spouse, and witnesses can be present.

At the hearing, the judge will listen to both sides, and either continue the protective order, or dismiss your petition. The judge can give you all of the above relief and, in addition, order temporary support from your spouse.

SOCIAL SECURITY

You need to be aware of the "ten year rule" for retirement, survivor, and disability benefits under Social Security. A marriage of at least ten years before your ex-spouse's retirement, disability, or death may entitle you to benefits based on your ex-spouse's Social Security account. Benefits are only payable to you if the benefits based on your own work record are less. There is also a family benefit cap.

RETIREMENT OR
DISABILITY

When your ex-spouse retires (or reaches age 62, whichever is first) or becomes disabled, in order to receive benefits as a divorced spouse you must:

- have been married at least ten years;

- be unmarried (if you remarried, you will still be eligible if the new marriage ended in death, divorce, or annulment before you apply for benefits);

- be age 62 or older; and,

- have been divorced at least two years ago.

DEATH

If your ex-spouse dies, in order to receive benefits as the surviving divorced spouse, you must:

- have been married at least ten years;

- be at least age 60 (or age 50 and disabled) at the date of death; and,

- be unmarried (or remarried under certain conditions).

So, if your marriage has lasted almost ten years, you may want to file your COMPLAINT FOR DIVORCE, discussed in Chapter 10, after your tenth anniversary.

GET THE FACTS 4

We have a saying in our law firm, "Get the facts first," meaning we cannot interpret or apply the law until we have the facts. If you have not done so already, start looking for evidence. Check desk drawers, safety-deposit boxes, bank boxes, or other places where documents might be hidden. It is a good time to visit with your family banker, stockbroker, or accountant to discuss the family financial situation, although you may not want to tell them about the divorce. First we will describe the documents you will want to gather for your divorce in any of the three jurisdictions. You will use these to complete FINANCIAL STATEMENTS for each jurisdiction, discussed in Chapter 26. We also have a cautionary word about snooping.

SNOOPING

The *Omnibus Crime Control and Safe Street Act of 1968* makes it a federal crime and a civil tort for anyone to listen in on a telephone conversation or to record any conversation if they are not a party to that conversation or do not have permission from someone who is a party.

Such recordings are not admissible as evidence. If you record your spouse's conversation with his or her "lover," you cannot use that tape in court and you could end up in a federal prison.

It is lawful for a person to record a telephone conversation or other conversation when both of the parties to the communication have given prior consent to record it. Maryland requires the consent of both parties. Virginia and the District of Columbia are "one party consent" jurisdictions—but do not risk it.

You can still be sued by your spouse for invasion of privacy. That is why an answering machine is a good idea—the caller knows they are being taped and, by speaking, gives permission.

You can use the information on a family computer as evidence in a divorce trial. The courts will usually permit you to discover electronic information such as email or other files retrieved from computers.

DOCUMENTS

You will want copies of the following documents:

- *Income tax returns.*

- *Financial statements.* These are most often filed when borrowing money and are very important.

- *Employment contracts.* Any explanations of benefits from you or your spouse's work.

- *Canceled checks and charge records.*

- *Retirement plans.* Include IRAs, 401(k), etc.

- *Deeds and other settlement papers.*

- *Real estate tax bills or appraisals.*

- *Insurance policies.* Include life insurance, medical insurance, health insurance, and homeowners' insurance.

- *Bank accounts and bank statements.*

- *Safety-deposit boxes.* You will want the bank to verify an inventory if possible.

- *Securities.*

- *Partnership agreements and/or corporate records.* Documents showing any business interests.

- *Any inheritance or trust interests.*

- *Wills by you or your spouse.*

- *Any written agreements or notes between you and your spouse.*

- *Any other evidence you have such as photographs, letters and emails.*

A good way to organize the financial facts of a case is to have our clients complete a financial statement, listing assets and liabilities, income, and expenses.. The courts have forms for this, which we reproduced in the appendices, and we will explain how to fill these out in detail in Chapter 26. Besides organizing your case, the court financial statements may be required when you file your divorce and should be helpful in negotiating a settlement.

SECTION 2:

SETTLEMENT OUT OF COURT

ALTERNATIVES TO TRIAL 5

You do not want to have a contested divorce trial if you can help it. Trials involve enormous expense, time, and uncertainty. If you do not have an attorney, you have to take time off from work and expert witnesses (for example, a therapist to testify about custody, an appraser to value real estate or a business, or a vocational rehabilitation expert to help establish alimony needs) may cost thousands of dollars.

Judges are strangers to your life and marriage and they are called upon to make a decision after hearing only a few hours or a few days of testimony about a marriage that may have lasted for years. Judges have no "truth detector" or "justice detector" at the bench and they may not always decide the right way. They are also limited by the legislature in how they must rule.

In every trial, there is a winner and a loser. And even if you win, you may lose, because attorney fees, witness fees, trustee fees, and division of income and property across two families will cost more than one family. However, there are several alternatives to litigating your case.

Only about 3% of divorces actually go to trial. But the lawyers have to spend 90% of their time preparing for trial. It makes more sense for all parties involved to work together in reaching a settlement. Here are some ways to settle your case out of court that are common to all three jurisdictions.

TALKING WITH YOUR SPOUSE

You and your spouse can try to work out an agreement. If you try to work something out with your spouse yourself, here are some useful tips.

Meet on neutral ground. Do not meet at her office or at his mother's home, but some place where both parties will feel comfortable.

Set aside time. A reasonable amount of time should be set aside to deal with the issues. If you leave to answer a telephone call just as you almost have things worked out, you may find that things have fallen apart when you get back. On the other hand, do not leave the meeting time open-ended. A meeting without a deadline will drag on and issues will not get resolved.

Set an agenda. Decide what will be dealt with at the meeting. "This week we will decide on custody and child support, next week we will decide on the house."

Do not "bog down." Try to talk about what you agree on. No matter how bad it is, there are some things you agree on ("the marriage stinks," or "the kid is cute"). If you hit a point that gives you trouble, move on to something else and come back to the problem after you have resolved some other issues.

Reschedule as needed. If things start to turn nasty, if someone gets angry, or if you are losing everything, re-schedule the meeting for another time. It is important that both of you feel that the agreement is a good thing.

Keep the kids out of it. Your children do not need to be involved in this. Do not have them around. They will interrupt you, and it will upset them. Do not discuss or complain about the divorce to the children. Reassure them that they will be provided for—even if you are worried about it.

Start talking early. Divorces usually settle early on when both parties feel guilty and are not locked into a position, or divorces settle after much litigation when the parties are too exhausted to fight anymore. Sometimes you can get more by talking than you can get at a trial.

Objectives. It is good to know what you want. We recommend writing down your objectives before you start negotiating.

Priorities. Assign priorities to your objectives, such as "strong interest, medium interest, weak interest." You also need to ask questions and learn what your spouse wants and what his or her priorities are.

Flexibility. Sometimes you have to be flexible, especially on items that are a strong priority for your spouse and a weak priority for you. We like to say "A good settlement is where each side gives up 60%."

This is the least expensive way to settle your case. But it is also difficult. (After all, if you could work things out with your spouse, you probably would not be getting a divorce.)

If you and your spouse work out something and you create and sign notes, this could be considered to be an agreement. If it is not correct legal language, you may be bound by something other than what you thought you agreed to, so you may want to have a lawyer review it at this point.

NEGOTIATION

You can hire attorneys to try to work out an agreement. The classic negotiation style is one party makes a proposal in writing (the *offer*) covering all issues of the marriage and divorce. The other party then responds in writing to the offer with their proposal (*counter-offer*) or with their specific objections to specific provisions of your proposal (*objections*).

These writings go back and forth, with compromises on the part of each until agreement is reached (or not, as the case may be.) Telephone calls and face to face meetings help answer questions or break an impasse during these negotiations.

It costs money every time you talk to your attorney and every time he or she writes a letter. It can easily cost several thousand dollars. However, if your spouse will not talk to you, this may be your only option.

MEDIATION

In mediation, a trained, neutral third party attempts to help the parties resolve their disputes through special techniques. The mediator does not represent either party, but guides the discussions, explores and offers options, explains the law, and facilitates an agreement. Mediators can be lawyers, psychologists, accountants, ministers or anyone else with proper training.

Mediators charge in a range from $50 to $200 an hour, but the fee is normally shared by both parties. You will go to the mediator's office for two or three hour "sessions" with your spouse. You will exchange financial information, and with the mediator's help, try to reach an agreement.

The agreement is not final or binding until it is put in writing and signed by both parties. You do not have to sign the agreement if you do not like it. You are encouraged to hire a lawyer to review the agreement before you sign. Once you do sign, the agreement will be binding and enforced by the court.

The advantage to mediation is usually lower cost and control over the outcome. But you cannot do mediation unless your spouse is willing. Also, the court requires litigating parties to go to mediation. Court-appointed mediators (sometimes called *facilitators*) can recommend solutions and do a little more "arm-twisting" than their private counterparts.

COLLABORATION

In *collaborative family law*, each party hires a lawyer trained in collaborative law to be their advocate. There are no neutral parties as in mediation. The lawyers and parties sign an agreement stating that both lawyers must withdraw if the case does not settle and goes to litigation. Everyone is committed from the beginning to settle the case and not litigate it, so the focus is on the settlement and not the trial.

Collaborative family law works through a series of four-way meetings with you, your spouse and the two lawyers. You are a full participant in the settlement process. You can speak face-to-face with everyone involved instead of having to communicate with your spouse through your lawyer who speaks to your spouse's lawyer, and vice versa.

The lawyers and parties also agree to provide full and early disclosure of all issues such as income and assets. The parties may agree to hire one or more experts for both (instead of the litigation model where each party hires competing experts). For example, the parties would hire one appraiser to value the house or one expert to value the business, or one therapist to design a parenting plan.

Collaborative lawyers can and do place value on long-term relationship issues that may be overlooked in the litigated divorce, where only financial and legal issues are considered. Collaborative law works well when you both want to settle and want to control the outcome of your divorce yourselves. You each have to pay your own lawyer, although fees may be reimbursed as a result of the final agreement. Regardless, you will save money as compared to litigation. But, if one of you wants to litigate, then both lawyers have to withdraw.

ARBITRATION

The parties can agree to submit their dispute to a third party for a binding or non-binding decision. The third party can be their mediator, a lawyer, a retired judge, or any other party. You can find an arbitrator through your attorney or the bar association for your city or county.

Usually, each party presents their case to the *arbitrator*, either in person, in writing, or both. Then, the arbitrator makes a decision. *Arbitration* works well if you need a quick decision and you are willing to take your chances with an arbitrator who is not the judge of your case. Arbitration has the advantage of speed and expense over a trial. It can also be used to decide limited issues when negotiation, mediation, or collaborative law reaches an impasse.

CHILDREN

The court will be the final decision maker on child custody, visitation, and child support. It cannot delegate this authority to the parties or a third party mediator or arbitrator. The court can consider the opinion of the parties and third parties, and often follows these recommendations. However, the court must make its own decision based on the best interest of the child. See Chapters 23, 24, and 25 for more information on child custody, visitation, and support.

DIFFERENT TYPES OF DIVORCE 6

There are two types of divorces in Maryland, Virginia, and the District of Columbia. In all three jurisdictions, you can either have a *contested* divorce or an *uncontested* divorce. The following descriptions apply to all three jurisdictions.

CONTESTED DIVORCE

Contested divorces are where the parties cannot resolve one or more of their disputes, such as custody, visitation, alimony, or property division. Each side is entitled to examine witnesses and present evidence. The parties then ask the judge to decide. Although judges are usually experienced and wise, they are only human. They do not have truth detectors in court. A marriage of some years is compressed to a few days and the judge makes a decision in a few minutes affecting the rest of your life. These trials take a lot more time, days or weeks, and cost a lot more money.

UNCONTESTED DIVORCE

Where the parties have reached an agreement on all issues, including custody and finances, they are entitled to uncontested divorce. This is a short hearing before the court that takes about ten minutes. The parties testify about the grounds for divorce and ask the court to approve their agreement and grant their divorce.

LENGTH OF TIME

In our experience, uncontested divorces usually take two to three months, after filing. If you need a faster divorce, say to get remarried, then you can shorten the time it takes if your spouse cooperates. You can file your papers together at the courthouse, explain to the clerk your circumstances, and see if you can get an early hearing. Judges normally like to accommodate settled cases because there are more case than there are judges, and settlement means one more case they can move off their desk.

Contested divorces can take up to two years or even longer in some cases. There is no right to a speedy trial in divorce cases like there is in criminal cases. The wheels of justice move slowly and even lawyers are frustrated sometimes by the time it takes to be heard by a judge.

COST

If you hire a lawyer, you can expect to pay between $2,000 and $5,000 for an uncontested case, depending on whether there are children, support, and property issues. The average contested case costs about $20,000, but could be much more, depending upon the issues, your spouse, and your spouse's lawyer.

SEPARATION AGREEMENTS

More divorce cases are filed each year than there are judges to try them. But ninety percent of the cases settle. Most contested divorce cases that are filed are settled before trial with an agreement. These agreements are called by various names such as *Voluntary Separation* and *Custody, Support and Property Settlement Agreement*. In this book, we will usually refer to them as *Separation Agreements* (although you do not necessarily have to be separated to have one).

The court encourages agreements and provides for ways to help you and your spouse settle during the litigation. You can propose or sign a *Separation Agreement* before you file for divorce. Or you can file for divorce first, and negotiations on the *Separation Agreement* can proceed on a parallel track with the divorce litigation. So it often happens, that a case filed as a contested divorce is amended to an uncontested divorce once a *Separation Agreement* is signed.

If you have a choice, you want an uncontested divorce. Therefore, you need a *Separation Agreement*, which is the covered in Chapter 7.

SEPARATION AGREEMENTS 7

Although not required by law, we always recommend a written *Separation Agreement*, even when there are little or no assets. In Virginia, *Separation Agreements* must be in writing to be enforceable by the court. This is not required, but it is desired, in D.C. and Maryland as well, because the parties usually never agree on what a verbal agreement says. The following describes *Separation Agreements* in general, and is applicable to all three jurisdictions.

THE ESSENCE OF DIVORCE

Because a *Separation Agreement* resolves all issues that otherwise would be resolved by the judge in a contested divorce, we sometimes say that reaching a *Separation Agreement* is the essence of your divorce. You do not have to be separated and you do not have to have grounds for divorce to have a *Separation Agreement*. There is no waiting period. You can sign one now.

Separation Agreements usually provide that the parties may live separate and apart as though unmarried. Therefore, issues such as adultery will no longer have any effect at the divorce trial because property division and alimony have already been decided. Once you both sign a *Separation Agreement*, you can date, contribute to your pension and savings, and buy property, all without worry that these things may impact your future divorce.

The *Separation Agreement* will be attached to your COMPLAINT FOR DIVORCE and you will ask the court to incorporate it into your Decree of Divorce. Essentially, it will substitute for the judge's findings after a long trial. You will be able to tell the court, we do not need a divorce trial because we have already resolved everything in a *Separation Agreement*.

In fact, once you have a *Separation Agreement*, you have almost everything that a divorce will give you, so you no longer even need a divorce. The only reason that you may want a divorce is to get remarried or for tax filing status.

A *Separation Agreement* has other advantages, in that it allows the parties to decide their future rather than the judge, who is a stranger to their lives and marriage. It can be a lot more detailed than a court order. And it can provide for things that a judge is limited by law from ordering.

WHAT TO INCLUDE

You will want to include many things in your *Separation Agreement*, because it will cover all of the issues of your divorce. Here is a checklist of items for you to cover:

❏ The Marital Residence and Other Real Property

- Who is leaving?
- Who will live where?
- How will the mortgage and other expenses be paid?
- Will the house be sold?
- How will the equity be divided?
- How will other real estate be divided?

❏ Bank Accounts and Stocks

- Who gets what?

❏ Personal Property

- Who gets which car, what appliances, and what happens to the sofa in the den?
- Who gets Rover? (You would be surprised how many people fight over the pets.)

❏ Retirement

- What happens to any retirement benefits that have accrued?

❏ Debts

- Who pays what?
- Should the debts be paid off by refinancing?

❐ Court Costs and Attorney's Fees

  • Who pays?

❐ Alimony

  • How much?

  • How long?

  • When and how is it paid?

  • When does it start?

  • How will it be modified?

❐ Custody

  • Should the children be split up between the parents?

  • Should any aspects of custody be shared?

  • Will joint custody work?

  • How will decisions be made about doctors, schools, discipline, religious upbringing, and who will have the final say?

  • How will day-to-day decisions be made?

  • Where will the children live?

  • What will be the schedule for seeing the other parent?

❐ Child Support

  • How much?

  • How long?

  • When does it start?

  • When is it due?

  • How will payment be made?

  • Is there a cost of living adjustment?

  • Who carries health or life insurance on children?

  • Who gets to claim the children as income tax deductions?

  • Private school or public school?

  • College tuition and costs?

  • Who pays for uncovered medical expenses?

  • Who pays for day care expenses, summer camp, extra-curricular activities, and baby sitters?

❐ Visitation

- Do you want a specific schedule or can you and your spouse be flexible and work together on it, especially as the children grow up and change?

- What will be the schedule for visitation?

- Daily and weekly?

- Holidays?

- Birthdays?

- School vacations?

- Summer vacations?

- When can a parent take a child out of the state?

- Out of the country?

- What notice need be given for a change in plans?

- How will visitation be changed if one parent moves?

❐ Life Insurance

- Who is insured?

- Who is the beneficiary?

- Term or cash value?

- How much?

❐ Health Insurance

- Who is covered?

    NOTE: *In many cases, an employee's spouse can be covered up to thirty-six months after the divorce by the employed spouse's insurance for an additional premium. Sometimes one parent's health coverage is cheaper than the other's and the cost differential can be reimbursed in other ways.*

❐ Other Provisions

- Security for obligations in the agreement, for wills, for death, and for taxes.

SAMPLE SEPARATION AGREEMENT

On the following seven pages is a sample *Separation Agreement*. Because every agreement is different, this agreement is not set up as a blank court form, but only as an "indication" of what one may *look* like.

$$\boxed{\text{SAMPLE}}$$

VOLUNTARY SEPARATION, SUPPORT AND
PROPERTY SETTLEMENT AGREEMENT

THIS AGREEMENT, the original of which being executed in quadruplicate, is made this 17th day of January, 2003, by and between Teddie Bear, whose Social Security Number is 123-45-6789, hereinafter referred to as "Wife" and Theodore Bear, whose Social Security Number is 987-65-4321, hereinafter referred to as "Husband."

WITNESSETH :

WHEREAS, the parties hereto were married on the 5th of March, 1993, in Your Town, Your State; and

WHEREAS, 2 children were born to the parties as a result of said marriage; namely Roberta, born April 4, 1996; and Roland, born June 26, 1999; and

WHEREAS, relations between the parties have been such that they have separated as of the 1st day of November, 2002; and they have mutually and voluntarily determined to live separate and apart and have mutually concluded that it is in the best interest of all concerned to live separate and apart for the rest of their lives; and

WHEREAS, in view of the foregoing, the parties desire to settle and determine their obligations to each other and to their children, including all of their property rights, the maintenance, and support of the parties and their children, and all rights, claims, relationships or obligations between them arising out of their marriage or otherwise; and

WHEREAS, each party hereto declares that he or she has had independent legal advice by counsel of his or her own selection or has been advised to obtain legal counsel; that each has made a full disclosure to the other of his or her financial assets and liabilities; that each fully understands the facts and all of his or her legal rights and obligations; and that after such advice, disclosure and knowledge, each believes this Agreement to be fair, just and reasonable and that each enters into same freely and voluntarily;

NOW, THEREFORE, in consideration of the premises, and the mutual covenants and agreements hereinafter contained, and in further consideration of the sum of ONE DOLLAR ($1.00), to each of the parties in hand paid by the other, the receipt whereof is hereby acknowledged, the parties hereto covenant and agree as follows:

SEPARATION

1. The parties mutually and voluntarily separated on <u>November 1</u>, <u>2002</u>, with the intention of ending their marriage. It shall be lawful for each party at all times thereafter to live separate and apart from the other party at such place or places as he or she may from time to time choose or deem fit.

2. Each party shall be free from interference, authority and control, direct or indirect, by the other, as fully as if he or she were single and unmarried. Neither party shall endeavor to compel the other to cohabit or dwell with him or her, nor in any manner or form whatsoever molest or trouble the other party.

3. Nothing herein contained shall be construed to bar or prevent either party from suing for divorce in any competent jurisdiction because of any past or future fault on the other party's part.

4. Henceforth, each of the parties shall own, have and enjoy, independent of any claim or right of the other party all items of property of every kind, nature and description, wheresoever situated, which are now owned or held by him or her with full power to him or her to dispose of the same as fully, effectively and effectually in all respects and for all purposes as if he or she were unmarried. Both parties agree to execute all necessary documents to carry out the terms of this Agreement.

CUSTODY AND VISITATION

5. The parties agree that it is in the best interest of the children for the Wife to have sole legal and physical custody.

6. The parties agree that it is in the best interest of the children for the Husband to have reasonable visitation, the exact dates and times to be agreed upon by the parties.

7. The parties agree to abide by the Any County Guidelines for Effective Parenting.

CHILD SUPPORT

8. Commencing and accounting from <u>February 1, 2003</u>, the Husband shall pay to the Wife for the support and maintenance of the parties' children, the sum of <u>one thousand</u> DOLLARS ($<u>1000.00</u>) per month, by mail, directly to the Wife in accord with the attached Child Support Guidelines Worksheet. Said child support payments shall continue on the first day of each month thereafter until the first to occur of the following: the death of a child, the death of the Husband, a child's marriage, when a child enters the armed forces, when a child no longer has her principal residence with the Wife; when a child obtains full-time employment (other than employment during school recesses); or when a child attains the age of eighteen (18); provided however, if a child has not graduated high school by his or her 18th birthday, child support shall continue until graduation or the 19th birthday of that child, whichever first occurs.

WAIVER OF ALIMONY

9. In consideration of the mutual agreement of the parties to voluntarily to live separate and apart and the provisions contained herein for the respective benefit of the parties, each party releases

and waives to the other any claim or right to temporary or permanent alimony, support or maintenance, whether past, present or future.

HEALTH INSURANCE LIFE INSURANCE

10. The Husband agrees to provide medical insurance coverage for the Wife until the date of divorce and the parties' children until age 23.

LIFE INSURANCE

11. To secure the payment of child support, the Husband agrees to acquire life insurance in the face amount of at least <u>two hundred thousand</u> Dollars ($<u>200,000.00</u>) with the Wife as beneficiary. The Husband will provide the Wife with evidence of such coverage on January 1 of each year. If such life insurance is not in effect and the Husband dies, then the Wife will have a claim against the Husband's estate for the face amount of the life insurance that should have been in effect.

REAL PROPERTY

12. The parties own no real estate.

MISCELLANEOUS PERSONAL PROPERTY

13. Furnishings and Miscellaneous Items. It is agreed that the parties have separated all their household furnishings, clothing, jewelry and similar items of tangible personal property to their mutual satisfaction, and all such property shall be and become the sole and separate property of the individual who has possession and control thereof.

14. Automobiles. The Wife will keep the <u>Chevy Sedan</u> and shall assume all financial responsibility for this vehicle. The Husband will keep the <u>Jeep</u> and shall assume all financial responsibility for this vehicle.

15. Bank Accounts. The parties have no joint bank accounts. Each party will keep the individual bank accounts that are in his or her own name.

16. Retirement Accounts. The parties have no retirement accounts, pension plans, profit sharing plans, Individual Retirement Accounts, 401(k) plans or similar retirement funds.

OUTSTANDING DEBTS

17. The parties have no joint credit card debt. Except as otherwise provided herein above, neither party has incurred any debts or obligations heretofore for which the other may be held liable. The parties agree that neither will incur hereafter any liability or obligation whatsoever upon the credit of the other, or for which the other might be held liable. Each party agrees to indemnify and hold harmless the other from any obligation, liability or expense incurred by the other by virtue of any breach of this paragraph, including attorney's fees he or she may necessarily incur in connection therewith.

TAXES

18. Each party may have certain tax liabilities resulting from separate returns filed by each of them. Each party agrees to be responsible for their own tax liabilities and indemnify and hold harmless the other from such liabilities.

19. The Wife shall take the son as an exemption each year and the Husband will take the daughter as an exemption each year.

LEGAL FEES

20. Each party agrees to be responsible for their own legal fees in connection with the negotiation of this Agreement and any action that either of the parties may undertake for either a limited or absolute divorce in whichever jurisdiction said action is ultimately filed. The parties also agree to divide the court costs and Master's fees equally between them in connection with any subsequent suit for divorce.

21. The reasonable cost of any legal services required in the Court enforcement of this Agreement will become the obligation of the person whose breach required the enforcement of the Agreement, provided the movant prevails and provided that the Court feels a legal fee should be awarded.

MUTUAL RELEASES

Except as otherwise provided in this Agreement:

22. Each party shall be fully released by the other from any obligation for alimony, support and maintenance, except as hereinabove set forth, each accepts the provisions hereof in full satisfaction of all obligations for support, or otherwise arising out of the marital relation of the parties, and relinquishes any right or claim to the earnings, accumulation, money or property of the other.

23. All property and money received and retained by the parties pursuant hereto shall be the separate property of the respective parties, free and clear of any right, interest or claim of the other party, and each party shall have the right to deal with and dispose of his or her separate property, both real and personal, as fully and as effectively as if the parties had never been married.

24. Provided all obligations hereunder have been performed, each party hereby releases and forever discharges the other, his or her heirs, executors, administrators, assigns, property and estate from any and all rights, claims, demands or obligations arising out of or by virtue of the marital relation of the parties, including loss of consortium, dower rights, curtesy, homestead rights, right of election regarding the estate of the other, or to take against the Will of the other, right of inheritance or distribution in the event of intestacy, right to act as administrator of the estate of the other, similar or related rights under the laws of any state or territory of the United States or of any foreign country, as such laws exist or may hereafter be enacted or amended. Nothing herein, however, shall constitute a waiver of either party to take a voluntary bequest or bequests under the Will of the other.

25. Except for any cause of action for divorce which either party may have or claim to have, and except for the enforcement of the provisions of this Agreement, each party does hereby release and forever discharge the other of and for all causes of action, claims, rights or demand whatsoever, in law or in equity, which either of the parties ever had or now has against the other.

INCORPORATION IN ANY DECREE OF DIVORCE

26. The parties hereto agree that any action for Divorce between them shall be subject to and governed by the terms of this Agreement, and that this Agreement shall be presented to the appropriate court for affirmation, ratification, and incorporation in any Decree of Divorce, Limited or Final, which may be entered in any action between the parties, but this Agreement shall be independent of and shall not depend for its effectiveness upon such affirmation, ratification and incorporation, shall not merge in the Decree, and shall survive execution of the Decree.

FULL DISCLOSURE

27. The parties warrant that they have fully disclosed their respective assets and liabilities to the other, and that the parties have no other assets and liabilities other than what they have disclosed. They have relied on the information obtained during marriage in valuing assets and not on the representations of counsel or any other person. They have been advised by counsel of their rights to obtain discovery and to have the assets valued by expert appraisers, and they have knowingly and voluntarily waived these rights. If assets of either party are discovered after the signing of this agreement, such asset(s) shall be divided between the parties in the following manner: forty percent (40%) of the value of each previously undisclosed asset shall be the property of the of the party failing to disclose the asset, and sixty percent (60%) of the value of each previously undisclosed asset shall become the property of the party to whom disclosure was not made. If liabilities of either party are discovered after the signing of this agreement, such liability(ies) shall become the sole responsibility of the party failing to disclose the liability(ies). The parties shall do any and all acts necessary to assign their interests and financial responsibilities in said asset(s) and/or liability(ies) accordingly.

GENERAL PROVISIONS

28. The parties agree that no provision of this Agreement, except as otherwise set forth herein, shall be modifiable by any court except by agreement of the parties. Any modification or waiver of any of the provisions of this Agreement shall be effective only if made in writing and executed with the same formality as this Agreement. The failure of either party to insist upon strict performance of any of the provisions of this Agreement shall not be construed as a waiver of any subsequent default of this same or different nature.

29. Each of the parties hereto shall, from time to time, at the request of the other, execute, acknowledge and deliver to the other party, any and all further instruments that may be reasonably required to give full force and effect to the provisions of this Agreement.

30. If any provision of this Agreement is held to be invalid or unenforceable, all of the other provisions shall, nevertheless, continue in full force and effect.

31. Failure to perform any of the obligations contained herein shall create a lien on the estate of the obligor.

32. This Agreement contains the entire understanding of the parties, and there are no representations, warranties, covenants, or undertakings of, by or between the parties other than those expressly set forth herein.

33. This Agreement shall be construed in accordance with the laws of the State of __Your State__ .

IN WITNESS WHEREOF, the parties being fully advised as to the matters herein set forth, have set their hands and affixed their seals on the date set forth below.

WITNESSES:

_John Jones_____   _____(SEAL)

_Bill Smith_____   _____(SEAL)

STATE OF <u>YOUR STATE</u>   )

COUNTY OF <u>YOUR COUNTY</u>   ) to wit:

     I HEREBY CERTIFY that before me the undersigned Notary Public, personally appeared <u>Teddie Bear</u>, known to me to be the person whose name is subscribed to the within instrument, who, after being sworn, made oath in due form of law under the penalties of perjury that the matters and facts set forth in the foregoing Agreement with respect to the voluntary separation of the parties are true and correct as therein stated and acknowledged said Agreement to be her act.

WITNESS my hand and official seal this <u>17th</u> day of <u>January</u>, 2003.

A. Fine Notary

Notary Public

My commission expires: <u>12/31/2005</u>

STATE OF <u>YOUR STATE</u>   )

COUNTY OF <u>YOUR COUNTY</u>   ) to wit:

     I HEREBY CERTIFY that before me the undersigned Notary Public, personally appeared <u>Theodore Bear</u>, known to me to be the person whose name is subscribed to the within instrument, who, after being sworn, made oath in due form of law under the penalties of perjury that the matters and facts set forth in the foregoing Agreement with respect to the voluntary separation of the parties are true and correct as therein stated and acknowledged said Agreement to be his act.

WITNESS my hand and official seal this <u>17th</u> day of <u>January</u>, 2003.

A. Fine Notary

Notary Public

My commission expires: <u>12/31/2005</u>

SECTION 3:
COURT PROCEDURES

THE LAW   8

You will find that most of the law, as it pertains directly to divorce, is written in four places: the Constitution, the Code, court cases, and in the various local rules.

CONSTITUTION

The United States and each state has a written Constitution that sets forth essential rights of the people. For example you have the right to due process of law and the right to pursue happiness. You can find these constitutions at the library or on the Internet. Lists of the Internet sites for each state are located in the appendices.

CODE

The legislature, elected by and representing the people, passes laws, also called *statutes*, each year. These are published in volumes called the *Maryland Code*, *Virginia Code*, and the *Code of District of Columbia*.

They are called *codes* because laws are meant to codify human behavior and reflect the will of the majority in our society. They are intended to be logical and practical, but you may not always find them to be so. Laws are supposed to be consistent with the Constitution of the individual state and the United States. You can find the code for each state at the law libraries or Internet sites we have listed in the appendices. We have also provided in the appendices a summary of divorce laws for each jurisdiction with code citations for your reference.

CASES

The appellate courts for each jurisdiction review the record of trial courts on a case-by-case basis when appeals are brought by the parties. The appellate court either affirms, vacates, modifies, or reverses the trial court. It usually explains its decision in writing and many decisions are published in books called *reporters*. These cases form a precedent for later trials and appeals. The court can interpret or even invalidate laws if they are unconstitutional. While the legislature reflects the will of the majority in writing general laws, the court can look at the facts of individual cases and make exceptions for the minority when the law would work an unjust result.

RULES

There is a *rules committee* in each jurisdiction that passes rules for the court that the parties and their lawyers must follow. The rules are published as: *Maryland Rules, Virginia Rules, and District of Columbia Rules.* These are very detailed and cover how pleadings must be presented and signed, time deadlines, how evidence is to be presented at trial, and many other subjects. In addition, some courts and some judges publish what are called *local rules*, which may be available only in a memorandum from the clerk or order from the judge. Finally, there are what lawyers refer to as *unpublished rules*, which are the customs and practices of various courts and judges, that you only know from experience.

WHERE TO FIND THE LAW

We have provided summaries of divorce laws with citations to the Codes of Maryland, Virginia, and the District of Columbia that will be helpful to you in your divorce. These summaries will point you in the right direction for research if you want to know more. Usually there is a law library at the courthouse available to the public. Also, many laws and cases are available for free on the Internet.

LEGAL REQUIREMENTS FOR DIVORCE 9

In this chapter, we discuss some of the preliminary legal requirements you must meet before going to court. These requirements are common to all three jurisdictions, but the details are different. We discuss the differences below and set forth the specific grounds for divorce (both final and limited or for a legal separation).

JURISDICTION

When a court has *jurisdiction*, it has the power to hear and decide a matter and bind the parties to its decision. If the court lacks jurisdiction, any order it enters in your divorce case is void and of no effect.

SUBJECT MATTER JURISDICTION
The Maryland, Virginia, and D.C. courts have *jurisdiction* over your marriage as long as one of the parties meets the residency requirements set forth in the law. In Maryland, the courts can also obtain jurisdiction if the grounds for divorce arose within the state. The power and authority to decide matters concerning your marriage and divorce is called *subject matter jurisdiction*.

PERSONAL JURISDICTION
The courts must also have the power to bind the parties to its decisions. This is called *personal jurisdiction*. The courts have jurisdiction over any person living in the state or served with process in the state. The court can also obtain personal jurisdiction over a non-resident by serving process outside the state in certain circumstances (known as *long-arm jurisdiction*). A person may submit to jurisdiction of the court by appearing in court or filing a pleading in the case.

VENUE

You may file a divorce in the county where you live or where your spouse lives or works. This is called *venue* (the place where you may properly bring a lawsuit). The parties may consent to a different venue. In Maryland or Virginia, if you file in the wrong county and your spouse objects on the basis of venue, you may simply ask the court to transfer venue to the right county. In D.C. there is only one court.

RESIDENCY   You or your spouse have to live in the jurisdiction (state) for a certain period of time before you can use the courts of that jurisdiction for a divorce. You can file for emergency relief, such as custody or support, before the residency period has run in all three jurisdictions.

In Maryland, the residency requirement is twelve months unless the grounds for divorce occurred in Maryland. (Maryland Code, Family Law Article, Sec. 7-101(a).)

In Virginia it is six months. (Virginia Code, Sec. 20-97.)

In the District of Columbia it is six months. (D.C. Code, Sec. 16-902.)

If your spouse contests your residency, you can prove it with items like a lease, utility bills, driver's license, or voter registration card. Once you establish your home in a jurisdiction, it stays there, even if you temporarily move elsewhere, as long as you have the intent to remain a permanent resident.

It is only necessary that you meet the residency requirements at the time of filing for divorce. Neither party has to be a resident at the time of the divorce.

You or your spouse may be able to file a complaint in more than one jurisdiction. Or you may be able to get a divorce faster by moving across the state line. So it is important to know the differences in the laws of each jurisdiction that we discuss in this book.

MOVING   Do different residency requirements and different grounds in the three jurisdictions mean that you can move to a different jurisdiction to get divorced faster? You bet! But you also have to consider the other differences in the divorce laws among the three jurisdictions in making the decision to move.

GROUNDS FOR DIVORCE

In order to file for a divorce, you must have good reasons for wanting a divorce, which are called *grounds*, and you have to prove these grounds to the court at your divorce trial. You must plead and prove your grounds even if your divorce is uncontested. It used to be that the only grounds for divorce were fault grounds, like adultery or cruelty. Now Maryland and Virginia accept *no-fault grounds*, such as separation for a certain period of time, in addition to fault grounds. D.C. has abolished fault grounds altogether and only has no-fault grounds.

DEFENSES TO GROUNDS

There are certain defenses to the various grounds for divorce that may be raised by your spouse in any of the three jurisdictions. For example, renewing physical relations starts the separation period over again. Another example is *condonation* as a defense to the claim of adultery (in Maryland and Virginia where adultery is grounds for divorce). Condonation means forgiveness, and is usually shown by sexual relations between spouses after the adultery is disclosed. The following are grounds for divorce and legal separation in each jurisdiction.

MARYLAND GROUNDS

ABSOLUTE DIVORCE

In Maryland, the grounds for an *absolute divorce* are:

- *A one year voluntary and mutual separation.* The parties must live under separate roofs for twelve consecutive months, without cohabitation or sexual relations. The time starts over if you have sexual relations, live together, or even spend one night under the same roof. The separation must be mutual and voluntary with the intention of ending the marriage, and there can be no reasonable expectation of reconciliation. A separation that begins as involuntary on the part of one spouse can become voluntary at a later date. A *Separation Agreement* can corroborate voluntariness if signed before a COMPLAINT FOR ABSOLUTE DIVORCE is filed.

- *A two year involuntary separation.* The parties must live under separate roofs for twenty-four consecutive months, without cohabitation or sexual relations.

- *Adultery.* Adultery means sexual intercourse with a person other than your spouse. Adultery is grounds for an immediate divorce and no sep-

51

aration is required. You can prove adultery by direct evidence, such as the admission of your spouse and the deposition or affidavit of the paramour. You can also prove adultery by circumstantial evidence indicating opportunity and predisposition. *Predisposition* means your spouse and another person act romantically. *Opportunity* means a specific chance to have sex with that person. So circumstantial evidence could be the testimony of a private detective that he saw your spouse holding hands with another person and watched them enter a hotel for a period of time.

- *Desertion for a year.* Desertion can be either *actual* or *constructive*.

  Actual desertion is when your spouse leaves the marital home without legal justification and ends cohabitation or sexual relations. The desertion must be for at least twelve months, be the deliberate and final act of the deserting party, and there must be no reasonable expectation of a reconciliation.

  Constructive desertion means that the behavior of your spouse is so harmful to your physical or mental well-being, that you are forced to leave. Again, the constructive separation must be for twelve months, without cohabitation or sexual relations, and no reasonable expectation of a reconciliation. This is harder to prove because the judge always wants to know why you did not leave sooner. In other words, what happened on the day you left that made you leave at that particular time?

- *Insanity.* This requires that your spouse be confined in a mental institution for at least three years, and the testimony of two psychiatrists that the insanity is incurable and there is no hope for recovery.

- *Imprisonment.* This requires that your spouse be in jail for one year under a sentence of three or more years.

- *Cruelty or excessively vicious conduct.* There is no waiting period for this ground. There must be no reasonable expectation of reconciliation. This ground requires a pattern of conduct and one incident is usually not enough, unless it was especially violent and your spouse intended to harm you. It is also hard to corroborate because often there are no witnesses besides the parties to domestic violence. Be sure you have your corroborating evidence. You do not want to get all the way through your trial and have the judge tell you that you have not made your case. It happens. (Maryland Code, Family Law Article, Sec. 7-103.)

LIMITED DIVORCE   A form of legal separation in Maryland is called a *limited divorce*. It also requires that you have grounds. The grounds for a limited divorce are different from the grounds required for an *absolute divorce*, and they are as follows:

- *Voluntary Separation.* Without reasonable expectation of reconciliation. (no minimum duration)

- *Desertion.* (no minimum duration)

- *Cruelty.*

- *Excessively Vicious Conduct.* (Maryland Code, Family Law Article, Sec. 7-102.)

VIRGINIA GROUNDS

FINAL DIVORCE   In Virginia, the grounds for a *final divorce* are:

- a six-month separation with a written *Separation Agreement* and no children;

- a one year separation;

- adultery;

- conviction of a felony and imprisonment for one year;

- cruelty continuing for one year; or,

- desertion or abandonment continuing for one year. (Virginia Code, Sec. 20-91.)

LIMITED DIVORCE   In Virginia, you may obtain a *limited divorce*, also called a *divorce a mensa et thoro* (from bed and board). A limited divorce also requires that you have grounds. The grounds for a limited divorce are different from the grounds required for a final divorce, and they are as follows:

- reasonable fear of bodily harm;

- desertion or abandonment (no minimum duration); and,

- cruelty. (Virginia Code, Sec. 20-95.)

DISTRICT OF COLUMBIA GROUNDS

ABSOLUTE
DIVORCE

In D.C., the grounds for an *absolute divorce* are:

- a six-month voluntary separation or,

- a twelve-month involuntary separation. (D.C. Code, Sec. 16-904(a).)

In D.C., you can be separated and still live together, meaning at least separate sleeping arrangements and a lack of physical relations; however, that makes it harder to prove in court. This is different from Maryland and Virginia, which define separation as living in separate places.

LEGAL
SEPARATION

A *legal separation* in the District of Columbia also requires that you have grounds. The grounds for a legal separation are different from the grounds required for an absolute divorce, and they are as follows:

- mutual and voluntary separation (no minimum duration);

- separation for one year;

- adultery; or,

- cruelty. (D.C. Code, Sec. 16-904(b).)

STARTING THE DIVORCE 10

A divorce action is started by filing a COMPLAINT FOR ABSOLUTE DIVORCE in Maryland, a BILL OF COMPLAINT FOR DIVORCE in Virginia or a COMPLAINT FOR ABSOLUTE DIVORCE in the District of Columbia. You file it with the court clerk at the courthouse in the county or city where you live or where your spouse lives. You do not have to file in the place where you were married.

THE COMPLAINT

In all three jurisdictions, your complaint is essentially a letter to the judge. The complaint starts with the caption that states the court and the names and addresses of the parties. There is a blank space for the court clerk to assign a case number. The party that files the complaint is called the *plaintiff* (or sometimes the *complainant* in Virginia) and the other party is the *defendant*.

No matter which jurisdiction, your complaint will contain certain statements, called *allegations*. First you state the jurisdiction of the court, and then facts about the parties, the marriage, the children, and grounds for divorce, as follows:

- where you and your spouse live;

- the date, city, and state of your marriage;

- names and birthdates of any children born or adopted as a result of the marriage;

- who the children are living with now;

- that it is in the best interest of the children that they live with you or that custody be shared;

- grounds for divorce; if separation, for example, date of separation; that it was mutual and voluntary or involuntary, and there is no hope or expectation of a reconciliation. You may have more than one ground for divorce;

- your income and your spouse's income if you are seeking support;

- property was acquired during the marriage and needs to be determined, valued, and distributed by the court;

- the house, furniture, and automobile may be family use property and you want use and possession of them;

- child support, including guidelines showing the needs of the children and your spouse's ability to pay;

- if there is an agreement, identify it by date, and attach a copy to the COMPLAINT as an exhibit;

- ask the court to incorporate, but not merge, your agreement in the final Decree of Divorce;

- you can ask the court to change your name back to your birth given name; and,

- if there is no *Separation Agreement*, you must ask the court to decide what you and your spouse cannot agree upon. If you do not include something in your prayer for relief, you may not get it. So be sure to ask for everything you want. The list may seem long to you, and the wording may seem strange, but it is a formal legal document and much of the language is required by law. If you are asking the court for spousal support or child support, you will have to attach a financial statement on the court's form, listing assets and liabilities, and income and expenses for you and your children.

The COMPLAINT is accompanied with an information form for the clerk. There is a filing fee and *master's fee* that ranges from $66 in Virginia to $95 in D.C. and $90 in some counties in Maryland. The clerk will start a court file and put the COMPLAINT in it. The outside cover of the court file will have an index of pleadings and dates.

The clerk will give you a copy of the COMPLAINT with related attachments, such as a *Summons*. These will be served on your spouse to give him or her notice of the divorce and a chance to respond. Besides the original COMPLAINT for the court file, and the copy to serve on your spouse, have an extra copy for your file. The clerk will stamp it with the filing date and write the case number on it. The following sections will describe how to complete the COMPLAINT for each jurisdiction.

MARYLAND COMPLAINT FOR ABSOLUTE DIVORCE (MARYLAND FORM 4)

To complete the COMPLAINT FOR ABSOLUTE DIVORCE, on page 234, complete the *case caption* by filling in the city or county of the court, then both your name, as plaintiff, and your spouse's name, as defendant. Provide current addresses and telephone numbers for both. The court clerk will fill in the case number when you file the COMPLAINT. Then complete the rest of the form as follows:

- ☛ *Line 1.* After printing your name in the space provided, fill in the month, day, and year of your marriage. In the second blank, fill in the city or county and the state where you were married. Circle whether you were married in a religious or a civil ceremony.

- ☛ *Line 2.* Check off all statements that apply in your case and fill in the blanks.

- ☛ *Line 3.* If you check off, "We have no children...," remember to skip lines 5 and 6. If you check off, "My spouse and I are the parents...," write in the full names of all the children you and your spouse had together and their dates of birth.

- ☛ *Line 4.* Fill in information about any court cases that have involved either yourself, the opposing party, or one of the children involved in this case. Provide information on cases that may have been handled by this court, or any other court, both in Maryland and outside the state.

- ☛ *Line 5.* Fill in the name of the person the children listed above live with now.

- ☛ *Line 6.* Check the box for the type of custody or visitation you have agreed upon and fill in the names of the children involved. For a contested case, you will mark the type of custody you want.

☛ *Line 7.* Circle whether or not you are seeking alimony. If you are seeking alimony, state "by agreement" or for a contested case state why you are seeking alimony.

☛ *Line 8.* Skip this if you have a *Separation Agreement* and an uncontested case. For a contested case, if you are asking the court to make a decision about your property, check off the kinds of property you and your spouse have. If you or your spouse have debts, you may check the box marked "Debts" and attach a list of the debts to this form.

NOTE: *Normally the court cannot order one party to pay the debts of another. However, the court may need to know what debts you have in order to determine the value of any marital property.*

☛ *Line 9.* Check each ground for divorce that applies and fill in the blanks. You may have more than one ground. Choosing a certain ground or grounds will not necessarily result in a divorce being granted because you must still prove and corroborate at least one ground at trial. For an explanation of each of the grounds for divorce in Maryland, see Chapter 10.

☛ On the third page of the form, in the blank space at the top, insert, "The parties have signed a Separation Agreement, dated (insert the date), resolving all issues between them."

☛ In the section that begins "FOR THESE REASONS. . .," insert your name change if you want it, then add after the last box, "The Separation Agreement be incorporated in, but not merged with, the Decree of Divorce." For a contested case, you will check off everything you want. If you fail to ask for alimony and/or property before the divorce, you will never be able to get it. However, the court will not necessarily give you what you asked for. You still have to prove your case and convince the Master or judge.

☛ Date and sign the COMPLAINT.

VIRGINIA BILL OF COMPLAINT FOR DIVORCE (VIRGINIA FORM 5)

Start your divorce by filing a BILL OF COMPLAINT in the circuit court for your city or county. The BILL OF COMPLAINT tells the court and the defendant what it is that the complainant (the person filing for divorce) wants and why the complainant is entitled to it. An example of a BILL OF COMPLAINT is in Appendix L. (see form 5, p.288.)

To complete your BILL OF COMPLAINT for divorce, you will make all of the following statements:

- ☞ a caption identifying the court followed by the names and addresses of the complainant and the defendant;

- ☞ a statement that the court has jurisdiction and the facts that give it jurisdiction. For example, the defendant is an actual and bona fide resident and domiciliary of this county and state and has been so continuously for the immediately preceding six months;

- ☞ a statement that both parties are over the age of eighteen and a statement of each party's military or non-military status;

- ☞ the date and place that the parties were married;

- ☞ the parties' children's names and dates of birth or a statement that no children were born to or adopted by the parties;

- ☞ a statement regarding who has custody and that that person is a fit and proper person to have custody;

- ☞ a statement of the facts constituting the grounds for divorce, generally either:

    a) the parties have lived separate and apart without cohabitation (without any sexual relations and without spending a night under the same roof) and without interruption for the twelve months immediately preceding the filing of the COMPLAINT with the intent to end the marriage on the part of at least one party, or

    b) the parties have lived separate and apart without cohabitation and without interruption for the six months immediately preceding the filing of the COMPLAINT with the intent to end the marriage the part of at least one party, no children were born to or adopted by the parties, and the parties have entered into a written agreement resolving all issues arising out of the marriage;

☞ that reconciliation of the parties is not probable;

☞ a statement that the parties have settled all matters arising out of the marriage and have put their agreement in writing and signed it, (or if the case is not settled, allegations regarding marital property, the parties' income and the need for and ability to pay support); and,

☞ a request stating what the complainant is asking the court to do. In an uncontested case, you ask the court to grant a divorce pursuant to Virginia Code, Section 20-91.9; ratify, approve, and incorporate but not merge the parties' agreement into the court's decree; and grant the complainant any other appropriate relief.

District of Columbia Complaint for Absolute Divorce (D.C. form 3)

The clerk of the Family Law Division at Superior court has divorce forms and instructions, called "Packets A through G," and will give you the correct one for your particular circumstance.

We will explain how to complete the forms in Packet D—Uncontested Divorce (Based on Six Months Mutual and Voluntary Separation with Children). We are modifying the court's form to include a *Separation Agreement*. This will give you enough information to complete any of the forms in whichever package applies to your situation. All forms must be typewritten. To prepare this COMPLAINT FOR ABSOLUTE DIVORCE (see form 3, p.339):

☞ At the top, fill in your name and address as the plaintiff and your spouse's name and address as the defendant. If you wish to keep your address secret because you believe that you will be harmed or harassed by your spouse or you spouse's family, you may provide an "in care of" name and address for someone to receive court papers for you. Mark it "SUBSTITUTE ADDRESS."

☞ The clerk will assign the case number when you file the COMPLAINT and pay the filing fee. Underneath the case number, write the numbers of any related cases, such as child support or domestic violence cases.

☞ Write your name in the first paragraph.

☞ Paragraph 1 recites the law that gives the court power to decide your case. This is *subject matter jurisdiction* explained in Chapter 9.

☞ To meet the residency requirement, either you or your spouse must be a resident of D.C. and lived there continuously for six months before filing the COMPLAINT. If you or both of you meet this requirement, write "Plaintiff" in paragraph 2. If only your spouse meets the requirement, write "Defendant" in paragraph 2.

☞ At paragraph 3, fill in your spouse's name and the date and place of your marriage. Check your marriage certificate to make sure it is the same.

☞ At paragraph 4, state the date you and your spouse stopped living together and were no longer having sexual relations.

☞ At paragraph 5, list each address where you lived after your separation, or if you did not move, give your current address. If you fear harm or harassment, you can explain here why you are using a substitute address in the COMPLAINT.

☞ At paragraph 6, insert the number and list the children who were born or adopted to you and your spouse together, either before or during the marriage. Give their birthdates and social security numbers. Do not list children from another relationship.

☞ At paragraph 7a, if the children live with you, put "Plaintiff" in the first blank. List the persons the children lived with and addresses for the last five years.

☞ At paragraph 7b, list any other cases involving the custody of your children. Give the type of case, case number, what type of order issued, date of the order, and what the order said. If there are no other cases, type "none."

☞ At paragraph 8a, circle whether there is a court order for child support and whether you receive public assistance. If there is a court order, list the case number, the city and state of the court that issued the order, and the amount of child support ordered to be paid by the plaintiff or defendant.

☞ Paragraph 8b states the terms of any agreement you have reached with your spouse about child support. Fill in who pays whom, for example, the defendant pays the plaintiff. Then put the amount and how often it will be paid. If there is a written *Separation Agreement*, insert at the end of the first sentence "pursuant to the Agreement of the parties dated [insert date]." The court will want to know that the child support is in accordance with the *Child Support Guidelines* so we usually attach the guidelines to the agreement. If the agreed upon child support is different from the guidelines, you will have to explain why the court should approve a deviation.

☞ Circle "IS" in paragraph 9 if you want child support.

☞ Paragraph 10 is a statement that your spouse can afford to pay child support.

☞ Paragraph 11 states that you have no property or debts for the court to divide. If you have a written agreement, then add "because the parties have entered into a written agreement dated [insert date] settling all issues between them." If you do have property or debts you want the court to divide, you must use a different packet.

☞ Paragraph 12 is a statement that you do not expect to get back together with your spouse.

☞ At paragraph 13, circle whether you want a former name restored and fill in the former name. You may use your birth given name or any name you have used in the past, but not a new name. You will need evidence of your use of a former name at trial.

☞ At paragraph 14, check the first box if there are no other cases involving the same issues as this case. If there are, check the second box and give the case numbers and a summary of the other cases.

☞ The WHEREFORE provision is your prayer for relief. This is where you tell the commissioner what you want the court to do.

☞ Section 1 asks for the divorce.

☞ In Section 2, write who gets custody of the children (plaintiff or defendant), and insert the names of the children.

☞ In Section 3, write who pays child support.

☞ If you have a *Separation Agreement*, strike through Section 4 and insert instead "The court incoporate and merge the parties' Separation Agreement dated [insert date]."

☞ In Section 5, write whether you want to restore a former name, and if so, write the name.

☞ Section 6 is a catchall provision that permits the court to do anything else it deems "just and proper."

☞ Sign and write your name, address, telephone, and fax number. You may use the substitute address if you do not feel safe providing yours. Print your name in the oath and sign below the oath. The oath swears that you are making true statements in your COMPLAINT under the penalties of making a false statement.

INFORMATION REPORTS 11

The clerk in each jurisdiction will require some form of an information report as a cover sheet to accompany your COMPLAINT FOR DIVORCE. This chapter explains how to fill them out.

MARYLAND CIVIL—DOMESTIC CASE INFORMATION REPORT (MARYLAND FORM 5)

- ☞ Fill in the city or county where the court is located at the top of the first page.

- ☞ In the first section, mark that the plaintiff is filing the COMPLAINT.

- ☞ The clerk will insert the *case number*.

- ☞ For *case name*, print your name as plaintiff and your spouse's name as defendant.

- ☞ Provide your name again as party, your address and telephone number. This is called the *case caption*.

- ☞ Mark the box that you are not represented by an attorney and supply the requested information for any related cases.

- ☞ Indicate whether you need an interpreter or other accommodation.

- ☞ Indicate whether alternative dispute resolution has been tried or requested and if so, provide details.

☛ Mark the box showing the case is uncontested (or indicate what issues are disputed if you have a contested case).

☛ Mark the box requesting an absolute divorce.

☛ You will leave the next three sections blank for uncontested divorces (and mark the appropriate issues in dispute for contested cases).

☛ On the second page (or reverse), repeat the case name, and put ten minutes in "time estimated for a merits hearing."

☛ Print your name and address.

☛ Sign and date the report.

VIRGINIA DIVORCE CASE COVER SHEET (VIRGINIA FORM 6)

Several counties require you to file a COVER SHEET with the BILL OF COMPLAINT to give the court a summary of information about your case in a convenient format. The court clerk will tell you whether a cover sheet is required.

To complete the COVER SHEET (form 6 in Appendix L), follow these instructions:

☛ Enter the date of filing where indicated.

☛ Leave the *case number* blank, the court clerk will enter it.

☛ Enter your full name and the defendant's full name where indicated.

NOTE: *Names on the cover sheet must agree with the names on the BILL OF COMPLAINT.*

☛ Check the block to indicate that the case is totally uncontested or, if not, check to appropriate contested blocks.

☛ Check the *Ore Tenus* block if you want to have your divorce hearing before a judge instead of a Commissioner.

District of Columbia Vital Statistics (D.C. form 4)

This **DC Vital Statistics** form is filed *with* the **Complaint for Absolute Divorce**. Although we have produced a copy of the form in this book, you will need to obtain the original, three part, tri-colored form from the clerk. Type the following information to complete the form:

☞ At the top left after "D" fill in the case number the clerk gives you for your **Complaint**.

☞ In the first section, for lines 1 through 4, provide the name, address, and date of birth for the husband.

☞ In the second section, provide the same information for the wife in lines 5a through 8.

☞ At line 9, fill in the date of the marriage.

☞ At line 10, list the names of the minor children of this marriage.

☞ For line 11, check whether the husband or the wife is the Plaintiff.

☞ At lines 12 and 13, give the name and address of the plaintiff's attorney if applicable.

☞ Skip the section entitled "Decree," lines 14 through 18, which will be completed by the clerk.

☞ At lines 19 through 22, provide statistical information on race and number of marriages for the husband and wife.

SERVICE OF PROCESS 12

SERVICE OF PROCESS IN GENERAL

Your spouse must have notice of your COMPLAINT. This gives your spouse an opportunity to defend and also satisfies the requirement of due process of law. It also gives the court personal jurisdiction over your spouse. This is accomplished by service of process, which means serving him or her with a copy of the COMPLAINT and *Summons*.

Service of process can be by certified mail or by personally handing a copy of the COMPLAINT and *Summons* to your spouse. But you cannot personally serve your spouse. You have to have a friend or a professional process server do it. The average cost of a process server is about $35. Once the complaint is served, the process server sends you an AFFIDAVIT OF SERVICE to file with the court.

If your spouse avoids service, you can file a motion with the court to serve him or her by alternative means, such as posting on the courthouse bulletin board or publishing in the local newspaper. Accompany your motion with an affidavit describing your unsuccessful attempts to serve. (You can also ask for service by publication if your spouse cannot be found.)

Your spouse can voluntarily submit to jurisdiction of the court by filing an ANSWER, and then you will not have to serve the *Summons* and COMPLAINT or file an AFFIDAVIT OF SERVICE.

If you do not know where your spouse is, contact his or relatives and last known employer. Check the Internet, phone book, military listings, and traffic and criminal records. After a diligent search, you can ask the court to permit service by alternative means such as publication in the newspaper or posting a notice on the courthouse bulletin board. Following are the rules and forms for service of process in each jurisdiction.

Maryland Service

Serve your spouse with the COMPLAINT, one copy of the *Summons* (provided by the clerk when you file the COMPLAINT), the CIVIL—DOMESTIC CASE INFORMATION REPORT you completed, and a blank CIVIL—DOMESTIC CASE INFORMATION REPORT. You can serve it by certified mail, return receipt requested, or by private process server, which means anyone over 18 years of age, except you.

AFFIDAVIT OF SERVICE BY CERTIFIED MAIL

If you use certified mail, when you get the return receipt, file it with the AFFIDAVIT OF SERVICE (CERTIFIED MAIL). (see form 6, p.239.) Fill in the case caption at the top and complete the rest of the form as follows:

☞ *Line 1.* Insert "Complaint for Divorce and Summons."

☞ *Line 2.* Enter your spouse's name.

☞ *Line 3.* Insert the date you mailed and the address you mailed to.

☞ *Line 5.* Fill in your spouse's name.

☞ Date, sign, and print your name, address and telephone number on the form.

☞ Attach the original return receipt and a copy of the summons.

☞ File this with the court.

AFFIDAVIT OF SERVICE BY PRIVATE PROCESS

If you serve by hand, the person you used as a process server will complete the AFFIDAVIT OF SERVICE (PRIVATE PROCESS). (see form 7, p.240.) Fill in the case caption at the top and complete the rest of the form as follows.

☞ *Line 1.* Print your spouse's name and time served.

☞ *Line 2.* Indicate the date served and address where served.

☞ *Line 3.* Insert "Complaint for Divorce and Summons."

☞ Have the server date, sign, and print his or her name, address, and telephone number on the form.

☞ Attach a copy of the *Summons*.

☞ File this with the court.

Virginia Service

After you file the BILL OF COMPLAINT and pay the filing fee, the court will issue a *Subpoena in Chancery*. The subpoena is a notice to the defendant that a lawsuit has been filed against him or her. It is your responsibility to have the *Subpoena in Chancery*, together with a copy of the BILL OF COMPLAINT served upon the defendant.

Service of process on a Virginia resident can be accomplished by personal service, which means handing the *Subpoena in Chancery* (prepared by the court) and BILL OF COMPLAINT to the defendant. This can be done by the sheriff or by an individual over the age of eighteen who does not have an interest in the lawsuit. That is, you can have a friend or a relative serve the defendant, but you cannot serve the papers yourself.

Actual receipt of the process does not by itself cure any defects in service of process. The defendant must have been served with process in one of the ways authorized by the statute or must have formally waived or accepted process.

If a resident defendant cannot be personally served, service can be accomplished by leaving the papers with a member of defendant's household who is at least sixteen years of age or, if that is not possible, by posting the papers at the defendant's front door. The complainant must show by the process server's affidavit that each method was attempted in the proper order. In an uncontested divorce case, service problems are needless opportunities for delay and additional expense.

The methods of service of process on a non-resident defendant depend upon the particular basis for jurisdiction. Generally, personal service by a law enforcement official authorized to serve process in the foreign jurisdiction is sufficient. Acceptance or waiver of process by the non-resident defendant is also effective.

RETURN OF SERVICE

Service by the sheriff is an effective and cost-efficient means to have a resident defendant served, and should be used in most circumstances. The sheriff will file a *Return of Service* with the court.

AFFIDAVIT OF SERVICE

If you have someone other than the sheriff serve the defendant, then you must file an AFFIDAVIT OF SERVICE with the court. (see form 8, p.293.) To complete the AFFIDAVIT OF SERVICE:

- ☛ The name of the court, the names of the parties and the case number must agree with those shown on other papers filed in the case.

☞ Enter the title of this paper below the caption. The title is "Affidavit of Service of Process."

☞ The process server should state his or her name, that he is over the age of eighteen and not a party to the case.

☞ State the date and the address where the defendant was served.

☞ State that the defendant acknowledged his or her identity, and give brief physical description.

☞ The process server should sign the affidavit before a notary or deputy clerk of court and have his or her signature notarized.

ACCEPTANCE/
WAIVER FORM

A defendant in Virginia can accept or waive service of process by signing the **ACCEPTANCE OF SERVICE OF PROCESS AND WAIVER OF NOTICE** ("the Acceptance/Waiver Form"). (see form 7, p.290.) Waiver of process also dispenses with the need to formally serve the defendant with notice of the divorce hearing. The form must be signed in front of a notary or other official authorized to administer oaths, and filed with the court. To complete this form:

☞ Fill in the blocks for case number, location of court and names of parties.

☞ In item 1, check the defendant block.

☞ In item 2, check Subpoena in Chancery block and Bill of Complaint block, and write in the additional documents, if any, you are sending to the defendant with these documents (such as exhibits to the complaint).

☞ In item 3, check blocks a through e.

☞ Check the defendant block under the signature line.

☞ Send the completed **ACCEPTANCE/WAIVER FORM** to the defendant along with the *Subpoena in Chancery*, **BILL OF COMPLAINT** and any other papers.

☞ The defendant then signs the **ACCEPTANCE/WAIVER FORM** before a notary and has his or her signature notarized.

☞ The defendant files the **ACCEPTANCE/WAIVER FORM** with the court and mails (or hand delivers) a copy to the plaintiff.

DISTRICT OF COLUMBIA SERVICE

Service of Process in the District of Columbia may be by:

- certified mail, return receipt requested;

- hand delivery to your spouse; or,

- hand delivery to someone at your spouse's home of suitable age or discretion.

PERSONAL
SERVICE

You may not personally serve the papers yourself. You can use any other person who lives or works in D.C., is over the age of 18, and is not a party to the divorce. You may use a special process server.

The process server hands the COMPLAINT and the "service copy" of the *Summons* that the clerk gave you to your spouse or someone in your spouse's home. The person in your spouse's home must be someone of suitable age and discretion, but not a young child or a visitor.

The *Summons* must be delivered within twenty days of issuance or it expires. If your *Summons* expires before you can have it served on your spouse, you can ask the clerk for a second summons (sometimes called an "alias Summons") for a fee of $10. You can have the *Summons* served anytime and anywhere (at work, home, or elsewhere).

Once the papers are served, the process server will complete the bottom portion of the "legal copy" of the *Summons* and have it notarized. The date and time of service will be stated and the name of the person served. File this copy with the clerk. Make a copy and have the clerk date stamp it for your records.

SERVICE BY
CERTIFIED MAIL

Instead of personal service, you can send the papers yourself to your spouse's home by certified mail, return receipt requested. When you receive the green return receipt card, attach it to the bottom of the legal copy of the *Summons*.

Prepare an AFFIDAVIT OF SERVICE BY CERTIFIED MAIL. (see form 6, p.349.) The *Affidavit* is your sworn and notarized statement of:

- the date you got the summons;

- the date you mailed it; and,

- the date your spouse received it.

If someone other than your spouse signed for it, you will have to state who that person is, and it must be someone who lives with your spouse, and who is of suitable age and discretion.

If you do not know the person who signed for it, you do not have good service, and you will have to try again by certified mail, or have it served by hand. If you are still living with your spouse, the court will not consider it good service if you sign the receipt for him or her.

Once you have obtained Service of Process, then the defendant has to file a response or be found in default. Chapter 13 explains what to do if you cannot find your spouse. Chapter 14 gives information on how to respond if you are the one who has been served with a COMPLAINT FOR ABSOLUTE DIVORCE. Chapter 15 tells you what to do if your spouse does not respond after you have served him or her with a COMPLAINT FOR ABSOLUTE DIVORCE.

FINDING YOUR SPOUSE 13

If you cannot find your spouse, or your spouse is avoiding service, you will have to ask the court for alternative service. Since this will slow your case down, you should make every effort to locate and serve your spouse first. The courts in Maryland, Virginia, and D.C. will require a good faith effort on your part, and records of your attempts to locate your spouse. Here are the procedures and forms for alternative service of process in each jurisdiction.

MARYLAND ALTERNATIVE SERVICE

ATTEMPTS TO LOCATE SPOUSE

To attempt to locate your spouse, your need to make diligent efforts, which may include the following:

- serve by certified mail at the last known address (save return receipts);

- send letters to relatives and friends (save copies of your letters and responses);

- write to the last employer (save copies of your letter and response);

- hire a private investigator to find him or her (save a copy of report);

- use a telephone directory, directory assistance, and the Internet (keep a record of your attempts to locate);

- call the Motor Vehicle Administration in Maryland for a current address;

- contact the Military Service Locator (see Maryland form 9) to see if he or she is a member of the armed forces;

- ask former neighbors;

- contact the local child support enforcement agency for any records of whereabouts; and,

- use any other method you can think of.

MOTION FOR
ALTERNATIVE
SERVICE

If you have tried all these means to locate or serve your spouse and are still unsuccessful, then you are ready to file a **MOTION FOR ALTERNATIVE SERVICE**. (see form 8, p.241.) First fill in the top section with the caption of your case. Then complete the rest of the form as follows:

☞ *Line 1.* Print your name.

☞ *Paragraph 1.* Write "Complaint for Divorce," the city or county of the court, and the date you filed.

☞ Date and sign the form.

☞ On the *Affidavit* portion of the form, put in the county where you are signing.

☞ Print your name where indicated.

☞ *Line 1.* Write "Complaint for Divorce," the city or county of the court, and the date you filed.

☞ *Line 2.* Check off all the boxes that indicate your attempts to locate or serve your spouse and attach supporting documents.

☞ *Line 3.* Indicate the last date you saw your spouse and check the appropriate boxes to indicate what you know about his or her whereabouts.

☞ Sign the form in front of a Notary Public and have the Notary complete the *Notarization* part of the form.

☞ Fill in the case caption of the Order for Alternative Service. The judge will complete the rest.

☞ Fill in the case caption of the *Notice*. The clerk will complete the rest.

File all of these documents with the clerk. There will be another filing fee for this motion. If the judge grants your motion and orders service by posting, the clerk will arrange to have the notice posted, usually on the bulletin board at the courthouse. If the judge orders service by publication in the newspaper, you will have to check to see whether the clerk will arrange this or it is your responsibility. In either event, you will have to pay the newspaper for publication.

Virginia Alternative Service

If your spouse is not a Virginia resident or you cannot locate your spouse after following the steps previously described, you can use the procedures for **Service by Publication**. The steps for **Service by Publication** are as follows.

AFFIDAVIT FOR SERVICE BY PUBLICATION

Complete and file an **Affidavit for Service by Publication** stating the reasons you are seeking to serve by publication. (see form 13, p.298.) Complete the affidavit by doing the following:

- ☞ Complete the *caption* as usual.

- ☞ Enter your name on the complainant line.

- ☞ Enter the your spouse's name on defendant line.

- ☞ Check the appropriate box to indicate whether the basis for publication is that your spouse is a non-resident, cannot be found, cannot be served by the sheriff, or other reason (and state the reason, if applicable).

- ☞ fill in your spouse's name and last known address where indicated.

- ☞ State any other information that is relevant to the need for an **Order of Publication**.

- ☞ Sign where indicated in the notarizing officer's presence.

- ☞ Have your signature notarized by a notary or deputy clerk of court.

ORDER OF PUBLICATION

Complete and file an **Order of Publication**. (see form 14, p.299.) Complete the order as follows:

- ☞ Fill in the caption.

- ☞ Check the appropriate box to indicate whether the basis for publication is that your spouse is a non-resident, cannot be found, cannot be served by the sheriff, or other reason (and state the reason, if applicable).

- ☞ Fill in your spouse's name and last known address where indicated.

☛ Sign where indicated and fill in your address and telephone number.

☛ If the judge signs the ORDER OF PUBLICATION, the clerk's office will arrange for publication of the order.

☛ Pay the clerk's office the cost of publication or your pro-rata share if two or more orders are combined in one publication.

DISTRICT OF COLUMBIA ALTERNATIVE SERVICE

If you do not know where your spouse is, you may ask for service by publication or posting.

MOTION TO SERVE BY PUBLICATION

Prepare a MOTION TO ALLOW SERVICE BY PUBLICATION (DC form 7), together with POINTS AND AUTHORITIES (DC form 10) and an AFFIDAVIT OF SERVICE BY CERTIFIED MAIL (DC form 6). This affidavit states your true belief that your spouse has lived outside the District of Columbia for the last six months and describes your diligent search for your spouse, including relatives, last known employer, telephone book, military listings, traffic and criminal records. Attach an ORDER PUBLICATION—ABSENT DEFENDENT (DC form 9). Sign the AFFIDAVIT OF SERVICE in front of a Notary. Then file all of these documents together with the clerk. It will be up to you to arrange for publication.

Responding to a Complaint for Divorce

14

If you are served, you have to respond to a **COMPLAINT FOR DIVORCE** within:

- thirty days in Maryland, but sixty days if served outside Maryland, and ninety days if served outside the country;

- twenty-one days in Virginia; or,

- twenty days in the District of Columbia.

Otherwise you will be in default and an order may be entered against you. It is possible to ask the court for an extension of time in which to respond, but it is safer to respond on time.

The response is usually in the form of an **ANSWER**, a formal legal pleading, in which the answering party, the defendant, either admits or denies each of the allegations of the complaint.

The defendant may also file a countercomplaint, saying it was actually the plaintiff that was at fault in the marriage. If the plaintiff decides to withdraw the complaint, or cannot prove all the elements at trial, then the defendant can proceed with the divorce on the countercomplaint without starting over in the legal process.

MARYLAND ANSWER (MARYLAND FORM 11)

Your spouse has thirty days (sixty days if served outside Maryland and ninety days if served outside of the United States) from the date of service to file an **ANSWER** or other response with the court. (see form 11, p.247.) Each calendar day is counted starting with the first day after you serve your spouse, except if the last day falls on a Saturday, Sunday, or holiday. Then the response is due on the next business day.

If you are the party who is being sued for divorce (the defendant), and you have been served with a COMPLAINT FOR ABSOLUTE DIVORCE, you must file an ANSWER if you want to participate in the case. The ANSWER is your letter to the judge, which either denies or admits each of the allegations in your COMPLAINT. If you do not file an ANSWER, the judge will not hear your side of the story and will probably give your spouse most or all of what he or she is requesting. Even if you have an uncontested divorce, filing an ANSWER will speed up the process.

To complete the ANSWER, fill in the case caption with the names exactly as they appear on the case caption of the COMPLAINT and copy the case number from the COMPLAINT and *Summons*. Complete the rest of the ANSWER as follows.

☞ In the title, mark the box that shows you are answering a complaint.

☞ In the first section, print your name and write "Complaint for Divorce" on the next line.

☞ *Lines 1 through 9.* Check whether you admit or deny each paragraph of the COMPLAINT, do not have enough information, or there is no such paragraph. Attach another page if there are more than nine numbered paragraphs in the COMPLAINT. Do not leave any sections blank and check only one block in each section. You may deny part and admit part of a paragraph. Attach additional pages if you run out of space. Do not write on the back of the form.

☞ *Line 10.* If there is any more information you think the judge ought to know about your case, write it here, attaching additional pages if you need more room.

☞ In the section that starts "FOR THESE REASONS," check the box asking the court to dismiss or deny the COMPLAINT if you are contesting it, or grant the relief requested in the COMPLAINT if you are not contesting it. If you are contesting part of the COMPLAINT, there is a box for that, too.

☞ Sign and date the ANSWER. Print your current address and telephone number under your name if it is different than that shown in the COMPLAINT.

☛ Fill in the *Certificate of Service* at the bottom of the Answer. You must mail a copy of everything you file to your spouse or your spouse's attorney if he or she is represented by counsel.

☛ File your Answer with the court clerk together with the Civil–Domestic Case Report (Maryland form 5). Make an extra copy for your files. If you are contesting your case, and you or your spouse is asking for alimony or child support, you will also have to file a Financial Statement on the Court (Maryland form 1).

☛ There is also space at the end of the Answer for you to file a counter-claim against your spouse, if you wish, by marking the appropriate boxes for what you want. You will have to attach other forms, the same as those required for a Complaint for Absolute Divorce (Maryland form 4) to complete your counterclaim. Complete the *Certificate of Service* at the bottom of the counterclaim as well.

☛ There is no fee to file an Answer or a counterclaim.

Virginia Answer (Virginia Form 15)

Once the Bill of Complaint is served upon the defendant, he or she has twenty-one days to file an Answer. To complete the Answer, the defendant will:

☛ Write the name and location of the court and the names of the parties (the parties' addresses are not necessary) at the top.

☛ Copy the assigned case number on the Answer.

☛ In an uncontested case, it is sufficient to state defendant admits the allegations of the Bill of Complaint and does not oppose the granting of the relief requested.

☛ Complete the *Certificate of Service*.

☛ Sign the Answer and *Certificate of Service*.

☛ File the Answer with the court clerk at the courthouse.

☛ Mail or hand deliver a copy of the Answer to the complainant.

DISTRICT OF COLUMBIA ANSWER (DC FORM 11)

Your spouse has twenty days from the date of service to file an ANSWER or other response with the court. Each calendar day is counted starting with the first day after you serve your spouse, except if the last day falls on a Saturday, Sunday, or holiday, then the response is due on the next business day.

If you are the party who is being sued for divorce (the defendant) and you have been served with a COMPLAINT FOR ABSOLUTE DIVORCE, you must file an ANSWER if you want to participate in the case. The ANSWER is your letter to the judge, which either denies or admits each of the allegations in your COMPLAINT. If you do not file an ANSWER, the judge will not hear your side of the story and will probably give your spouse most or all of what he or she is requesting. Even if you have an uncontested divorce, filing an ANSWER will speed up the process.

Use the uncontested ANSWER in Appendix R only for an uncontested divorce.

☞ Fill in the case caption at the top of the form with the names exactly as the appear on the case caption of the COMPLAINT and copy the case number from the COMPLAINT and *Summons*.

☞ Put your name in the first paragraph.

☞ Paragraph 1 is the D.C. law that gives the court jurisdiction to hear the case.

☞ Paragraph 2 is the six month residency requirement. If you or both of you meet this requirement, write "Plaintiff." If only you meet the requirement, write "Defendant."

☞ Paragraph 3 is a statement that you are married to the plaintiff.

☞ Paragraph 4 states that you agree with all the statements in your spouse's COMPLAINT FOR ABSOLUTE DIVORCE.

☞ Paragraph 5 states that you do not expect to get back together with your spouse.

☞ At paragraph 6, circle whether you want to change your name to a former name, and if so, give the former name.

☞ The WHEREFORE clause tells the court what you want, that is an absolute divorce and any other relief the court finds proper. Indicate in line 3 if you want a name change or not.

☛ Sign your name to the ANSWER.

☛ Complete the affirmation with your name and signature, which indicates that your ANSWER is true under penalties of perjury.

☛ Fill in the information in the *Certificate of Service* and sign your name.

☛ You must mail or hand deliver a copy of your ANSWER to your spouse or your spouse's attorney.

DEFAULT DIVORCE 15

If your spouse fails to file an ANSWER or other pleading within the required time, or after the time passes that is set forth in the judge's *Order for Alternative Service*, you may seek a divorce by default in any of the jurisdictions in which you filed your COMPLAINT FOR DIVORCE.

MARYLAND DEFAULT

If your spouse has failed to answer the COMPLAINT in the required time in Maryland, file a REQUEST FOR ORDER OF DEFAULT (Maryland form 10). To complete the REQUEST, fill in the case caption at the top and then:

- ☞ Print your name on the first line.

- ☞ Print your spouse's name on the second line.

- ☞ On the third line, write "Complaint for Divorce."

- ☞ Insert your spouse's last known address on the fourth line.

- ☞ Sign and date the REQUEST.

- ☞ On the *Non-Military Affidavit*, put your spouse's name.

- ☞ Sign and date the *Affidavit*.

- ☞ On the next page, fill in the case caption on the *Order of Default* and the judge will complete the rest.

Once you receive an ORDER OF DEFAULT, you will need to contact the court clerk to schedule an uncontested divorce hearing.

Virginia Default

If the defendant does not file an timely ANSWER within twenty-one days of service, you can proceed with the divorce by default. Count the time by counting the first day after the day of service as one and counting each calendar day thereafter. If day twenty-one falls on a weekend or holiday, then the defendant has until the next business day to answer.

The default procedures contain safeguards to ensure that the defendant is given notice and an opportunity to appear and defend. The safeguards create potential for mistakes by the complainant that will prevent entry of the Decree of Divorce until complainant goes back and corrects the mistake. In short, like service of process problems, the default procedure is full of opportunities for needless expense and delay. If the parties to an uncontested divorce want to obtain a divorce without needless delay and expense, the defendant has to file a timely ANSWER.

If the defendant is on active duty in the Armed Forces of the United States, you cannot proceed by default.

District of Columbia Default

If you file and serve the COMPLAINT properly, but the defendant does not file an ANSWER within twenty days, you can ask the court to enter a default against the defendant and to set a hearing for *ex parte* proof. *Ex parte* means one-sided, that is you get to tell your side of the story and the defendant does not.

PRAECIPE FOR DEFAULT AND *EX PARTE* HEARING

First, file a ***PRAECIPE* FOR DEFAULT AND *EX PARTE* HEARING** asking the court to determine whether it is necessary to appoint an attorney for the defendant. (see form 12, p.360.) If the court determines it is not necessary to appoint counsel for the defendant, file a praecipe asking the court to enter a default and set a hearing.

AFFIDAVIT IN SUPPORT OF DEFAULT

File your **AFFIDAVIT IN SUPPORT OF DEFAULT** with the praecipe. (see form 13, p.361.) Complete it as follows.

- ☞ Fill in the case caption and case number at the top.

- ☞ Print your name on the first line after the title.

- ☞ If you do not have an attorney, you will want to strike the words "the attorney of record for."

☞ Fill in the date of service of process.

☞ Sign the AFFIDAVIT before a notary or a clerk at the courthouse and substitute "Plaintiff" for "Attorney" under your signature.

SOLDIERS AND SAILORS AFFIDAVIT

You will also need to complete and file a SOLDIERS AND SAILORS AFFIDAVIT (see form 14, p.362) with your PRAECIPE FOR DEFAULT. Complete the caption, insert your name, and sign the AFFIDAVIT before a notary.

DEFAULT ORDER

Finally, attach to the PRAECIPE FOR DEFAULT a proposed DEFAULT ORDER for the judge to sign after your hearing. (see form 15, p.363.) Complete the proposed order as follows.

☞ Fill in the case name and number.

☞ Fill in the day your spouse was served.

☞ Fill in the day you are filing the PRAECIPE FOR DEFAULT.

☞ Fill in your spouse's name.

☞ The judge will complete the rest.

You have six months from the time you file the COMPLAINT to process your default or bring the case to issue (meaning an ANSWER is filed by the defendant). Otherwise the court will dismiss your case and you will have to start over by filing a new COMPLAINT.

SECTION 4:
UNCONTESTED DIVORCE

MARYLAND UNCONTESTED DIVORCE 16

You can file a COMPLAINT FOR ABSOLUTE DIVORCE in Maryland if you or your spouse meet the residency requirement of one year prior to filing, or the grounds for divorce (such as adultery) arose within the state. You must also have one of the grounds for either an absolute or limited divorce that were described earlier. A case is uncontested if you have a comprehensive *Separation Agreement* in writing and signed by both parties. In other words, to have an uncontested case, you and your spouse must be in agreement on grounds, custody, child support, alimony, and property distribution.

Sometimes a client will tell us they have an uncontested case, but when we ask they have no *Separation Agreement*. After we prepare a *Separation Agreement*, the other spouse wants to negotiate it. After a lot of negotiation, we finally come to terms and sign the negotiated agreement. Then we file a COMPLAINT for an uncontested divorce.

So, you can do your arguing before the trial and reach a comprehensive *Separation Agreement* to present to the court in an uncontested divorce. Or you can do your arguing before the judge or Master and he or she will decide. That is a *contested* divorce, which we will discuss in Chapter 21 and 22.

REQUIRED FORMS

To begin an uncontested divorce in Maryland, you'll need to file the following with the court clerk:

- CIVIL—DOMESTIC RELATIONS CASE INFORMATION SHEET (Maryland form 5);

- COMPLAINT FOR ABSOLUTE DIVORCE (Maryland form 4);

- *Separation Agreement*; and,

- filing fee.

If you are seeking alimony or child support you will also be required to file a FINANCIAL STATEMENT (Maryland form 1). Later you will file a JOINT REQUEST FOR AN UNCONTESTED DIVORCE HEARING (Maryland form 12). At the final hearing you will need:

- a *Report of Absolute Divorce* (the "Blue Form" for statistical information) (sample Maryland form 13);

- a copy of your marriage license (or witness present at your marriage);

- *Child Support Guidelines* (if there are children);

- Witness Identification Information;

- *Separation Agreement* (if you did not file it with your Complaint); and,

- SUBMISSION TO JUDGMENT (for waiving appeals) (Maryland form 14).

The following sections will describe the uncontested divorce process and the required forms.

FILING A COMPLAINT

File your COMPLAINT (Maryland form 4) and CIVIL-DOMESTIC CASE INFORMATION SHEET (Maryland form 5) with the clerk's office at the courthouse in the county where you live or where your spouse lives. If you are requesting alimony or child support, you also have to file a FINANCIAL STATEMENT (Maryland form 1). There is a filing fee of about $215 depending upon the county where you are filing. The clerk will process your COMPLAINT, give it a case number, open the court's file, and return it to you with two copies of a *Summons*.

SERVICE OF PROCESS

Serve the COMPLAINT and *Summons* on your spouse by certified mail or by personal service. Remember you cannot personally serve your spouse. You have to have a friend or a professional process server do it. Once the COMPLAINT is served, file the AFFIDAVIT OF SERVICE with the court (Maryland form 6 or 7).

ANSWER

Once served, your spouse has to respond to your COMPLAINT, with an ANSWER or other pleading, within thirty days (sixty days if served outside Maryland and ninety days if served outside of the United States) or he or she will be found in default.

SCHEDULING CONFERENCE AND ORDER

Once an AFFIDAVIT OF SERVICE or an ANSWER has been filed, the court will send you *Notice of a Scheduling Conference*. At the scheduling conference, the master will call your case. Step forward and the Master will ask you to introduce yourself.

Bring your calendar. The court will set a schedule for your case, and give you a *scheduling order*, with dates for parenting classes, custody mediation, alternative dispute resolution, discovery cut-off, and a pre-trial conference. Do not take these deadlines lightly. Put them on your calendar now, because they may be strictly enforced.

If your case is contested, you will need to request certain things from the master at this scheduling conference, as follows:

- ☞ a *Pendente Lite Hearing* to determine temporary alimony, child support, visitation, legal fees and expert fees, as applicable;

- ☞ custody evaluation;

- ☞ custody assessment;

☞ *guardian ad litem;*

☞ attorney for the children; and,

☞ *Nagel v. Hooks attorney.*

Failure to ask for these things at the scheduling conference, or to have them included in the scheduling order, may prevent you from obtaining them later.

JOINT REQUEST TO SCHEDULE AN UNCONTESTED DIVORCE HEARING

Attached to the *Notice of a Scheduling Conference*, will be a JOINT REQUEST TO SCHEDULE AN UNCONTESTED DIVORCE HEARING. (see form 12, p.250.) If your spouse answers and admits all the allegations of your COMPLAINT, the divorce is uncontested. You may file a JOINT REQUEST signed by both of you.

To complete the JOINT REQUEST, state your grounds for divorce—usually one year voluntary separation or two years separation in an uncontested divorce. Then check the following items, if applicable.

☞ Check line 1b if custody and visitation have been agreed to.

☞ Check line 2 if child support has been established in compliance with the child support guidelines.

☞ Mark line 3 if all parties speak English.

☞ Mark line 4 if there are no pension or any pension rights have been waived.

☞ Check line 5 if there are no support or property rights to be adjudicated.

☞ Attach a completed CHILD SUPPORT WORKSHEET (Maryland form 2 or 3). This is required for an uncontested hearing if you have minor children of the marriage. (Child support is discussed in Chapter 25.)

Once you file the JOINT REQUEST, the scheduling conference will not be held and you will not be scheduled for any other hearings except your divorce hearing.

VIRGINIA 17
UNCONTESTED
DIVORCE

Once you meet the residency requirements and have grounds for divorce, you may file for an uncontested divorce in Virginia.

Residency in Virginia means that one party is an actual and bona fide resident and domiciliary of the state for at least six months before filing the complaint. This means someone who has established a residence in the state with the intent to remain indefinitely. Special statutory provisions cover military personnel. Persons in the military who are stationed in Virginia for six months are presumed to be Virginia residents and domicilliaries.

Once you meet the residency requirement so the court has subject matter jurisdiction over your marriage, the court has the power to grant you a divorce. However, if you want the court to decide custody, support, or property, it will have to have personal jurisdiction over the defendant. The court will have personal jurisdiction if the defendant is properly served with process and:

- he or she is a Virginia resident at the time the suit for divorce is filed;

- the parties lived in Virginia at the time of the separation that is the grounds for divorce;

- the defendant lived in Virginia at the time the grounds for divorce arose;

- the defendant maintained a marital home in Virginia at the time the suit is filed;

- the defendant executed an agreement in Virginia to pay support to a Virginia resident;

- the defendant has previously ben ordered to pay support by a Virginia court that had jurisdiction over him; or,

- the defendant fathered or conceived a child in Virginia.

REQUIRED FORMS

To begin an uncontested divorce, you will need to file the following with the court clerk:

- BILL OF COMPLAINT FOR DIVORCE (see form 5, p.288);

- DIVORCE CASE COVER SHEET (if required) (see form 6, p.289);

- *Separation Agreement* (if you have one); and,

- filing fee.

Later, you will file:

- AFFIDAVIT OF SERVICE (see form 8, p.293) (unless the sheriff serves the papers on the defendant); or,

- REQUEST FOR ORDER OF PUBLICATION (see form 9, p.294) and

- AFFIDAVIT IN SUPPORT OF ORDER OF PUBLICATION. (see form 10, p.295, form 11, p.296, or form 12, p.297—whichever is appropriate to your situation.)

You will also file a *Praecipe* requesting an uncontested divorce hearing.

The defendant will file:

- ACCEPTANCE/WAIVER FORM (see form 7, p.290) and,

- ANSWER to the BILL OF COMPLAINT FOR DIVORCE (see form 15, p.300).

At the final hearing you will need:

- a VITAL STATISTICS FORM VS-4 (see form 17, p.302);

- a copy of your marriage license (or witness present at your marriage);

- Child Support Guidelines (if there are children);

- *Separation Agreement* (if you did not file it with your COMPLAINT);

- corroborating witness; and,

- FINAL DECREE OF DIVORCE. (see form 20, p.305 or form 21, p.307.)

The following will describe the uncontested divorce process in Virginia and explain the required forms.

FILING YOUR BILL OF COMPLAINT

File an original and one copy of the BILL OF COMPLAINT (see form 5, p.288) at the clerk's office at the courthouse. Bring an extra copy for you to keep. The clerk will stamp it "filed" and note the case number on it. Pay the filing fee of $66, plus an additional $19 if a change of name is required. You will also have to pay for the cost of service of process if you want the sheriff to serve it.

REQUEST FOR *ORE TENUS* HEARING

Once the defendant has filed an ANSWER (Virginia form 15), or been placed in default, the case is "at issue" and the clerk's office will schedule a hearing upon request.

You can have a hearing scheduled by filing a request, called a REQUEST FOR *ORE TENUS* HEARING. You will in some counties, also be required to file a completed VITAL STATISTICS FORM VS-4 (see form 17, p.302), and a FINAL DECREE OF DIVORCE. (see form 20, p.305 or form 21, p.307.)

To complete the REQUEST FOR *ORE TENUS* HEARING (see form 16, p.301):

- ☛ Enter the name of the court, the names of the parties, the case number and the title of the paper (*Request for Ore Tenus Hearing*) as usual.

- ☛ Fill in your name and check complainant.

- ☛ Fill in your address and telephone number.

- ☛ Check the appropriate attachments and list any other attachments to your request.

- ☛ Send a copy of the REQUEST FOR *ORE TENUS* HEARING to the defendant and complete and sign the *Certificate of Service* if the defendant has not filed an ACCEPTANCE/WAIVER (see form 7, p.290) in the case.

District of
Columbia 18
Uncontested
Divorce

You can file a COMPLAINT FOR ABSOLUTE DIVORCE in the District of Columbia if you or your spouse meet the residency requirement of six months prior to filing and have one of the grounds for either an absolute divorce or legal separation that were described in Chapter 9.

A case is uncontested if you have a comprehensive *Separation Agreement* in writing and signed by both parties. In other words, to have an uncontested case, you and your spouse must be in agreement on grounds, custody, child support, alimony, and property distribution.

If you have a *Separation Agreement* with your spouse, and you are both cooperating, it is possible to obtain an uncontested divorce in the District of Columbia in three to six weeks.

REQUIRED FORMS

To begin an uncontested divorce, you will need to file the following with the clerk:

- *Vital Records Collection Form*;

- *Intake/Cross Reference Sheet*;

- *Vital Statistics Form* (see sample form 4, p.345);

- COMPLAINT FOR ABSOLUTE DIVORCE (see form 3, p.339);

- *Separation Agreement*;

- FINANCIAL STATEMENT (if you are seeking alimony or child support) (see form 1, p.333);

- *Notice of Hearing* and *Order to Appear* (if child support is contested); and,

- filing fee.

Later you will file a PRAECIPE FOR AN UNCONTESTED DIVORCE. (see form 16, p.364.) At the final hearing you will need:

- a certified copy of your marriage license;

- *Child Support Guidelines* (if there are children);

- *Separation Agreement* (if you did not file it with your COMPLAINT);

- CONSENT FORM (see form 17, p.365);

- FINDINGS OF FACT, CONCLUSIONS OF LAW AND JUDGMENT FOR ABSOLUTE DIVORCE (see form 18, p.366.); and,

- JOINT WAIVER OF APPEAL. (see form 19, p.372.)

The court in the District of Columbia runs a free divorce clinic, which you can register for with the clerk. The clerk also has forms for an ANSWER, an UNCONTESTED PRAECIPE, and the VITAL STATISTICS FORM; however, the clerk does not have packages of forms for a contested divorce or for a *Separation Agreement*. Be sure to ask the clerk for a copy of the court's divorce booklet. If your spouse cooperates, you can file all of these forms at once to expedite your divorce. Be sure to let the clerk know that you have an uncontested divorce and are filing the COMPLAINT, ANSWER and UNCONTESTED PRAECIPE at the same time. The following sections will describe the uncontested divorce process, explain the required forms, and give you instructions for completing the forms.

FILING YOUR COMPLAINT

File your COMPLAINT (see form 3, p.339) and the associated documents with the clerk of the Domestic Relations Branch of the Family Court.

Clerk of Domestic Relations Branch
Family Court
Room 4230
D.C. Superior Court
Carl Moultrie I Courthouse
500 Indiana Avenue N.W.
Washington, D.C.

Business hours are from 9:00 A.M. to 4:00 P.M. Monday through Friday. There is a filing fee of $80. The clerk will process your COMPLAINT, give it a case number, open the court's file, and return it to you with two copies of a *Summons*.

SERVICE OF PROCESS

Serve the COMPLAINT and *Summons* by certified mail to your spouse or by hand delivery to your spouse or someone of suitable age and discretion living at your spouse's residence. Remember you cannot personally serve your spouse. You have to have a friend or a professional process server do it. Once the COMPLAINT is served, file the AFFIDAVIT OF SERVICE with the court.

ANSWER

Once served, your spouse has to respond to your COMPLAINT, with an ANSWER (see form 11, p.357), or other pleading, within twenty days, or he or she will be found in default. There is no form ANSWER for a contested divorce. If you are the one served with a COMPLAINT, and you want to contest it, you will have to prepare your own ANSWER admitting the statements in your spouse's COMPLAINT you agree with, and denying those you do not. You may also bring to the court's attention facts in your ANSWER that you think your spouse omitted in the COMPLAINT.

PRAECIPE FOR UNCONTESTED DIVORCE

If your spouse is cooperating, both of you can file a PRAECIPE FOR UNCONTESTED DIVORCE. (see form 16, p.364.) A *Praecipe* is a letter to the clerk asking him or her to do something. In this case you are asking the clerk to set a hearing date on your divorce as soon as possible, since it is uncontested. To complete the form:

- ☛ Put the case number where it says "Jack No." and fill in the date at the top of the form.

- ☛ Fill in the names of the plaintiff and defendant as they appear on the COMPLAINT on the next lines of the form.

☛ Provide name, address, telephone number, and signatures at the bottom. The plaintiff completes the box on the left and the defendant completes the box on the right.

To speed things up, the COMPLAINT, ANSWER, and *PRAECIPE* FOR UNCONTESTED DIVORCE can all be filed at the same time. You should draw the clerk's attention to the fact that the COMPLAINT, ANSWER and *PRAECIPE* are being filed, and the case is ready to be scheduled for an uncontested divorce.

Preparing for the Uncontested Divorce Hearing

There are certain things you need to know and forms you must fill out before your uncontested divorce hearing in each jurisdiction. This chapter will explain the steps you must take before your hearing.

Maryland Uncontested Divorce

In an uncontested divorce case in Maryland, the plaintiff needs to appear in court to testify. The defendant need only appear if it is what he or she wants to do so. Uncontested divorces are heard by a *family law master*. At the hearing for an uncontested divorce, you must have:

- *Witness Information Form.* Have your witness print his or her name and address on it and mark whether the witness is for the Plaintiff or Defendant.

- REPORT OF ABSOLUTE DIVORCE OR ANNULMENT OF MARRIAGE. This is statistical information for your divorce. (see form 13, p.251.) The form is reproduced in this book for your information, but the court will not accept a copy, because the original is blue in color. You must obtain an original blue form from the court. Because the form says it must be typewritten, you need to request it before the hearing. Complete this form as follows:

  - ☛ *Lines 1–4.* Write the husband's name, address, birthplace and age.

  - ☛ *Lines 5–8.* Provide the same information for the wife and maiden name.

- ☞ *Lines 9–10.* Place and date of marriage.

- ☞ *Line 11.* Date of separation.

- ☞ *Line 12.* Number of children.

- ☞ *Line 13.* Indicate whether the husband or wife is the Plaintiff.

- ☞ *Line 14.* Name and address of Plaintiff's attorney if applicable.

- ☞ *Line 15.* How custody is being awarded.

- ☞ *Line 16.* Grounds for divorce.

- ☞ *Line 17.* Title and county of Court.

- ☞ *Lines 18–23.* Will be completed by the Clerk.

- ☞ *Lines 24–26.* Number of marriages, date of divorce of previous marriage, race, and education for husband and wife.

- *Separation Agreement* (if you have not filed it with the COMPLAINT).

- *Marriage License.* A certified copy of your marriage license or a witness present at your wedding.

- SUBMISSION TO JUDGMENT. If you and your spouse want to waive the ten day period for filing exceptions so that your divorce becomes final earlier, you can file a SUBMISSION TO JUDGMENT. (see form 14, p.252.) Complete the SUBMISSION TO JUDGMENT by filling in the case caption and signing it as plaintiff or defendant. Both parties must sign for this form to be accepted, so if your spouse will not be present at the hearing, you must obtain his or her signature in advance.

CORROBORATING WITNESS

Whenever you must prove something in court, you need witnesses. In divorce cases, you need to have corroboration (support) of your proof, even if your spouse is not disputing the grounds. Corroboration usually means another witness other than your spouse in addition to yourself. You need to prove and corroborate every allegation in your COMPLAINT.

You can request a subpoena for witnesses from the court clerk. The subpoena will help the witnesses get time off work to appear in court. If the witnesses do not appear in court, and you did not subpoena them, you cannot necessarily have the case put off until you can get them to appear in court. Your case could be dismissed.

Virginia Uncontested Divorce

Unlike other lawsuits, even an uncontested divorce in Virginia requires a hearing at which the complainant must prove the essential facts of the case that show complainant is entitled to a divorce. The hearing can be in front of a specially appointed commissioner or in front of a judge (referred to as an *Ore Tenus Hearing*). It is also possible to obtain a divorce by taking testimony of witnesses at a deposition. (We do not recommend divorce by deposition.)

- **Decree of Reference.** (see form 18, p.303.) If a hearing before a commissioner is desired and available, complainant should file a DECREE OF REFERENCE. The commissioner procedure requires the payment of the commissioner's fee and the court reporter's fee, which will usually total several hundred dollars. To complete this form:

  - Enter the name of the court, the names of the parties, and the case number.

  - Enter the title of the pleading, "Decree of Reference."

  - The first paragraph states the procedural history of the case to date, that is, that complainant filed a BILL OF COMPLAINT and had the BILL OF COMPLAINT served upon the defendant and the defendant filed an ANSWER.

  - The second paragraph states that the court concludes that the case has matured and can be referred to a commissioner in chancery.

  - The next paragraph is the court's order, leave the space for the commissioner's name blank. This chapter explains how to conduct your uncontested divorce hearing in Virginia.

- VITAL STATISTICS FORM **VS-4.** Form VS-4 gathers statistical information about divorces. (see form 17, p.302.) Complete the form using a typewriter or printing in permanent black ink as follows:

  - *Line 1.* Enter Court location.

  - *Lines 2–8.* Enter husband's full name, social security number, place of birth, date of birth, race, number of this marriage for husband, number indicating husband's highest educational level attained, and husband's home address.

☛ *Lines 9–15.* Enter wife's full name, social security number, place of birth, date of birth, race, number of this marriage for wife, number indicating wife's highest educational level attained, and wife's home address.

☛ *Line 16.* Enter place of marriage.

☛ *Line 17.* Enter date of marriage.

☛ *Line 18.* Enter number of children under 18 in the family.

☛ *Line 19.* Enter who was awarded custody of the children, or how many to each spouse, if appropriate.

☛ *Line 20.* Enter date of separation.

☛ *Line 21.* Check block to indicate who is the plaintiff (complainant).

☛ *Line 22.* Check block to indicate to whom the court granted the divorce.

☛ *Line 23.* State the grounds, for example one year separation.

☛ *Line 24.* Sign where indicated, enter your name and address and check Petitioner block.

● FINAL DECREE OF DIVORCE. (see form 20, p.305 or form 21, p.307.)

The decree is the court's decision and order granting your divorce. When a party files a proposed decree, the party prepares the decree to say what the party wants the court to rule. In your divorce case, there are certain findings and decisions you want the judge to make and there are certain things that the law requires to be in the decree. If you and your spouse have children, there are very specific statutory requirements the decree must meet with respect to the child support provisions.

To complete the FINAL DECREE OF DIVORCE:

☛ The decree has a caption, style of the case, case number, and heading like other court papers.

☛ The text of the decree begins with an introductory statement that explains what happened in the case before the hearing: a bill of complaint was filed, properly served or service was accepted or waived and an answer was filed.

☛ The next part of the decree sets forth the judge's findings of fact. It is traditionally introduced by the phrase "IT APPEARING THAT." This section relates the statements of fact in your complaint regarding residency, age, social security or DMV number, military status, date and place of marriage, children's names and dates of birth, date of separation, that at least one party intended that the separation be permanent, no reasonable likelihood of reconciliation, and that the parties entered into a written agreement, if applicable.

☛ In cases involving child support or spousal support, the law requires that detailed notices and information be in the decree. This section of the decree should be reproduced and filled in exactly like the form in the Virginia forms appendix. Do not paraphrase or summarize. All required information must be set forth even if it seems to be inapplicable to your case. To complete this portion of the decree:

☛ At paragraph 3, list the required information regarding children.

☛ At paragraph 4, check the person responsible for paying support and list all the information regarding both spouses' employment (or state none) even though only one spouse is responsible for paying support.

☛ At paragraph 5, fill in the information regarding occupational licences or check the line indicating neither party holds such licence.

☛ At paragraph 7, check the appropriate line.

☛ The next section is the court's decisions and orders in the case. Each paragraph contains one decision or order and is introduced by the (traditionally) capitalized phrase "ADJUDGED ORDERED AND DECREED." In an uncontested divorce, there will be at least two such ordering paragraphs, one granting the divorce and one affirming and ratifying the agreement and incorporating it into the decree.

☛ The last section of the decree informs the clerk's office whether the case should be closed or held open for further proceedings.

☞ There is signature line for the judge.

☞ At the bottom left, the decree has signature lines for the party seeking the decree or both parties below the phrase "I (WE) ASK FOR THIS:" If the defendant has not waived service of process and will not be at the hearing, it is important that he or she endorse the proposed decree. If not, complainant must serve notice of the divorce hearing upon the defendant in the same manner as original process is served.

DISTRICT OF COLUMBIA UNCONTESTED DIVORCE

Usually *Commissioners* preside over uncontested divorces in the District of Columbia. However, both you *and* your spouse must sign a CONSENT FORM agreeing to have your case heard by a commissioner instead of a judge.

● CONSENT FORM. You will both need to appear at the hearing where the clerk will give you a Consent Form, or if only one of you will be there, you need to bring the CONSENT FORM to the hearing signed by both of you. (see form 17, p.365.) You will also need the original or a certified copy of your marriage certificate. (The court clerk will ask for these documents together with FINDINGS OF FACT (see following paragraph) just before the hearing. If you do not have them, you probably will have to come back another day.)

● FINDINGS OF FACT, CONCLUSIONS OF LAW AND JUDGMENT FOR ABSOLUTE DIVORCE. This will become your Decree of Divorce after you give your testimony and evidence to the commissioner at the uncontested divorce hearing and prove all the statements in your COMPLAINT. The court will mail you a copy signed by the commissioner after the clerk enters it in the court files. To complete the FINDINGS OF FACT, CONCLUSIONS OF LAW AND JUDGMENT FOR ABSOLUTE DIVORCE (see form 18, p.366):

☞ Use the same names, addresses and case number as the COMPLAINT, and social security numbers for you and your spouse, to fill in the top section of the form.

☞ The first part of the form is entitled "FINDINGS OF FACT."

These are the facts about your marriage and divorce that the commissioner will find to be true from your testimony and evidence. The commissioner will fill in the blanks in the first paragraph with the date of the hearing.

☛ At paragraph 1, either you or your spouse must have been a resident of D.C. when you filed the COMPLAINT, and lived there continuously for the previous six months. If you or both of you meet this requirement, write "Plaintiff." If only your spouse meets the requirement, write "Defendant."

☛ At paragraph 2, fill in the date and place of your marriage, making sure it matches with your marriage certificate.

☛ At paragraph 3, state the date you and your spouse stopped living together and were no longer having sexual relations together.

☛ At paragraph 4, fill in the number of children born or adopted to you and your spouse together (but not children from other relationships), and list their names and birthdates.

☛ At paragraph 5, if there have been any earlier orders concerning the children, such as custody, visitation, or child support orders, provide the case numbers, dates and what the orders stated.

☛ At paragraph 6, if the children are living with you, insert "Plaintiff." If they are living with your spouse, and that is what you have agreed, write "Defendant."

☛ At paragraph 7, if your spouse has visitation with the children, write "Defendant." If you have visitation, write "Plaintiff." Write the agreed upon visitation schedule, or if you have not agreed, you may leave this blank for the commissioner to complete.

☛ Paragraph 8 states the terms of any agreement you have reached with your spouse about child support. Fill in who pays whom. For example, if your spouse has agreed to pay you, then fill in the blanks to show that the "Defendant" will pay the "Plaintiff." Then put the amount and how often it will be paid.

☛ Paragraph 9 states there are no property rights for the court to decide. If you have a *Separation Agreement*, add to the end of this sentence "because the parties have entered into a written Agreement dated [insert date] settling all issues between them."

109

☞ Paragraph 10 states that there is no reasonable prospect of your getting back together with your spouse.

☞ Fill in paragraph 11 if you want the court to restore your birth name or prior name.

☞ The second part of the form is entitled "CONCLUSIONS OF LAW." This is where the court finds you are entitled to a divorce based upon the "FINDINGS OF FACT."

☞ The third part of the form is entitled "JUDGMENT." These are the orders of the court concerning your divorce. The commissioner will fill in the dates in the first paragraph.

☞ Paragraph 1 grants your divorce. Fill in the present married names of you and your spouse, which should be the same as the caption of the COMPLAINT.

☞ Paragraph 2 orders custody and visitation. Fill in whether you (Plaintiff) or your spouse (Defendant) will have custody, list your children's names, and then the party having visitation. If the party with custody is you (Plaintiff) then your spouse (Defendant) will have visitation. Set out the visitation schedule if you have a *Separation Agreement*, or leave it blank if you do not.

☞ Paragraph 3 orders child support. Fill it out the same as you did paragraph 8 in the "FINDINGS OF FACT." If your spouse is paying you child support, put "Plaintiff" in the last blank. Put "Defendant" if you are paying your spouse child support.

☞ Paragraph 4 does not require anything.

☞ If you want a name change, fill in paragraph 5 the same way as you did paragraph 11 in "FINDINGS OF FACT." Otherwise leave it blank.

☞ Under "Copies to:" fill in the names and addresses for you and your spouse.

THE 20
UNCONTESTED
DIVORCE
HEARING

Court is a formal place. In this chapter we will discuss some general rules for appearing your best in court in any of the three jurisdictions. Then we explain in detail the courtroom procedures for each jurisdiction.

COURTROOM BEHAVIOR

Dress neatly, modestly and nicely for all court appearances. It is unfortunate that people judge other people by the clothes they wear, but they do. If you want the master to think you are one of the "good guys," then dress like a good guy. Women should wear little or no makeup or jewelry. Men should wear suits and ties.

Do not chew gum or smoke. Walk and stand erect. Do not slouch in the witness stand or slur your words. Be serious and forceful. Do not cover your mouth or avert your eyes.

Look at the master, commissioner, or judge when you talk. Remember, you are trying to convince the master, commissioner, or judge, so talk to him or her and not to your spouse or your spouse's attorney.

Be polite. It makes a good impression on the court. Answer "Yes sir" or "Madam" and address the master, commissioner, or judge as "your honor."

PUBLIC RECORDS

All papers filed in your case and all testimony in your case are theoretically matters of public record, and the public has a right to see or hear it. However, the only people you are likely to see at court are other people who are getting divorced themselves that day, and they are far more concerned with their own problems than with your case. Following are the specific courtroom procedures for each jurisdiction.

MARYLAND

The Master's clerk will call your case by name and number. You and your witness will come forward to the tables in front of the master's bench.

The Master will ask you to introduce yourselves and then raise your right hands to be sworn in. The Master will ask you to prove, and your witness to corroborate, by your testimony and documents, the allegations in your COMPLAINT.

At the end of the hearing, the Master will give his or her findings and recommendations that you be divorced. Once these are signed by the judge, they become your *Decree of Divorce*. It will be entered on the court docket and mailed to you a couple of weeks later.

VIRGINIA

This section explains how to conduct your uncontested divorce hearing in Virginia.

The clerk's office can tell you whether there are Commissioners appointed to hear divorce cases in your county. Where it is available, the Commissioner procedure has several advantages. One advantage of this procedure is early and easier scheduling. Another advantage is that many Commissioners will conduct the hearing and ask all the questions. If so, the complainant only has to appear with the witness and listen to the questions and answer them truthfully.

Once the Commissioner is appointed, call his or her office to schedule the hearing and find out whether the Commissioner will conduct the examination of the witness. If not, you have to prepare your questions in advance. The hearing is usually in the Commissioner's office, not in court.

After the hearing, the Commissioner will prepare and file a written report and send you a copy. If all has gone as expected, the Commissioner will report facts entitling the parties to a divorce.

Be sure to review the report carefully to make sure that the essential facts are correct. Check spellings of names, dates of marriage, birth and separation, etc. If there is a problem, contact the Commissioner's office and request that it be corrected. If it is not corrected several days before the objection period runs, you may file an objection to the report. After the Commissioner's report is filed and the objection period has run, file the proposed FINAL DECREE OF DIVORCE with the clerk of the court. (See Chapter 19, Preparing for the Uncontested Divorce Hearing.)

APPEARING
BEFORE A JUDGE

When no Commissioner is appointed, you have more work to do in preparing for and conducting the divorce hearing. First, the complainant should prepare a proposed final decree. (See Chapter 19, Preparing for the Uncontested Divorce Hearing.) The facts that the final decree recites as "appearing" are the facts to be proven at the hearing. You and your witness will testify to these facts. Also, write out a list of questions for which those facts are the answers.

The facts must be proven by the testimony of complainant and a corroborating witness, not the defendant. In selecting a witness, the complainant should choose an adult who can testify to all the essential facts from personal knowledge. Pick a person who will take the matter seriously, will listen carefully to you before the hearing and at the hearing, and will appear on time and testify truthfully.

Be sure to ask the corroborating witness all these questions before the hearing so that you know what the witness will answer. If the witness does not know the answer or remembers the events differently from you, check to make sure your memory is correct and refresh his or her memory before the date of trial or, if necessary, find another witness.

In addition to witnesses, two exhibits are generally required, the marriage certificate and the *Separation Agreement*.

You can give your own testimony in short declarative sentences. You can write these out or, if you are comfortable with it, use a copy of the decree as your talking points for your testimony. Be careful not to leave out any essential facts.

Arrive at the courthouse well before the time your hearing is scheduled and take care that your witness does so as well. If you are late and miss your call, you will have to sit through the entire docket before your case is called again. In some courts, this could include sitting through hearings on contested motions or even, trial of contested cases. Go into the courtroom and observe a few cases if possible.

When your case is called, go to the appropriate table or lectern or approach the judge's bench, depending on what you have observed. When you address the judge, be serious and respectful. State your name and that you are the complainant in the case. You will be sworn in and then may proceed with your case. Tell the judge you are your first witness. The judge may or may not direct you to the witness seat. In either case give your testimony in a serious business-like way.

Look at the judge when you give your testimony, but you can refer to the proposed decree or other prepared notes. Identify the agreement and the certificate of marriage by telling the judge what they are. When testifying try to stay "in character" as a witness and not the person conducting the case. When you are through testifying, indicate this to the judge and return to your role as the person conducting the case. Ask the judge to accept the agreement and the certificate of marriage into evidence. Then call your corroborating witness to testify.

Ask the witness the questions in the order you asked them before court and use the same words. If the witness is nervous and cannot remember something, you can probably get away with what lawyers call *leading questions*. A leading question is one that suggests the answer, e.g. "Isn't it true that ..." When you are finished with your questions to the corroborating witness, tell the court that concludes your case.

Ask the court to grant your divorce and to ratify and approve the agreement and incorporate but not merge it into its decree. If appropriate, ask the judge to restore you to the use of your given name.

FINAL DECREE
OF DIVORCE

After the judge gives his or her ruling, thank the judge. In most counties, the judge will sign the Decree at the conclusion of the hearing if the divorce is granted. You may be able to walk the file to the clerk's office and leave with two certified copies of the FINAL DECREE OF DIVORCE that day. Ask the clerk's office prior to the hearing whether you can do this. If so, ask the judge after he signs the Decree. Once the FINAL DECREE OF DIVORCE is signed by the judge and entered into the court's records, you are divorced.

DISTRICT OF COLUMBIA

You will receive a notice of the hearing date in the mail. The plaintiff has to move the case forward and provide evidence so he or she needs to be there. The defendant is invited to the hearing, but does not have to attend.

No
Corroborating
Witness

You do not need a corroborating witness in the District of Columbia, but you must prove your case. The plaintiff can testify to prove his or her six month's residency in D.C., but if the **Complaint** is based on the defendant's residency in D.C., you may need a witness to corroborate that if the defendant is not present. The marriage license can corroborate your marriage. If you do not have it, then you need a witness who was at your wedding. The plaintiff can prove the other issues through his or her testimony, such as the separation and the agreement. You do not need to have the *Separation Agreement* at court, but we usually introduce a copy of it as an exhibit to corroborate your testimony. If there are no children, alimony, or property issues to be decided by the court, you can simply say that.

Hearing

The Commissioner's clerk will call your case by name and number. Come forward to the tables in front of the Commissioner's bench. The clerk will ask you to raise your right hand and be sworn in. The Commissioner will ask you to introduce yourself. The Commissioner will ask you questions and you will give testimony to prove the allegations in your **Complaint**.

The Commissioner will then give his or her findings, usually reading from the proposed order that you have submitted. The Commissioner will sign the order, and you are divorced. A copy will be mailed to you after the clerk enters it on the court records.

SECTION 5:
CONTESTED DIVORCE

PREPARING FOR A CONTESTED DIVORCE TRIAL 21

A contested case begins the same way as an uncontested divorce in all three jurisdictions—with a COMPLAINT, SERVICE OF PROCESS, and an ANSWER by your spouse. If the ANSWER from your spouse denies any allegation of your COMPLAINT, then you have a *contested* case. Preparing for a contested divorce trial is similar in the three jurisdictions, and where there are differences, we point them out in this chapter.

SETTLEMENT NEGOTIATIONS

As you read this, keep in mind that settlement negotiations can go on simultaneously with litigation, and over 90% of contested cases settle and turn into uncontested cases before trial. While it is not impossible for you to try a contested case without a lawyer, this is the time to consider hiring one.

SCHEDULING CONFERENCE
The court will notify you of a *Scheduling Conference* in Maryland and Virginia, or an *Initial Conference* in the District of Columbia, as soon as the AFFIDAVIT OF SERVICE or ANSWER has been filed. At the Scheduling Conference, the court will set various dates for your trial. The court will not hear argument about your case.

CUSTODY DISPUTES
If custody is disputed, the court may divide the case into two trials and give you two schedules. The first trial will be the custody trial, and it will determine all issues related to the children, such as child custody, visitation and support. The other trial, called the merits trial, will determine everything else including the remaining financial issues, such as alimony and property division, as well as grounds for divorce.

PARENTING
CLASSES

The court may order *parenting classes* if custody is contested. These are usually taught by mental health professionals for two evening sessions in a classroom setting.

CUSTODY
MEDIATION

The court will order two sessions with a custody *mediator* if custody is contested. The mediators are mental health professionals on the court staff ad they have a high rate of success in settling custody cases.

ALTERNATIVE
DISPUTE
RESOLUTION

The court may also require you to participate in *Alternative Dispute Resolution (ADR)* unless there has been domestic violence or you both agree that it would be futile. ADR facilitators are experienced family lawyers who will attempt to help you settle the financial issues in your case.

PENDENTE LITE
HEARING

If you need temporary support, you will need to work with the master or commissioner to set a *Pendente Lite* Hearing. The lawyers and master or commissioner may refer to this as a "P.L. Hearing." Be sure to tell the master or commissioner the temporary relief you need, such as visitation, child support, spousal support, expert witness fees, and/or attorney fees.

SCHEDULING
ORDER

At the end of the Scheduling Conference, the clerk will usually give you several papers about your case, including a Scheduling Order. Check the Scheduling Order before you leave the courtroom to make sure that everything you asked for is listed.

The Scheduling Order will also set dates for identification of expert witnesses, cut-off of discovery, and a pre-trial hearing. You will need to tell the other side, in writing, the names, addresses and telephone numbers of your expert witnesses, and what they will be testifying about.

PENDENTE LITE
RELIEF

The master or commissioner may send you to an attorney facilitator at the Scheduling Conference to see if a settlement can be reached as to *pendente lite* relief. If you can settle with the facilitator, you can avoid the Pendente Lite Hearing.

EXPERTS

Expert witnesses may be desirable in many contested cases. For example, a vocational expert can testify about potential earning ability of a spouse seeking alimony. An appraiser may testify about the value of a house, furniture or a business (although an owner may testify as to his or her opinion of values too). An appropriate therapist may testify as to grounds for divorce or custody and visitation. A financial planner or accountant may testify as to financial needs.

DISCOVERY

Discovery can be described as interrogatories, document requests, requests for admissions, and depositions. These must all be concluded within a certain time, typically three to six months, unless extended by the court. You have to ask for discovery. Then, if your spouse fails to respond to discovery or responds inefficiently, you may ask the court for an order compelling your spouse to respond. If your spouse still fails to respond, you can ask for sanctions, such as striking your spouse's pleadings and attorney fees if you have an attorney.

Each party may discover information about the other party's case. Discovery responses are due within thirty days from when they are served in Maryland and D.C., and twenty one days in Virginia, plus three days if they are mailed. Time is counted by counting the day after service as day number one. If the last day is a weekend or holiday, then you have until the next business day.

Interrogatories. Interrogatories are written questions that must be answered under oath. Parties are limited to thirty interrogatories in Maryland and Virginia, and forty interrogatories in D.C.

Requests for Documents. You can ask that your spouse produce, for your inspection and copying, documents related to the issues in your divorce, for example, bank and business records.

Requests for Admissions. You can ask your spouse to admit facts.

Depositions. You can ask oral questions of your spouse under oath. A court reporter will prepare a transcript for use in court.

PRE-TRIAL CONFERENCE

The pre-trial conference is when the master, commissioner, or judge sets the trial date. The parties are required to present pre-trial statements in Maryland, which inform the court about such matters as mediation, discovery, pending motions, disputes, agreements, trial exhibits and trial witnesses. The master, commissioner, or judge will also usually ask about the possibility of settlement. In the District of Columbia, you are required to meet with the opposing counsel two weeks before the pre-trial. You are also required to exchange copies of exhibits and an exhibit summary one week before trial.

Maryland Joint Statement of Parties Concerning Marital and Non-Marital Property. In Maryland (but not Virginia or D.C.), you are required to file a JOINT STATEMENT at the pre-trial conference. (see form 15, p.253.) This form is very important because the judge will use it at trial as a checklist to divide your property.

Prepare your own version of the JOINT STATEMENT before the pre-trial conference and mail it to your spouse. Send it with a transmittal letter inviting your spouse to sign, and keep a copy. If your spouse does not cooperate in preparing a statement, then file the one you prepared at the pre-trial conference.

To complete the JOINT STATEMENT, you will need the information from the FINANCIAL STATEMENT that you complete in Chapter 26. Then follow these steps:

☞ Fill in the top part of the form with the court, names and addresses of you and your spouse, and the case number.

☞ In section 1, list all property in the right hand column from your FINANCIAL STATEMENT that you and your spouse agree is marital property. In general, this includes any property acquired during the marriage. The exceptions are listed in section 2 of the form. Include, if applicable, real estate, bank accounts, stock, automobiles, furniture and furnishings, jewelry, and any other property.

☞ In the second column, write how the property is titled. You may write "J" for jointly held, "H" for held in the husband's name, or "W" for held in the wife's name. There is a place for your assertion and your spouse's assertion. You can either give your opinion of value or have the property valued by an appraiser.

☞ In the third column, put your assertion of value and your spouse's assertion. It is acceptable to write "unknown" for your spouse's assertion or leave it blank if you do not know. You should place your best estimate of value in the space for your assertion.

☞ In the fourth column, fill in any debt directly attributable to an item of property, for example, the balance remaining on your mortgage goes on the line with your house, and the balance of your automobile loan goes on the line with your automobile.

☞ In section 2, list in the right-hand column, all property that you and your spouse agree is non-marital, which means any property that is

• acquired by one of you before the marriage;

• an inheritance or gift from someone other than your spouse;

• excluded by agreement; or,

• directly traceable to one of these sources.

☞ For the remaining columns in section 2, follow the instructions in section 1.

☞ In section 3, list in the right-hand column, any property that you and your spouse have a dispute about whether it is marital or non-marital property.

☞ For the remaining columns in section 3, follow the instructions in section 1.

☞ Sign and date the form as plaintiff or defendant as the case may be.

TRIAL PREPARATION TIPS

We are all afraid of things we do not understand. Here are a few tips to help your prepare for trial:

● Prepare a "trial notebook" before trial. Write out your opening statement, all your questions for witnesses, and your closing argument. You can have a section on discovery and a section on legal research. Attorneys who do not prepare like this rely on thinking on their feet and are said to "shoot from the hip." Do not try this yourself.

● Review any documents you will refer to during your testimony.

● Review any statement you made.

● Visiting the court before your case may make you more comfortable about your court appearance. After you watch a few cases, you will see that no one dies or is seriously injured when testifying. You will feel better when it is your turn.

● Try not to discuss your case with anyone before trial if you can help it. One of the best ways for the opposition to trip you up is to get a statement you made before trial especially to so called "mutual friends" that does not coincide exactly with your testimony at trial.

● It is a good idea to call the court clerk a couple of days before court to make sure your case will be heard. Often cases are continued by the court for one reason or another, and you do not want to waste a trip if it is avoidable.

THE 22 CONTESTED DIVORCE TRIAL

This chapter will describe the basics of a contested divorce trial. The procedures for a contested divorce trial are basically the same in Maryland, Virginia, and the District of Columbia, with the exception of the MARYLAND JOINT PROPERTY STATEMENT. However, each court and each Judge will do things a little differently.

ELEMENTS OF THE TRIAL

At trial, the parties present witnesses, testimony, and documents called *exhibits*. The plaintiff goes first and then the defendant. Each side can ask questions (*cross-examine*) of the witnesses of the others. At the conclusion of the trial, the judge will usually grant a divorce and give a decision as to custody, visitations, child support, alimony, property, and legal fees.

RULES OF EVIDENCE

The court uses the *Rules of Evidence* at trial. These are intricate legal rules to which volumes of books are devoted. You will generally be able to maneuver these rules in a divorce if you remember that only testimony based on personal knowledge is permitted. You cannot testify about what someone else told you ("hearsay").

NOTE: *An important exception to this rule is that you can testify about what your spouse said.*

Documents like letters, reports, and appraisals require special treatment at trial. They may be objected to by the other side if there is not a live witness at court to authenticate them. The proper way to handle a document is to have the clerk mark it as an exhibit (e.g. "Plaintiff's Exhibit No. 1"). Show it to the other side. Ask the witness to identify it. Say to the judge, "Your Honor, I move the admission of Plaintiff's Exhibit No. 1 into evidence." The judge cannot base his or her decision on an exhibit you fail to move into evidence.

A contested trial starts with the clerk calling the case name and number. The judge will ask both parties to introduce themselves and inquire as to whether they are ready for trial.

PRELIMINARY MATTERS

Preliminary matters, which would include any unresolved motions, are first. The rule on witnesses, which you usually must ask for to get, requires all witnesses except the parties to leave the courtroom until they are called. That is so they cannot listen to the testimony and be tempted to change theirs.

OPENING STATEMENTS

The judge will then ask for *opening statements*. The plaintiff goes first and the defendant follows. Use the opening statement to give the judge a summary of your case. Tell him or her the important issues and what evidence you will present. We always start our statements like this, "Good Morning, Your Honor. May it please the court, the evidence will show..."

THE PLAINTIFF'S CASE

The plaintiff's case begins next and the plaintiff calls the first witness, usually the plaintiff. The following will describe a contested trial from the plaintiff's point of view.

DIRECT EXAMINATION

You will take the stand and be sworn in by the court clerk. This is called *direct examination*. If you do not have an attorney, the judge may ask you questions or allow you to speak in a narrative and tell your story. Your testimony will generally follow this outline:

- the parties (your name, age, address, how long you have lived there, and occupation, your spouse's name, age, address, and occupation);

- the marriage (date, place, your marriage certificate, your children (names and birthdates) and which parent the children are residing with);

- grounds for divorce;

- your financial statement;

- the joint property statement, and your opinions and evidence of values of property;

- your contributions to the marriage, monetary and non-monetary; and,

- tell the judge what you want in the way of custody, visitation, child support, alimony, property division, and legal fees.

CROSS
EXAMINATION

The defendant or his or her attorney will then cross-examine you. They can ask you questions about your testimony and try to undermine it. Listen to the question and keep your answers short.

YOUR TESTIMONY

Here are a few tips for *your* testimony.

- Stay calm and make all your remarks to the judge, not your spouse or your spouse's attorney, no matter how provoked you may be by the other side.

- Do not be a smart-aleck, or appear nervous, scared, argumentative, or angry. If your adversary baits you into becoming angry, he or she is probably trying to set you up for a trap, so keep your cool. (Lose your temper, and you may lose your case.)

- Tell the truth. It is going to come out eventually anyway, and it is better coming from you than from the other side. (If the other side catches you in a lie, you may lose your case.)

- Listen carefully to all questions. Pause, make sure you understand the question, then take your time and answer that question. You cannot give a truthful and accurate answer if you do not understand the question. If you ask, the attorney will repeat the question.

- Do not tell the court "I think" or what it "must have been." The court does not normally care what you think or what could have happened. It wants to know what actually happened. However, if you estimate a time or a cost, make sure the court knows it is an estimate. If you make a mistake during your testimony, correct it as soon as possible. Politely say something such as, "May I correct something I said earlier?"

- When the other side asks you a question you do not know the answer to, say "I do not know." Witnesses are often trapped by being led into areas about which their knowledge is inadequate. They try to save face and end up making a statement that is incorrect. This gives the other side what it needs to shoot them down. You can usually avoid the problem by saying "I do not know." In cross-examinations, most questions can be answered with "yes," "no," "I do not know," or with a simple sentence.

- Do not try to play with words. When you say things like "to the best of my recollection," people may think you are getting ready to lie to them. Do not volunteer information. Do not let the other attorney pull you into testifying more than you need to by standing there looking at you, waiting for you to add material. When you are finished with your answer, stop talking.

- One of the oldest tricks in the book is for the other side to ask you if you have discussed the case with anyone else. If the other sides asks you, then tell the truth—you have. The other side is not asking you if you have fabricated the story, but it is asking you if you have talked about it. Only a fool would go to court without having discussed the case with his or her witnesses.

- Do not let the other side trick you by asking you if you are willing to swear to what you are saying. You already did when you took the oath as a witness.

REDIRECT
EXAMINATION

You can then ask the judge for permission to explain any answer you gave on cross-examination. This is called *redirect examination.*

WITNESSES

Next you present and question your corroborating *witness* and any expert witnesses. Again, the other side will cross-examine your witnesses and you may conduct redirect examination.

If you are seeking support, you need to provide your spouse's income. Call the defendant as a witness and ask him to identify his financial statement or tax return. Then tell the judge that is your case or say, as our lawyers do, "Your Honor, that submits the plaintiff's case."

THE DEFENDANT'S
CASE

The defendant will then present his or her case, and you will have the opportunity to cross-examine the defendant and the defendant's witnesses.

REBUTTAL

At the close of the defendant's case, you can present witnesses to *rebut* anything the defendant's witnesses said.

CLOSING
ARGUMENTS

Both sides then make a *closing argument* to the judge summarizing the evidence in their favor. The plaintiff goes first, defendant follows, and then the plaintiff can respond to the defendant's argument.

DECISION

The judge will usually announce a *decision* right away ("from the bench") or may need some time in more complex cases ("taken under advisement"). You may not like the judge's decision. The judge may not always believe everything you said, may not understand part of your case, or may just disagree with you. Judges are not always right, but we pay them to be the decision makers. And we have a Court of Appeals to look over their shoulder if they do make a mistake. Now you have a decision—you can accept the judge's decision or you can appeal it.

SECTION 6:
CHILDREN

CUSTODY 23

During or after your divorce you may encounter disagreement over custody. Custody cases are the cruelest and most destructive of litigations. Be sure that the children would be significantly better off with you than the other parent before you get involved in a custody fight. Custody cases are expensive in both emotional cost and in legal cost. A custody case will automatically double your legal fees. The damage caused by winning a custody case is great; the damage caused by losing is terrifying.

LEGAL CUSTODY AND PHYSICAL CUSTODY

In Maryland, Virginia, and the District of Columbia, all parents, separated or not, have joint custody of their minor children until and unless the court orders otherwise. However, the court can determine custody and issue a custody order in a divorce. Custody consists of two parts, *legal custody* and *physical custody*. The following discussion describes custody law common to all three jurisdictions and points out where they differ. For example, the custody factors the court must consider are slightly different in each jurisdiction. Finally, we will describe custody trials and parenting plans in a discussion that is applicable to the three jurisdictions.

LEGAL CUSTODY

Legal custody means long-term parenting decisions such as education, medical, discipline and religious decisions. Legal custody can be joint, meaning both parents make decisions mutually, or the court can grant one parent sole legal custody, which means that parent makes the final long-term parenting decisions. The District of Columbia has enacted a presumption in favor of joint legal custody, except in cases of domestic abuse. Maryland and Virginia look at various factors, such as ability of the parties to agree on parenting issues, to determine the best interest of the child.

PHYSICAL CUSTODY   Physical custody means where the child lives most of the time. It is sometimes referred to as residential custody. Sometimes we avoid the term altogether and just say the children will have their primary residence with one of the parents.

BEST INTEREST OF THE CHILDREN

The legal standard in deciding who will get custody is what is in the *best interest of the children*. Every judge sees it differently. There are no courts in Maryland, Virginia, or the District of Columbia where the mother has an automatic edge in litigation. Fathers win in at least half of the litigated cases, except when the children are very young.

There are also certain doctrines and presumptions in all three jurisdictions (but not inflexible rules or requirements) that aid the court in determining the best interest of the child.

Parental rights. Parents must be shown to be unfit before the children will be given to someone else, such as grandparents.

Continuity of placement. If children are doing well where they are, do not mess things up by moving them.

Children's preference. A judge will consider who the children want to live with. The judge may talk with the child in private. The judge is not bound by what the child wants.

Other. The court can consider the custodian's age, health, wealth, religious beliefs, conduct, type of home, psychological evaluations; the location of the residences of the child's siblings; the child's school performance; or anything else the court considers important.

Because the factors the court will considered in determining custody are similar, but with slightly different nuances in each jurisdiction, we set them out in detail below.

Maryland Custody Factors

In determining whether to award joint legal custody in Maryland, the court will consider the following factors:

- capacity of the parents to communicate and to reach shared decisions affecting the child's welfare;

- willingness of the parents to share custody;

- fitness of the parents;

- relationship established between the child and each parent;

- preference of the child;

- potential disruption of the child's social and school life;

- geographic proximity of parental homes;

- demands of parental employment;

- age and number of children;

- sincerity of parent's request;

- financial status of the parents;

- impact on state and federal assistance;

- benefit to parents; and,

- any other factor or circumstance related to the issue. *(Taylor v. Taylor, 306 Md. 290, 508 A.2d 964 (1986).)*

Virginia Custody Factors

In Virginia, the court is required to consider the following factors in determining best interests of a child for custody arrangements:

- the age and physical and mental condition of the child, giving due consideration to the child's changing developmental needs;

- the age and physical and mental condition of each parent;

- the relationship existing between each parent and each child, giving due consideration to the positive involvement with the child's life, the ability to accurately assess and meet the emotional, intellectual and physical needs of the child;

- the role that each parent has played and will play in the future, in the upbringing and care of the child;

- the propensity of each parent to actively support the child's contact and relationship with the other parent, including whether a parent has unreasonably denied the other parent access to or visitation with the child;

- the relative willingness and demonstrated ability of each parent to maintain a close and continuing relationship with the child, and the ability of each parent to cooperate in and resolve disputes regarding matters affecting the child;

- the reasonable preference of the child, if the court deems the child to be of reasonable intelligence, understanding, age, and experience to express such a preference;

- any history of family abuse; and,

- any other factors that the court deems necessary and proper. (Virginia Code, Sec. 20-124.3.)

DISTRICT OF COLUMBIA CUSTODY FACTORS

There is a rebuttable presumption that joint legal custody is in the best interests of the child; unless child abuse, neglect, parental kidnaping or other intrafamily violence has occurred. The court may order the parents to submit a written parenting plan for custody. The court will award custody, without regard to a parent's sex, sexual orientation, race, color, national origin, or political affiliations, based on the following factors:

- the preference of the child, if the child is of sufficient age and capacity;

- the wishes of the parents;

- the child's adjustment to his or her home, school, and community;

- the mental and physical health of all individuals involved;

- the relationship of the child with parents, siblings, and other significant family members;

- the willingness of the parents to share custody and make shared decisions;

- the prior involvement of the parent in the child's life;

- the geographical proximity of the parents;

- the sincerity of the parent's request;

- the age and number of children;

- the demands of parental employment;

- the impact on any welfare benefits;

- any evidence of spousal or child abuse;

- financial capability of providing custody; and,

- the benefit to the parties. (D.C. Code, Sec. 16-911(a)(5).)

CUSTODY TRIAL

If there is custody litigation in Maryland, Virginia, or the District of Columbia, you must be able to show the judge that the child is better off with you. Photographs of you and your child having a good time doing things together is useful evidence. Make sure you know the names of your children's teachers, coaches, doctor, dentist, and best friends. It does not hurt to know your children's shoe sizes, clothing sizes, favorite pajamas, and bed time story, because opposing counsel may ask you.

This is a good time to subscribe to publications such as *Parents* magazine. Buy some books about children, parenting, and getting children through divorce. Attend seminars and keep the brochures and literature. The point is to do these things for your child and yourself, not just to impress the judge.

Divorce proceedings are very emotional, and parties sometimes use children to seek revenge. Try to keep the children out of this. If they must be involved, prepare them properly without poisoning their minds about your spouse. Obtain professional advice if possible, but do not try to use your child's therapist to gain an advantage in a custody battle. Tell the children that the divorce is not their fault and that they will still have both parents.

When you discuss issues like support and property division with your spouse, do not use the children as messengers. Make a special effort to spend time with your children during this difficult time. Give them your full attention. Reassure them that both parents love them. Give them extra love now—they need it.

PARENTING PLANS

Although you may be ending your relationship as husband and wife, you will still be partners in the business of raising your children for the next several years. Just like any other business, you need a plan.

You can settle custody and avoid a custody trial in any of the three jurisdictions. These settlement agreements are often called *parenting plans*. They can be a part of a *Separation Agreement* resolving your whole divorce, or they can be stand-alone agreements before you reach a global settlement.

Parenting plans are an infinitely better resolution of custody disputes than a custody trial. Parenting plans provide much more detail than a custody order from the court. Because they are designed by the parties and not the judge, they can be much more specific about plans for parenting the children.

VISITATION 24

If the mother and father can agree on visitation, the courts of Maryland, Virginia, and the District of Columbia will usually approve their schedule. If you are able to handle visitation without dispute, sometimes the agreement will just say reasonable or liberal visitation. However, you can avoid any future disputes by having a specific visitation schedule. In this chapter, we describe visitation in general, and discuss any differences among the three jurisdictions.

TYPICAL VISITATION SCHEDULES

The sample *Guidelines for Effective Parenting* at the end of this chapter, is an example of a visitation schedule that will work in any of the three jurisdictions. The visitation schedule provides for alternating weekends, a weeknight every two weeks, two consecutive weeks in the summer, and alternating holidays.

The children are also with the mother on her birthday and Mother's Day, and with the father on his birthday and Father's Day. The children alternate spending their birthdays with each parent.

The example holiday schedule works like this: In even-numbered years, the residential parent has the children for Memorial Day, Labor Day, Halloween, Christmas Eve and Christmas morning for the winter school break. The non-residential parent has them for President's Day, Easter (spring break), Fourth of July, Thanksgiving and Christmas afternoon and evening through New Year's Day for the winter break. The schedule is reversed in odd-numbered years. Parents are encouraged to make other arrangements for other religious holidays.

If the parties are far apart, this pattern will not work. If the parties are more than 100 miles apart, the sample parenting plan then calls for fewer but longer visitation periods. The example schedule then becomes one weekend a month, seven weeks in the summer, and alternating Thanksgiving and spring vacations. You must also deal with who will provide or pay for transportation.

VISITATION DISPUTES

The courts of all three jurisdictions encourage visitation (and we do, too) except in very extraordinary circumstances. Sometimes when parents fight about visitation, they are very upset about something else that they do not believe they can fight about. It may be because they feel angry at the other spouse for leaving or it may be that they feel they gave up too much in the divorce agreement. But for whatever reason, they are involved in an argument about the children. Remember that the parent who visits regularly tends to be the parent who pays support regularly. Children benefit from having two parents.

If your approach does not seem to be working for you, then we recommend a provision in the parenting plan appointing a *parenting coordinator* or requiring a certain number of hours of mediation before going back to court. Many visitation disputes are minor, and the court is an expensive and cumbersome way to resolve whether your child was returned on time from visitation.

WITHHOLDING VISITATION

Withholding visitation from the children of the noncustodial parent pits you against the child's imagination. If the children do not see the noncustodial parent, they may begin to blame you for the noncustodial parent's having left. Also, withholding visitation to coerce the payment of child support is illegal in Maryland, Virginia, and the District of Columbia, and it never works.

The child's imagination is then on the other parent's side. The children dream about a perfect parent, and since they do not see the absent parent they do not see any flaws in that parent. You might win against many things, but you will lose against your child's imagination. A bad former spouse is not necessarily a bad parent. It may be hard to remember this, but they are two separate issues. The court can find you in contempt for withholding visitation and even change custody to the other parent.

GRANDPARENT VISITATION

Grandparents can petition the court for visitation in Virginia and Maryland. The courts will usually grant reasonable visitation with grandparents if it is in the best interest of the grandchildren. However, if the parents have a different visitation schedule than the grandparents, the United States Supreme Court has ruled there is a presumption that the parent's schedule is in the best interest of the child. This presumption can be overcome in certain circumstances, for example, when the parent is refusing any visitation with the grandparents at all.

The District of Columbia is the only jurisdiction in the United States where the courts have ruled that visitation is a right that is attached to custody. So D.C. grandparents, since they do not have custody, do not have automatic visitation rights. They must rely on the agreement of the parents to have visitation with their grandchildren.

┌─────────────────┐
│   SAMPLE   │
└─────────────────┘

MONTGOMERY COUNTY
GUIDELINES FOR EFFECTIVE PARENTING

I. Preamble

Maryland has established the public policy that it is in the child's best interest to maintain contact with the non-residential parent through liberal and meaningful visitation. However, portions of these guidelines may not apply to (1) a child from birth to age three or (2) to a child who, for whatever reason, has been separated from the non-residential parent for a significant period of time.

II. General Rules

1. Each parent (and any subsequent spouse) will refrain from exercising undue influence over the child with regard to the other parent, criticizing the other parent in the presence of the child, inducing the child to challenge the authority of the other parent, or encouraging the child to request a change of custody or to resist visitation. Neither parent will interrogate the child about the other parent.

2. Each parent will refrain from interfering with the custody or visitation rights of the other parent and will take steps to ensure that any parent's subsequent spouse or partner so refrains.

3. Parents will communicate directly with each other concerning the child, and will not require the child to deliver messages (including child support payments) to the other parent. Parents will ensure that their respective subsequent spouses do not interfere with the parents in matters concerning the child.

4. Each parent has the right and responsibility to make decisions concerning the child's daily routine when the child is in that parent's care. Parents with joint legal custody have an equal right and responsibility to make long-range decisions concerning the child, including, without limitation, education, religious training, discipline, medical care, and other matters of major significance concerning the child's life and welfare. The parent without legal custody of the child retains the authority to consent to emergency surgery or other necessary medical care for the child while in his/her care when there is insufficient time to contact the parent with legal custody.

5. Each parent is permitted access to all school and medical records of the child.

(A) The parent with legal custody shall take the necessary action with the authorities of the school in which the child is enrolled to:

(1) List the other parent as a parent of the child;

- 2 -

(2) Authorize the school to release to the other parent any and all information concerning the child;

(3) Ensure that the other parent may receive copies of any notices regarding the child.

(B) The parent with legal custody shall be the parent to authorize participation in school activities, sign permission slips, request excusal from school activities and early departure. The parent without legal custody shall be permitted to authorize the same only when the child is in that parent's care and only with the consent of the parent with legal custody.

(C) If not already furnished by the child's school, the parent with legal custody will promptly transmit to the other parent any information received concerning parent-teacher meetings, school programs, athletic schedules, and any other school and extra-curricular activities in which the child may be engaged or interested. Each parent is permitted and encouraged to attend.

(D) If not already furnished to the other parent by the child's school, the parent with legal custody will promptly, after receipt of the same, furnish to the other parent a photocopy of the child's grades or report, and copies of any other reports concerning the child's status or progress.

(E) The parent with legal custody will notify the other parent of all parent-teacher conferences, which whenever possible shall be arranged at a time when both parents can attend.

(F) The parent with legal custody will authorize medical providers to release to the other parent copies of any and all information concerning medical care provided to the child and will execute any medical release form necessary for the other parent to obtain such information. The parent with legal custody will promptly inform the other parent of any illness or injury of the child which requires medical attention. Emergency surgery necessary for the preservation of the child's life or to prevent a further serious injury or condition may be authorized by either parent provided that the other parent is notified as soon as possible. Elective surgery for the child may be authorized by the parent with legal custody after notification to the other parent.

6. Under Maryland law, a move out of state with the minor children by the parent with legal custody constitutes a change in circumstances that warrants a review of the residential arrangements. Therefore, the parent with legal custody shall notify the other parent at least 45 days in advance of any contemplated move (and sooner if possible), and the parents shall cooperate to work out a new visitation schedule. In the event that a new visitation schedule cannot be agreed upon by the parents, the parents shall promptly submit the issues raised by relocation to mediation.

- 3 -

7. The parent with legal custody will encourage free communications between the child and the other parent and will not do anything to impede or restrict communications by phone or mail between the child and parent. This rule applies equally to the parent without legal custody, most especially when the child is on extended visitation with that parent.

(A) Unless specifically permitted by the Court to withhold such information, each parent will provide the other parent with the following information in advance whenever the child is with him or her: a telephone number and an address where the child may be reached, as well as the name, address and telephone number of any regular child-care provider.

(B) Unless otherwise ordered by the Court, mail between the child and parent is strictly confidential between the child and that parent, and shall not be opened or read by the other parent or any other person.

(C) One of the following rules shall apply as agreed upon by the parents, or ordered by the Court, considering the circumstances of the parents and child:

(1) Each parent is entitled to reasonable telephone access to the child during those times when the child is with the other parent. Such telephone conversations shall be private, unrecorded, and take place out of the other parent's presence, limited only by the child or the calling parent terminating the telephone call; or

(2) At the request of either parent, telephone communications between parent and child shall be at set times agreed to by the parents, taking into consideration the regular routine of the child and the child's age. Such telephone conversations shall be private, unrecorded, out of the presence of the other parent, and limited only by the child or the calling parent terminating the telephone call.

8. Neither parent shall attempt to modify the religious practice of the child as established prior to the parents' separation without first consulting with the other parent. If after consultation the parties are unable to agree, the decision of the parent with sole legal custody shall prevail. If the parents share joint legal custody, the issue shall be submitted to mediation.

9. A decision to maintain, initiate or terminate therapy for their child should be made after discussion and following an agreement by the parties, but, if they are unable to agree, the parent with sole legal custody shall make the decision, or, if the parents share joint legal custody, the issue shall be submitted to mediation.

10. The parents will schedule weekend and holiday visitation on a regular basis. The following provisions assume that the parent with legal custody is the primary "residential" parent and that the parent without legal custody is the "non-residential" parent.

- 4 -

(A) The non-residential parent will give the residential parent notice of any change to the time of pick up and return of the child for regular weekend and holiday visitation at least 48 hours before a scheduled visit, except in the case of emergency and circumstances beyond the non-residential parent's control, in which case notification of the time of exchange will be made as soon as possible.

(B) The residential parent shall furnish the non-residential parent with any prospective plans for the child's summer camp/activity schedule as soon as it is available to the residential parent. The non-residential parent will notify the residential parent of summer vacation plans with the child as soon as his/her employment schedule permits.

(C) Parents shall not ask the child to communicate with the other parent regarding visitation arrangements.

(D) The residential parent, non-residential parent, and subsequent spouses, will be diligent in having the child ready and available at the appointed times for visitation and return from visitation. The transporting parent will be prompt in picking up and delivering the child within the grace periods set out on the applicable visitation schedule.

(E) Holiday visitation commences at the regular hour as set for the commencement of weekend visitation and ends at the regular hour set for the evening of weekend visitation. Holiday visitation will have precedence over the regular visitation schedule, but will not result in weekend visitation more than three (3) weekends in a row.

(F) The residential parent will send with the child on visitation sufficient clothing and outerwear appropriate for the season to last the period of visitation. For example, in the case of an infant, the residential parent will send with the child sufficient bottles, formula and diapers necessary to last one (1) day of the visitation period. The non-residential parent will provide any additional formula and diapers necessary. The non-residential parent shall return all such clothing and other reusable items sent with the child. Soiled clothing including cloth diapers shall be laundered before return.

(G) Each parent shall provide a car seat as required by law to transport the child.

(H) The residential parent will send with the child sufficient medication for a weekend or holiday visitation period and any necessary prescription for medication necessary for the first week during an extended summer visitation. The non-residential parent will provide any additional medication necessary.

(I) No alcoholic beverage may be consumed by either parent prior to operating a motor vehicle in which the child is riding. No illegal drug may be taken by either parent at any time. As a general practice, visitation does not include picking up the child and leaving the child

-5-

with a non-family member while the visiting parent pursues personal activities. The children may be picked up by a designated family member or others acceptable to either parent and may spend a portion of the visitation time with members of the respective parent's family, including resident partners not married to that parent. Visitation does not include taking the child to a non-restaurant type bar.

(J) As much as possible during visitation, the child's customary activities will be continued. The residential parent will make every effort not to schedule activities or appointments during the other parent's visitation period. The non-residential parent shall make every effort to support the child's interests and activities, including, without limitation, sports practice and games, medical appointments, dancing and music lessons and recitals, church, school, extracurricular, parties and other social gatherings, scouting and club activities. Both parents are encouraged to attend such activities, whether scheduled during visitation or at other times, but, when such activities occur during visitation, the other parent will be respectful of the visiting parent's time.

(K) When one parent is not available to take care of the children during his or her regularly scheduled time (e.g., business trip, weekend out of town) for more than one day, that parent is encouraged to give the other parent the opportunity to take the children rather than placing the children with a third party. Such an opportunity, however, is not obligatory; nor is it to be used by either party to interfere with the other party's scheduled visitation time.

11. Extended visitation does not terminate or reduce child support for that period except on specific Order of the Court, as the child support formula amount has been calculated to take into account periods of visitation. CHILD SUPPORT AND VISITATION ARE NOT MUTUALLY DEPENDENT UPON THE OTHER. CHILD SUPPORT IS PAYABLE REGARDLESS OF VISITATION. VISITATION IS PERMITTED REGARDLESS OF THE PAYMENT OF CHILD SUPPORT.

12. Repeated violations by either parent of any of the Guidelines for Effective Parenting may constitute a material change in circumstances and may be cause for granting modification of the custody or visitation Order, changing custody, curtailing or expanding visitation, implementing a visitation adjustment policy, or instituting contempt procedures, as the situation may warrant.

III. VISITATION SCHEDULES

Parents are encouraged to establish more convenient visitation schedules by agreement.

- 6 -

VISITATION SCHEDULE A

Schedule A contemplates the parents living one (1) hour or less apart driving door to door, and includes the General Guidelines for Effective Parenting listed earlier. Schedule A provides the minimum visitation, and parents are encouraged to agree on additional visitation.

(A) Visitation by the non-residential parent on alternate weekends from Friday at 7:00 p.m. to Sunday at 7:00 p.m. (the beginning and ending times may be varied to accommodate the work schedule of the parents). Visitation on one evening during one of the weekdays between alternate visitation weekends from _____ p.m. to _____ p.m. (one hour prior to the child's normal bedtime).

(B) Mother's Day the child will be with the mother; Father's Day the child will be with the father. In the event this provision requires the child to be with the residential parent when it is the non-residential parent's normal weekend visitation, the non-residential parent will return the child by 10:00 a.m. on that day. In the event that this provision requires the child to be with the non-residential parent on a day not falling within the non-residential parent's visitation weekend, the non-residential parent may have visitation from 9:00 a.m. to 7:00 p.m.

(C) The parents will alternate having the child with him or her on the child's birthday, and each parent shall be entitled to have the child with him or her on that parent's birthday.

(D) The parents will have the child on holidays as follows: (Holiday visitation will commence and end at the regular hour set for weekend visitation, except as otherwise set forth here.)

- 7 -

EVEN-NUMBERED YEARS

RESIDENTIAL PARENT

Memorial Day:
Friday night through Monday
night.

Labor Day:
Friday night through Monday
night.

Halloween:
Halloween Day afternoon
from after school through
the morning after.

Christmas/winter break:
Christmas Eve, 9:00 a.m.
through Christmas Day,
2:00 p.m.

NON-RESIDENTIAL PARENT

President's Day:
Sunday night until Monday night.

Easter/spring break:
To coincide with vacation from
school; for example, Friday,
7:00 p.m. through week off until
Sunday, 7:00 p.m.

Fourth of July:
Night before through morning
after, except when the 4th falls on
Friday, Saturday, Sunday or Monday,
in which case visitation will commence on
Friday night and continue to the end
of the weekend or end of holiday,
whichever is later.

Thanksgiving:
To coincide with vacation from
school; for example, Wednesday
7:00 p.m. until Sunday 7:00 p.m.

Christmas/winter break:
Christmas Day, 2:00 p.m.
through New Year's Day,
7:00 p.m.

Parents will make appropriate provisions for other holidays and religious observances
regularly observed by the parents and child: example, Hanukkah and Rosh Hashanah.

ODD-NUMBERED YEARS

The above schedule is reversed as to residential parent and non-residential parent unless
otherwise indicated.

ADDITIONAL GENERAL GUIDELINES FOR VISITATION SCHEDULE A

1. Each parent shall have a period of two consecutive weeks with the child in the summer. Regular visitation shall be suspended during this period if the parent and child travel out of town. Each party should notify the other of his or her choice of the two-week period as early as possible each spring so that any conflicts can be resolved, if not by agreement of the parties, then by mediation or a Court Order.

2. The transporting parent for visitations may have a grace period of fifteen (15) minutes for pick up and delivery where the parents live within a distance of thirty (30) miles from each other. Where the one-way distance to be traveled is in excess of thirty (30) miles, the grace period is thirty (30) minutes. In the case where the visiting parent suffers an unavoidable breakdown or delay en route, the visiting parent shall promptly notify the other parent by phone of the delay.

CHILD SUPPORT 25

Maryland, Virginia, and the District of Columbia have enacted child support guidelines. In this chapter we explain the general concepts of child support, child support guidelines, and point out the differences in the three jurisdictions.

GENERAL OVERVIEW

GUIDELINES   The child support guidelines are based on the "income shares" model in Maryland, Virginia, and the District of Columbia. This model is a formula based on the relative and combined income of the parties, the number of children, and the time spent with the children.

Although the guidelines are based on gross income, a rough rule of thumb is that you probably will not have to pay more than half of your net income in combined alimony and child support. Net income is total income less taxes and child support payments from any prior cases.

The guidelines provide for an adjustment for health insurance, day care for the children, and assume that the non-custodial parent pays for the children when they are with him or her during normal visitation. If there are any extraordinary expenses (medical, educational, etc.), then the support could be higher than the guidelines. In addition to child support, the court can order you to provide such things as health insurance and can allocate tax exemptions.

Child support will be deducted from your paycheck through a wage withholding order, and paid through the registry of the court, unless there is a compelling reason to do otherwise. Child support is not taxable to the recipient nor deductible to the payor. The obligation to pay child support cannot be discharged in bankruptcy.

NON-GUIDELINE CASES

Most cases are decided by using the guidelines. But the guidelines only go up to a certain amount of combined income. The top combined income on the guidelines is $120,000 per year in Maryland and Virginia. In the District of Columbia, the guidelines go up to $75,000 per year for the payor. When the guidelines do not apply or would not result in a fair amount of child support, the court will look at the needs of the children; and the financial assets, earnings, and needs of each parent.

LENGTH OF CHILD SUPPORT

In Maryland and Virginia, the court can require support of a normal child only until age eighteen. If the child is still in high school and living at home at age eighteen, then child support will run until graduation from high school or the nineteenth birthday, whichever comes first. In the District of Columbia, the court can order child support until age twenty-one. If you have a child with a mental or physical disability, it may be possible to have support continue after this child becomes an adult.

CHILD SUPPORT MODIFICATIONS

Child support always remains subject to the court's jurisdiction to modify it. The court will modify a prior support order if there has been a material change in circumstances and modification is in the child's best interest.

Many things can amount to a material change in circumstances. Some of the more common changes are a child reaches the age at which support ends, a child changes residences from one parent to the other, one parent's income increases, or decreases substantially, or the custodial parent moves to an area with a substantially higher, or lower, cost of living.

Try to obtain your spouse's agreement to the modification before filing your request with the court. Even if the modification is agreed to, it should be put in the form of a Consent Order and filed with the court.

COLLEGE EXPENSES

Maryland, Virginia, and the District of Columbia do not require a parent to put a child through college. You can provide for college, but you must do so by agreement as the court cannot order it. If the children's needs or the parent's ability to pay support substantially changes, then child support can be raised or lowered.

Maryland Guidelines

The **Child Support Guideline Worksheets** are used to calculate the proper amount of child support. The guidelines are presumptively correct and must be followed by the master, commissioner, or judge unless there are some special circumstances that would justify deviation from the guidelines.

Sole Custody Worksheet A

The **Sole Custody Worksheet A** is used when one parent has less than 128 (35%) overnights of visitation during the year. (see form 2, p.230.) For purposes of child support calculations only, this is called *sole custody*. It results in higher child support than **Worksheet B—Shared Custody**, so there is often a struggle over the 128 overnight visitation. For example, a visitation schedule of three overnights every other weekend, one overnight in alternating weeks, alternating holidays, and several weeks in the summer usually results in more than 128 overnights.

NOTE: *That all figures requested are monthly amounts.*

Complete the worksheet (form 2, p.230) by following the line-by-line instructions that are stated on the form. (We have added some instructions for lines that are fairly complex. You may want to use this information *in addition* to the instructions with the form.)

- ☞ Complete the top portion of the form with the case caption by filling in the court, the case number, and the names of the parties.

- ☞ In the next lines, fill in the names and birth dates of your children.

- ☞ Complete all lines 1–3 as directed.

- ☞ At line 4, for the *Basic Child Support Obligation*, go to the child support tables at Appendix A. These tables show what the legislature has determined to be the costs of raising children for people at various income levels. Find the combined income from line 2 in the first column, then read across the row for the number of minor children of your marriage. Where the row and column intersect will give you the *Basic Child Support Obligation*. Put that amount in the third column of line 4.

☞   At line 4(a), put any day care or other child care expenses that are required by work.

☞   At line 4(c), you may add any additional expenses for the children that you would like the court to consider.

☞   Complete lines 5–7 as directed

☞   There is a space for comments, calculations, rebuttals, or adjustments for direct payments of extraordinary expenses by the non-custodial parent.

☞   Print your name and date the form.

SHARED CUSTODY
WORKSHEET B

The **SHARED CUSTODY WORKSHEET B** is used when the non-custodial parent has more than 128 overnights (35%) of visitation a year. (see form 3, p.231.) To complete **WORKSHEET B**:

☞   Complete the top portion of the form with the case caption by filling in the court, the case number, and the names of the parties.

☞   In the next lines, fill in the names and birth dates of your children.

☞   Complete all lines 1–4 as directed on the form.

☞   At line 5, multiply the *Basic Child Support Obligation* on line 4 by one and a half (1.5). This is because the legislature has determined that it costs one and a half times as much to raise children in a shared custody arrangement as it does when one parent has primary custody. The result is called the *Adjusted Basic Child Support Obligation.*

☞   Complete line 6 as directed.

☞   At line 7, determine the percentage of overnights with each parent by dividing line 6 by 365 and multiplying the result by 100. If either column is less than 35%, then you must use **WORKSHEET A** instead.

☞   Complete lines 8–10 as directed.

☞   For certain *Expenses* on line 11(a), (b) and (c), see the instructions for line 4(a), (b) and (c) on **WORKSHEET A**. If you pay these expenses in any other percentage than indicated on line 3 (your percentage share of income), then you will have to adjust them on the third page of **WORKSHEET B**, entitled *Adjustment Worksheet*, before you can go on. There are detailed instructions on the *Adjustment Worksheet* on how to make the adjustment calculations.

☛ Take the result from the *Adjustment Worksheet*, go back to the second page of **WORKSHEET B**, and place it on line 12, entitled *Net Adjustment*.

☛ Complete lines 12–14 as directed on the form.

☛ There is a space for comments, calculations or rebuttals including direct payments by the non-custodial parent.

☛ Print your name and date the worksheet.

NOTE: *The court may impute income to a party who voluntarily impoverishes himself or herself. This rule does not apply in the case of a mother of the child of the parties for two years from the date of birth.*

VIRGINIA GUIDELINES

In Virginia, child support is determined by using the statutory child support guidelines. The guidelines take account of the number of children, the parties' incomes, a child's extraordinary medical/dental expenses, day care and similar expenses incurred to enable a custodial parent to work, and the cost of health care coverage attributable to the children. The parties' incomes are adjusted for spousal support payable between the parties and the expenses associated with "other children", children whom a party supports who are not children of both parties.

The starting point for the calculation is finding the amount of basic child support on a schedule based on the combined income of the parties and the number of children. Extrapolate at incomes between those listed on the chart to determine the exact guidelines amount. The schedule lists the amount of basic support for combined monthly gross income of up to $10,000.

For combined monthly gross incomes above $10,000, the basic support amount must be computed by multiplying the income that is over $10,000 by the appropriate percentages and adding that result to the basic support amount for $10,000 of combined monthly gross income. These percentages are as follows:

Combined monthly income between $10,000 and $20,000

One Child	Two Children	Three Children	Four Children	Five Children	Six Children
3.1%	5.1%	6.8%	7.8%	8.8%	9.5%

Combined monthly income between $20,000 and $50,000

One Child	Two Children	Three Children	Four Children	Five Children	Six Children
2.0%	3.5%	5.0%	6.0%	6.9%	27.8%

Combined monthly income over $50,000

One Child	Two Children	Three Children	Four Children	Five Children	Six Children
1.0%	2.0%	3.0%	4.0%	5.0%	6.0%

Example: There are two children. If Father earns $6,000.00 a month and Mother earns $9,000.00 a month, their combined monthly income is $15,000.00. This is over the $10,000 limit from the basic child support table by $5,000. So you would use the maximum from the basic child support table, which is $1,577.00. Find the percentage from the above table to apply to the amount by which they are over $10,000.00 in combined income. The correct percentage from the table is 5.1%. 5.1% of $5,000.00 is $255.00. Child support is then the basic amount of $1,577.00 plus the overage of $255.00, for a total combined child support obligation of $1,832.00.

Extraordinary medical/dental expenses, work-related child care expenses, and the cost of medical insurance (assuming all these are paid by the custodial parent) are added to the basic child support to arrive at total child support. Responsibility for total child support is allocated between the parents in proportion to their incomes. The custodial parent is presumed to spend his or her share on the children directly, the noncustodial parent pays his or share to the custodial parent.

The amount determined by application of the guidelines is presumed to be correct. You may be able to overcome this presumption by showing that additional factors in your case cause the guidelines amount to be an unfair amount of child support. The additional factors that Virginia courts have recognized as warranting departure from the guidelines are discussed on the following pages.

SOLE CUSTODY
WORKSHEET

Use the **CHILD SUPPORT GUIDELINE WORKSHEET** to compute child support payable under the guidelines. (see form 2, p.282.) Complete the child support guidelines worksheet for sole custody with no spousal support, or spousal support separately computed.

☛ For the caption, enter the names of complainant and defendant, the case number, and enter the date.

☛ Complete lines 1–6 using the directions on page 283.

☛ At line 7a, look up the schedule amount of basic child support for the parties combined gross income and number of children (see Appendix H, on p.283) and enter it here.

☛ Complete lines 7b–12d using the directions on page 283.

DEVIATION FROM
GUIDELINES

The following are some of the factors listed in Virginia law as reasons for a deviation in an appropriate case:

● a written agreement of the parties for child support;

● high debt incurred during the marriage for the benefit of the children;

● imputed income to a party who does not work or does not work full time when family and other circumstances indicate that he or she can;

● extraordinary capital gains;

● tax consequences of exemption and child care expenses;

● disposition of marital property;

● age, physical, and mental condition of children;

● independent financial resources of the children; and,

● any other factors necessary to do equity.

SHARED CUSTODY
WORKSHEET

If the child or children spend more than ninety days per year with the parent with less custody, the shared custody child support guidelines apply. In addition to the factors that affect child support under the sole custody guidelines, the shared custody child support guidelines take account of the increased cost of maintaining two households with children and the ratio of the time the children spend with each parent.

Complete the **SHARED CUSTODY CHILD SUPPORT GUIDELINES WORKSHEET**. (see form 3, p.284.)

☞ At the top section, enter the names of complainant and defendant, the case number, and enter the date.

☞ Complete lines 1–14 by following the directions on page 285.

☞ At line 15, check the schedule amount of basic child support for the parties combined gross income and number of children in the child support tables in Appendix H and enter it here.

☞ Complete lines 16–40 (the remainder of the form) by following the directions on page 285.

SPLIT CUSTODY
WORKSHEET

The term *split custody* refers to the situation where each parent has custody of one or more children of these parents. Child support is computed for each household using the procedures discussed previously under *Sole Custody,* or *Shared Custody* if appropriate for the children in one or both households. The amount the father owes the mother is netted against the amount the mother owes the father and the child support order is entered for the difference.

Complete the SPLIT CUSTODY SUPPORT GUIDELINES WORKSHEET. (see form 4, p.286.)

☞ At the top, fill in the *caption* by entering the names of complainant and defendant, the case number, state whose worksheet this is, and enter the date.

☞ Complete lines 1–7 by following the directions on page 287.

☞ At line 8a, check the *Schedule Amount for Basic Child Support* for the parties' combined gross income and the number of children living with the mother and the number of children living with the father in the child support tables in Appendix H and enter it here.

☞ Complete lines 8b–12e (the remainder of the form) by following the directions on page 287.

See the discussion on page 133 under the sole custody guidelines for a list of factors that are listed in Virginia law as reasons for a deviation from the guidelines in an appropriate case.

NOTE: *If custody of the children in one or both households is shared, you cannot use the split custody worksheet. Use a sole custody worksheet to compute the support payable by one parent, and a shared custody worksheet to compute the support payable by the other parent, or two shared custody worksheets if appropriate. Then subtract the smaller support obligation obtained from the larger.*

DISTRICT OF COLUMBIA GUIDELINES

The District of Columbia child support guidelines use a formula that depends on the age of the children, the number of children, the gross income of both parents, and the actual gross earnings of the noncustodial parent. A Commissioner may award support that differs from the guidelines by plus or minus three percent for unusual circumstances. For example, a Commissioner might add three percent on a finding that the children have moderately more than average needs. Child support may be ordered to be paid through the clerk of the court.

MASTER CHILD
SUPPORT
WORKSHEET

The District of Columbia worksheet uses annual figures. (see form 2, p.335.) To complete the worksheet for D.C. child support:

- ☛ Put the case number in the upper left hand corner.

- ☛ For CP, write the name of the custodial parent (the parent the children live with most of the time). For NCP, write the name of the noncustodial parent.

- ☛ In the upper right hand corner, write the number of children resulting from your marriage and the age of the oldest. Do not include any children from other relationships.

Section I is to determine income for the custodial parent.

- ☛ Complete line 1 as directed on the form.

- ☛ On line 2, write the date and annual amount of child support paid by you for children not living with you.

- ☛ Complete lines 3–7 as directed.

Section II is to determine income for the noncustodial parent.

- ☛ Complete lines 8–9 as directed on the form.

- ☛ Line 10 is a deduction for health insurance premiums paid by the non-custodian. (You will have to complete Form A to the Master Worksheet to obtain this amount, and check it as an attached form at the top of the Master Worksheet.)

Section III shows the actual calculation for support.

- ☛ At line 12, look up the *Basic Guideline Percentage* from the tables in Appendix N. Put it as a decimal on line 12.

- ☛ Complete lines 13–23 as directed on the form.

157

DEVIATION FROM
GUIDELINES

The guidelines are presumptively correct and the Commissioner cannot deviate more than plus or minus three percent unless the application of the guideline would be unjust or inappropriate in the circumstances of a particular case. Then the Commissioner must set forth and explain in writing the reason for the deviation.

There are eight factors that may be considered to overcome the presumption:

1. the needs of the child are exceptional and require more than average expenditures;

2. the gross income of the noncustodial parent is substantially less than that of the custodial parent;

3. a property settlement provides resources readily available for the support of the child in an amount at least equivalent of the formula amount;

4. the noncustodial parent supports a dependant other than the child for who the custodial parent receives credit in the formula calculation and application of the guideline would result in extraordinary hardship;

5. the noncustodial parent needs a temporary period of reduced child support payment to permit the repayment of a debt or rearrangement of his or her financial obligations. A temporary reduction may be included in a child support order if:

   • the debt or obligation is for a necessary expenditure of reasonable cost in light of the noncustodial parent's family responsibility;

   • the time of the reduction does not exceed twelve months; and,

   • the child support order includes the amount that is to be paid at the end of the reduction period and the date that the higher payments are to commence;

6. the custodial parent provides medical insurance coverage for the child at an additional cost to the custodial parent's medical insurance coverage and the additional cost is significant in relation to the amount of child support prescribed by the guideline;

7. children of more than one noncustodial parent live in the custodial parent's household receive a child support payment from the noncustodial parent, and the resulting gross income for the custodial parent and the children in the household cause the standard of living of the children to be greater than that of the noncustodial parent; or,

8. any other exceptional circumstance that would yield an unfair result.

SECTION 7:
OTHER FINANCIAL ISSUES

FINANCIAL STATEMENTS 26

The court's Financial Statement is a convenient way of organizing the financial facts in your case. It may help you to work out a *Separation Agreement* with your spouse so that your case becomes an uncontested case.

MARYLAND (MARYLAND FORM 1)

The Court Rules require that you file a FINANCIAL STATEMENT on the court's form with your COMPLAINT if you are seeking alimony or child support. If you fail to do so, your spouse's attorney may file a *Motion to Dismiss* your COMPLAINT, where the court will simply throw out your COMPLAINT without considering it.

To complete the MARYLAND FINANCIAL STATEMENT (long form) (see form 1, p.221), follow these directions:

☛ Fill in the top part of the form with the name of the court, the names of the parties and the case number. If you do not have a case number yet, leave it blank.

☛ Put your name in the title of the form.

☛ List the names and ages of all children born or adopted as a result of the marriage.

☛ The next section of the form calls for monthly expenses in various categories. The easiest way is to determine annual expenses in each category from your check book and divide by twelve for an average month.

Then allocate expenses between you and your children. If there are two children, many expenses may be allocated one third to you and two thirds to the children. But some expenses, like rent or mortgage may not lend themselves to this type of allocation and probably should be allocated more to you. Others, like school expenses, for example, should be allocated all to the children. Total the two columns in the third column and subtotal the three columns in each category of expenses.

☞ On page 6, total the three columns and write the number of dependent children you have.

☞ Page 7 is the Income Statement. Put your gross monthly wages from your pay stub in the first line. If you get paid biweekly (as, for example, do government workers), you will have to multiply by 26 and divide by 12 to get your gross monthly wages.

☞ There are spaces for your monthly deductions, such as federal withholding, state withholding, Medicare, F.I.C.A. (Social Security), and retirement. Use the above formula if you get paid twice a week.

☞ Subtract total deductions from your gross pay to get net income from wages.

☞ Fill in any other gross income, such as alimony, part-time jobs, rentals, etc., and any deductions you have against this income. Subtract these deductions from other income for your net other income.

☞ Add your net wage income and your net other income to obtain your total monthly income.

☞ Assets and liabilities, sometimes called a balance sheet, are set forth on page 8. In the first section, list all of your assets, starting with the fair market value of any real estate owned. Then list the value of your furniture in the marital home, bank accounts, bonds, stocks and other investments, personal property, jewelry, automobiles, boats, and anything else you own. List everything you can think of owned by you or your husband. If you do not know the value, you can say "unknown" or you can estimate. You can also include footnotes if you need to explain anything to the court. Total your assets.

☞ Liabilities are debts you owe. This includes the principal balance of the mortgage on your house, automobile loans, notes payable to relatives (if someone loans you money for your divorce, be sure to document it with a promissory note and include it here), bank loans, taxes owed, and credit cards. Total the liabilities.

☞ Subtract assets from liabilities for your total net worth.

☞ Subtract total income from total expenses for the excess or deficit.

☞ Sign and date the form. Notice that by signing, you are affirming the form is true under penalties of perjury.

VIRGINIA (VIRGINIA FORM 1)

While Virginia has no state-approved financial statement form for divorce cases, some counties have their own local forms. A sample MONTHLY INCOME AND EXPENSE STATEMENT is given on page 281. This form contains only summary information regarding liquid assets and no information regarding assets such as real property, vehicles, and business interests. (It could be useful for contested child support and alimony cases.)

Complete the MONTHLY INCOME AND EXPENSE STATEMENT as follows:

Introductory Information

☞ Enter your name, date of the statement, and case number (Chancery No.) where indicated.

☞ Enter your employer's name and address, your occupation, pay period, next payday, salary/wage, and number of exemptions where indicated.

☞ List your children's names and ages.

Average Gross Pay Per Month

☞ Calculate your average gross pay per month and enter it where indicated. If you are employed, start with your pay statement. Use gross income not income subject to federal tax. Monthly income is 4.33 times weekly income. Monthly income is bi-weekly income multiplied by 26, then divided by 12. All income counts including overtime and part time jobs. If your pay varies substantially, use the year-to-date figures divided by the number of months to date in the year. If it is early in the year, use last year's divided by 12. If you are self-employed, last year's tax return is a good starting point.

☛ Calculate and enter your monthly deduction (or expense if self-employed) for: federal taxes, state taxes, FICA, health insurance, life insurance, and required retirement.

☛ Calculate average monthly net pay by deducting the amount of each of the forgoing expense categories from average gross pay per month and enter it in the block.

☛ Calculate and enter your average monthly other income. Include any money your spouse pays you and any unearned income such as interest, dividends, and capital gains.

☛ Calculate monthly net income by adding average monthly net pay and monthly other income and enter the result in this block.

Expenses

The next section of the form concerns various categories of expenses. Use your check register or print a report from your household financial management software program. If you charge living expenses to a credit card, use the credit card statements in preparing your monthly income and expense statement.

For expenses that vary monthly, it is best to use an average of the most recent twelve months. However, if an expense has changed significantly, you bought or leased a car, a child started college and you are paying tuition, do not include the months before the change in the average.

Once you have computed your actual expenses, enter that amount. The MONTHLY INCOME AND EXPENSE STATEMENT must reflect your actual expenses. If your expenses "seem high," it is you adversary's task to bring that up. If your expenses "seem low" and will hurt your arguments for support, it is up to you to prove that future expenses will be higher and explain why that is so.

Include the full amount of the expenses you incur for yourself or your children in your custody even if your spouse reimburses you, or pays the expense directly. Include your spouse's reimbursement or direct payment under other income.

Household

☛ Enter the monthly average of each of these household expense categories. If there are deferred maintenance and repairs that need to be done, or if you have recently moved and have not furnished your new home, you may want to add a footnote explaining that the expense will increase.

Utilities

☞ Enter the monthly average of each of these utility expense categories. Be sure to use a twelve-month average for electricity and gas/heating oil.

Food

☞ Enter the monthly average of each of these food expense categories. Be careful to include the cost of all the food items you pay for in cash— like your lunches, children's lunches and fast food meals. Check credit card statements for charged meals or groceries.

Automobile

☞ Enter the monthly average of each of these automobile expense categories. Include the cost of public transportation and cab fare under other transportation. If you have no car payment but you have an old car that will need replacing soon, you may enter an appropriate monthly amount under payment/depreciation.

Children's Expenses

☞ Enter the monthly average of each of these children's expenses categories. Do not be limited by the printed categories. Carefully review your expenditures over the last year to make sure that you calculate and enter all of your children's expenses.

Clothing

☞ Enter the monthly average of each of these clothing expense categories. Be sure to use a twelve-month average for new clothing purchases.

Health Expenses

☞ Enter the monthly average of each of these health expense categories. Include health insurance premiums here unless they are deducted from your paycheck. This is another category where it is important to use a twelve-month average. If you are paying off an existing doctor or dentist bill, include the monthly payment for past services as well as any current expense.

Dues

☞ Enter the monthly average of each of these dues expense categories.

Miscellaneous

☞ Enter the monthly average of each of these miscellaneous expenses categories. Do not be limited by the printed categories. Carefully review your expenditures over the last year to make sure that you calculate and enter all of your miscellaneous expenses.

Fixed Debts with Payments

☞ Enter the balance and monthly payment for any fixed debt of yours that is not a mortgage payment or car note and is not included and claimed in one of the other foregoing expense categories.

Charge Account Debt

☞ Enter the balance and average monthly payment on each of your charge account debts. Remember that you should include your average monthly charges of expenses in the appropriate categories listed above. Here you should list payment of existing balances. Do not list payment of the previous month's charges of your expenses that have been included above. That would be double-counting.

If your charge account payments are comprised of both payment of current charges and payment on existing debt, calculate the amount to enter on monthly debt payment for each as follows:

1. Add all payments on the card during the last twelve months.

2. Add all charges on the card that were claimed as expenses in the expense categories discussed on page 164.

3. Subtract the result in 2. from the result in 1., divide the remainder by 12 and enter as your monthly payment for the card. If 1. is less than 2. you have no debt payment cash expense because your debts are increasing. In this case, you can still claim the monthly average of the interest added to your account balance as an expense.

Totals Per Month

If you have a computer software spreadsheet program, you can use it to calculate the totals. Otherwise a calculator will be useful for the following calculations.

☞ Calculate subtotals for each expense category and record them in pencil on the form or elsewhere. Add the expense category subtotals and enter the result in subtotal expenses.

☞ Calculate subtotals for fixed debts with payments and for charge account debt, and record them in pencil on the form or elsewhere. Add the debt category subtotals and enter the result in subtotal debt payments.

☞ Add subtotal expenses and subtotal debts and enter the result in the total expenses block.

☞ Bring down the entry in monthly net income and enter it again in the total net income block.

☞ Subtract total expenses from total net income.

If total net income exceeds total expenses, enter the result in the balance (+) block.

If total expenses exceed total net income, enter the result in the balance (-) block.

Liquid Assets on Hand

☞ Add the current balances of your checking and savings accounts and all currency not in an account and enter the result in the Cash/Checking/Savings block. You can use your checkbook balance, that is, deduct checks you have written and mailed that have not cleared the bank.

☞ Add the balances or values of all other liquid assets and enter the result in the Other Liquid Assets block. *Liquid assets* are those that are immediately convertible into cash without significant loss of value. The current value of 100 shares of IBM stock is a liquid asset. The current value of shares of stock in the corporation through which the family business is owned and operated is not a liquid asset. A Treasury Note is a liquid asset. The note you had your brother sign to make sure he repays the money you loaned him once he graduates college and finds a job is not a liquid asset (unless he has graduated, found a job, and started repaying you).

Submitted

☞ Print or type your name under the line and sign on the line.

DISTRICT OF COLUMBIA (DISTRICT OF COLUMBIA FORM 1)

The court publishes a financial form, but it is no longer *required* by many of the judges in the new District of Columbia Family Court. However, we believe it is a good idea to complete it, because it helps you, as well as the court, focus on the financial issues in dispute.

To complete the District of Columbia FINANCIAL STATEMENT (see form 1, p.333):

☛ Put the case number and date at the top. If you do not have a case number yet, leave it blank.

☛ Put your name, Social Security number, and occupation in the boxes on the first line.

☛ Fill in the name and address of your current employer and the number of tax exemptions you claim in the boxes on the second line.

☛ Income information is on the left side of the first page. At line 1, state your monthly gross wages. If you get paid every two weeks, multiply your pay stub by 26 and divide by 12 to get monthly figures.

☛ At line 2, fill in deductions from your pay.

☛ At line 3, subtract deductions on line 2 from your gross wages on line 1 to get Monthly Net Wages.

☛ At line 4, fill in any other income you have.

☛ At line 5, fill in any deductions you have against the income on line 4.

☛ At line 6, subtract other deductions on line 5 from other income on line 4 to get Monthly Net Income from All Other Sources.

☛ At line 7, add the net incomes on lines 3 and 6 to get Total Monthly Net Disposable Income. Also put this number on line 9 in the Summary Section at the bottom of the form on the left.

☛ At line 8, add the gross incomes on lines 1 and 4 to get Total Monthly Gross Income.

☛ Now go to the right hand section of the first page and itemize your Average Monthly Expenses. If you have children, you will allocate each line of expense between you and the children. Be sure to include credit card payments under periodic payments. If you have a lawyer, do not forget to include legal fees, or loan payments if you have borrowed money for your legal fees.

☞ At the bottom left, total your monthly expenses. Also put this number in line 10 in the Summary on the bottom right of the form.

☞ At line 11 of the summary section, subtract expenses on line 10 from income on line 9 and fill in the difference. If you make more than you spend, it will be a positive number. If you have shortfall each month, it will be a negative number.

☞ On page two of the form, the first section is for liabilities. For each item that you owe, state the type of debt, to whom it is owed, the date it was incurred, the total amount, the amount you have paid to date, and the balance due. In type of debt, also indicate whether it is joint name or your name alone. Although there is no space for it, add up the total amount of debt and put the number at the end of the column.

☞ In the second section, the left side is for assets. For everything you own, you will put the value in the column marked Separate or Joint depending on how it is held. Include cash, automobiles, bank accounts, bonds, notes, real estate, stocks, personal property and any other items. Add up the total assets in each column.

☞ In the summary on the right side, you will fill in total assets from the assets side. Then divide the total amount of debt into debt in your name and joint debt, and use those numbers for total liabilities in the summary section. Subtract total liabilities from total assets in each column to get your net worth.

☞ Sign the form in front of a notary public and attach a copy of your most recent paystub.

ALIMONY 27

Alimony is *spousal support* paid by one spouse to the other. In this chapter, we first discuss different alimony issues common to all three jurisdictions. Then we discuss the differences between the jurisdictions concerning *rehabilitative* and *permanent* alimony. Finally we set forth the similar, but different factors for determining alimony in each jursidiction.

GENERAL INFORMATION

In Maryland, Virginia, and the District of Columbia, alimony is based upon the relative needs and resources of the parties. If you do not get alimony at the time of the divorce, you cannot get alimony later on. (It is possible for either spouse to receive alimony.)

TAXES AND BANKRUPTCY
There are certain important things to know about alimony. Alimony can be deducted from your paycheck by an *Earnings Withholding Order* directed to your employer. Also, alimony is taxable to the person receiving and deductible to the person paying, unless otherwise agreed. Finally, alimony is not a debt that can be descharged in bankruptcy.

REHABILITATIVE OR INDEFINITE
Alimony can be *rehabilitative* or *indefinite* in Maryland and Virginia. In D.C. there is no rehabilitative alimony, so the Court either awards indefinite alimony or no alimony. (D.C. Code, Sec. 16-912.)

Rehabilitative alimony. Rehabilitate means to restore a party to an economic functioning level, such as earning a reasonable living. The public policy is to assist the former spouse to be self-supporting. Rehabilitative alimony is temporary, so it is set for a specific time period.

Indefinite alimony. If rehabilitative alimony cannot bring about rehabilitation, for example when a spouse has a disability, then the court can, in proper circumstances, order alimony on a long-term or indefinite basis. In Maryland and Virginia, indefinite alimony may also be granted when one spouse is disabled or the incomes of the spouses are "unconscionably disparate" (meaning far apart).

Indefinite alimony is granted less often these days, except in D.C. where that is the only type of alimony available. Indefinite alimony can be raised or lowered over time if there is a change of circumstances. Indefinite usually means until you die, your spouse dies, or your spouse remarries (although alimony can continue even past remarriage in some cases).

PENDENTE LITE

You can also ask the court for *pendente lite* alimony, meaning temporary spousal support during the litigation. The test for *pendente lite* alimony is more strict than permanent alimony. It is based on the needs of the party seeking alimony and ability of the other party to pay. *Needs* is defined as necessities and suit moneys in Maryland. In Virginia it is sums necessary for maintenance and support and to enable a spouse to carry on the suit. In the District of Columbia it is that which will prevent you from becoming a ward of the state, meaning the government would have to provide welfare assistance to you.

TERMINATION

Living with someone after the divorce, regardless of whether you have sex or not, may cause indefinite alimony to be lowered or stopped. Death of one of the persons paying or receiving alimony or marriage of the person receiving alimony will terminate alimony unless the *Separation Agreement* provides otherwise.

ALIMONY FACTORS

The legislature has set out specific criteria for the court to consider in alimony awards in all three jurisdictions. Because they are similar, but with subtle differences, we set them forth below in detail.

NOTE: *They are different from the standards for pendente lite alimony.*

MARYLAND

In Maryland, the court must consider the following factors in awarding alimony:

- income from salaries, investments, etc.;

- pension, profit-sharing, and retirement plans;

- education and ability of the parties, as well as opportunities for additional education;

- length of the marriage;

- age, physical condition, and mental condition of the two parties;

- children;

- whether one of the parties should stay at home with the child of the parties instead of working;

- separate property a person has;

- marital property a person has;

- standard of living the parties enjoyed during the marriage;

- tangible and intangible contributions of a homemaker;

- the tangible and intangible contributions of one party to the education, age, or increased earning power of the other party;

- fault of one of the parties (if the court desires);

- tax consequences; and/or,

- other factors that the court considers appropriate. (Maryland Code, Family Law Article, Sec. 11-016(b).)

VIRGINIA   In Virginia, the alimony factors are:

- need for support and ability to pay;

- standard of living during the marriage;

- length of marriage;

- parties' age and health;

- effect of a child's or children's age and health on a party's ability to work outside the home;

- contributions to the family during the marriage;

- property of the parties;

- division of marital property;

- education and training, prospects for future earnings;

- time and expense involved in a party's appropriate additional training or education;

- effect of parties' decisions regarding their education, employment and parenting on the parties' current and future earning potential;

- extent to which one party has contributed to the other's education and career; and/or,

- other factors, including tax consequences, necessary to make an equitable alimony decision. (Virginia Code, Sec. 20-107.1(E).)

In Virginia, unlike Maryland and the District of Columbia, alimony may *not* be awarded to a spouse who commits adultery when that is grounds for divorce, unless *manifest injustice* would result. The judge determines what manifest injustice may be, based on the facts and circumstances of each case.

DISTRICT OF COLUMBIA

In D.C., the alimony factors are:

- length of the marriage;

- age and health;

- respective financial positions;

- need for support;

- ability to pay;

- contributions to the family during marriage; and/or,

- prospects for future earnings. (*McEachnie v. McEachnie*, 261 A.2d 169 (D.C. App. 1966).)

Unlike Maryland and Virginia, fault (for example, adultery) is not a factor for the court to consider in awarding alimony in the District of Columbia.

PROPERTY 28

The legislatures in Maryland, Virginia, and the District of Columbia have set out a process for property division by the divorce court called *equitable distribution* in all three jurisdictions. Equitable means fair, which does not necessarily mean equal. We explain in this chapter how property is equitably distributed between the spouses by the court. We then point out the differences in distribution among the three jurisdictions. Finally, we set forth in detail the similar factors in each jurisdiction the court must consider in distributing property.

EQUITABLE DISTRIBUTION

Property in all three jurisdictions includes assets and liabilities; real estate; and personal property—both tangible and intangible. Property can include houses, pensions, businesses, coin collections—almost anything. This is how the courts of Maryland, Virginia, and the District of Columbia distribute property.

1. First, the court finds and values the property (equity in the house, value of pensions, value of antique furniture).

2. Next, the court determines whether the particular piece of property is separate or non-marital property and remains with the person who owned it.

3. Then the court distributes the marital property.

If you and your spouse can agree on how things will be divided and if your agreement is reasonable, it will be approved by the court, even if it does not follow this process. If you cannot agree, the court will divide the property, provided you can prove grounds to divorce.

NON-MARITAL
PROPERTY

Non-marital, or *separate property* is usually acquired before the marriage or outside the marriage (such as by gift or inheritance), or is excluded by a valid agreement. A gift from a spouse is marital property, however. And non-marital property can be converted into marital property, for example, by mingling marital and non-marital accounts, or changing the title on premarital accounts from sole to joint.

MARITAL
PROPERTY

Marital property is usually acquired during the marriage, no matter whose name is on the title. This comes as a surprise to many of our clients. They believe that because they have worked hard or their name is on a business or stock account or pension, that it belongs to them. We have to explain that all the work efforts of each party, all the income earned, and all the assets acquired during the marriage are marital property.

Different clients see contributions to the marriage differently. When we asked one spouse about his contribution, he said that he did everything—worked late hours and weekends to provide financially for the family, while his spouse did nothing but stay at home.

When we asked his spouse about contributions during her deposition, she said she did everything—raised the kids, helped them with their homework, fed and bathed and clothed them, and kissed away their tears, while her husband contributed nothing at all because he was always working.

That is why, in dividing property, the court can look at monetary and non-monetary contributions.

DATE OF
VALUATION

In Maryland, Virginia, and the District of Columbia, the court determines the value of property on the date of the divorce; however in Virginia, pensions are valued at the date of separation. And in Virginia, you may try to convince the court that another valuation date is more appropriate than the trial date if you have good cause to do so.

DEBT

Despite an agreement for one spouse to pay a debt that is in both parties' names, if the party responsible for the debt does not pay the debt, the other party can still be sued for the debt.

Example: Mary gets the house and her husband, George, agrees to pay the mortgage. George files for bankruptcy. Mary may or may not be able to sue George. In any case, the mortgage company can foreclose on the house if the payments go unpaid and sue Mary for any unpaid balance after foreclosure. The best way to protect Mary in this case would be for George to refinance the property and to remove Mary from the debt if possible. Sometimes this is financially impossible for large debts such as houses, but can still be done with smaller debts, such as second mortgages and charge accounts.

The court can distribute *marital debt*. Marital debt is defined as that which is used to acquire a marital asset, like a mortgage or a car loan. The court can also order one party or the other to pay a certain debt, or consider debt in making a marital award. In practice, however, the court will usually leave credit card debt, school loans, and loans from family and friends alone, and may not even mention the debt in the final order.

HIDING PROPERTY

Do not hide assets. These assets are usually found and if they are, you will look like a crook to the court. The judge will have trouble believing what you say about anything after that, and the judge will not have too much trouble assessing attorney's fees against you for your behavior.

USE AND POSSESSION

If you jointly own your house, you cannot force your spouse to leave. If you change the locks, you spouse can hire a locksmith and change them again, or call the police who will probably force you to let your spouse back in. There are two exceptions to this:

- the court can order a spouse to leave for domestic violence or,

- the court can give exclusive use and possession of a house, furniture and automobile, to a parent with primary custody of the children.

The Maryland courts can order use and possession for up to three years after the divorce. The Virginia courts can only order *pendente lite* (temporary) use and possession in cases of domestic violence. The District of Columbia does not have a use and possession statute.

PETS

Some people think of their pets as children. They get into custody and visitation fights over them. However, the courts tend to view pets as personal property like a table or a lamp. You have no custody or visitation rights in a table or a lamp. If you want to make sure there are no disputes over Rover, you can put a provision in a *Prenuptial Agreement* or *Separation Agreement*.

EQUITABLE DISTRIBUTION FACTORS

In all three jurisdictions, to determine who gets what marital property, the court will consider certain factors as set forth in the following sections.

MARYLAND

In Maryland, the court will consider:

- length of the marriage;

- age, health, skills, and abilities of the parties;

177

- amount of separate property owned by each spouse;

- relative ability of the parties to acquire property in the future;

- financial needs and liabilities of the parties;

- contribution to the education or to the earning power of the other;

- contribution to the value of the marital property or the separate property;

- premarital property and postmarital property;

- financial conditions of each party;

- tax consequences;

- use and possession—allowing the custodial parent and children to continue to live in the home permanently or for a period of time (the Maryland statute permits up to three years following divorce); and/or,

- other factors that the court considers appropriate. (Maryland Code, Family Law Article, Sec. 8-205(b).)

The court must divide joint accounts equally. The court cannot change title to property (except pensions). Therefore, jointly owned items such as the house and furniture, or even a jointly owned home if there is no use and possission order, are ordered sold by a trustee and the proceeds divided equally. After calculating what marital property will be in the hands of each party, the court can then make a marital award to adjust the amounts divided equitably. A marital award is usually reduced to a *judgment*. A judgment, however, is not the same as getting cash. You may then have to *enforce* the judgment to obtain payment, which means additional legal proceedings after your divorce.

The court can distribute *marital debt* in Maryland, which is debt used to acquire marital property.

VIRGINIA   In Virginia, the factors considered are:

- contributions to family unit;

- monetary and non-monetary contributions to acquisition and maintenance of property;

- length of marriage;

- parties' age and health;

- circumstances contributing to dissolution (i.e. fault);

- how and when property was acquired;

- the parties' debts, what was received for the debt and property securing the debt, if any;

- character of property, whether it is liquid or illiquid;

- tax consequences; and/or

- other relevant factors that the court considers appropriate. (Virginia Code, Sec. 20-107.3.)

Unlike Maryland, the Virginia court can transfer title to property if it is jointly owned.

DISTRICT OF COLUMBIA

In D.C., the factors are:

- duration of the marriage;

- any prior marriage of either party;

- age;

- health;

- occupation;

- amount and sources of income;

- vocational skills;

- employability;

- assets (including non-marital property);

- debts;

- needs of each party;

- custody;

- alimony;

- future income and asset opportunity;

- contribution to assets; and/or,

- contribution as a homemaker. (D.C. Code, Sec. 16-910(b).)

This list is not exclusive, and the court must also consider all other relevant factors, such as fault and taxes. The court can transfer title to property and distribute debt in D.C.

PENSIONS

Pensions can be divided by the court by entry of a *Qualified Domestic Relations Order* (QDRO). Having a QDRO drafted, approved by the pension administer, and entered by the court is not an easy task. The stakes are usually high. If your spouse has a substantial pension earned during the marriage, you probably should hire a lawyer.

AFTER THE DIVORCE 29

Most clients think it is over when the judge grants your divorce. Divorce lawyers know better. Here is a list and explanation of possible post-divorce issues. There are the slight differences in appeal procedures between Maryland, Virginia, and the District of Columbia, but the rest (reconciliation, records, changes, bankruptcy, and the post-divorce checklist) applies to all three jurisdictions.

FINANCES

After the divorce you and your ex-spouse will have two separate households. You will have to maintain those two homes on the money with which you maintained one earlier. "Two" cannot live as cheaply as "one," especially when "two" are two separate households.

DIFFICULT FORMER SPOUSE

Furthermore, if your spouse has been a difficult person all of his or her life, it is very unlikely that going through a divorce will make him or her a less difficult person. After the divorce, you may be separated, but still connected by visitation, child support, alimony, or debt payments. In that case, you will still have to deal with the problems together.

If your spouse is difficult, then no matter how hard you tried or how well you succeed, your spouse will probably still be difficult.

APPEALS

MARYLAND

In Maryland, if your case is heard by a Master, the Master will provide *Findings and Recommendations*. You then have ten days to file *Exceptions* with the clerk. Exceptions must be in writing and state the errors you assert with particularity. You also need to order a transcript of the hearing before the master from the clerk and file it with the court.

If you request a hearing, the court will hold one within sixty days of filing your exceptions. The hearing is before a judge who will listen to your argument and make an independent decision on your case.

You then have thirty days from the date of the judge's order to file a *Notice of Appeal*. If you did not take exceptions, then you have waived your appeal rights. Once you file your Notice of Appeal, you must transmit the record of your case to the appeals court. You will then receive a briefing schedule from the appeals court. If there is no appeal, your divorce will be final thirty days after the judge signs the final decree.

VIRGINIA

You may be able to appeal from a decision in your case if you are not satisfied with the outcome. If the trial judge made an error in finding the facts or applying the law that affected the outcome, your appeal may be successful. If not, appealing to a higher (appellate) court probably will not do you any good.

The appellate courts do not rehear all the evidence. They decide based on the record of the trial court hearing, whether the trial judge made one or more mistakes and, if so, whether they were important enough to warrant changing the decision or sending the case back to the trial judge.

If your case is heard by a Commissioner and you are not satisfied with the Commissioner's report, you have ten days to file *exceptions to the report*. If a party files exceptions, the court will schedule a hearing before a judge. File the exceptions with the clerk of court, mail a copy to the opposing party and file a *Certificate of Mailing*.

If you want to appeal the decision of the trial court judge in your divorce case to the Court of Appeals, you must file a *Notice of Appeal* in the circuit court, mail a copy to the opposing party, and file a certificate listing the names, addresses, and telephone numbers of the parties and lawyers, stating that a copy of the *Notice of Appeal* has been sent to the opposing party or lawyer, and stating that a transcript of the hearing has been ordered, if one will be filed. You must also file copies of the *Notice* and *Certificate* in the Court of Appeals and pay a $25 fee. There are detailed rules about filing the trial court record, the form and content of appeal briefs and the schedule for filing briefs. There may or may not be oral argument before the Court of Appeals.

If you want to petition the Supreme Court to review your case, you must file a *Notice of Appeal* within thirty days of the date of the trial court or Court of Appeals judgment. You must obtain and file a transcript of the trial court hearing. There is no automatic right to Supreme Court review. You must file a *Petition for Appeal* in the Supreme Court within three months of the date of the circuit court judgment or thirty days from the date of the court of appeals judgment.

Your petition should be about why your case is important and ought to be heard, not just about why you should win. The opposing party can file a brief in opposition and you can file a reply brief. The Supreme Court will decide, based on the briefs and maybe oral argument, whether it will hear your appeal. If the Supreme Court decides to hear your appeal, the process continues under detailed rules of procedure similar to the rules for the court of appeals.

DISTRICT OF COLUMBIA

In the District of Columbia, you have ten days to request a review of the commissioner's decision by a judge. The ten days starts counting from the entry of your Divorce Decree on the court docket by the court clerk. A judge can extend the time by another twenty days for good cause. A judge may also review any decision on his or her own within thirty days of docketing. After the judge has reviewed the commissioner's decision and issued a decision of his or her own, you may appeal to the Court of Appeals of the District of Columbia. If there is no appeal, your divorce is effective thirty days from entry on the court record.

CHANGES

If you and your spouse or ex-spouse agree to change the terms of a court order (*Temporary Support Order*, *Final Decree*, or what have you), you must change it with another Order. If your spouse says, "You do not have to pay alimony for the next year if you will take the children to Disneyland this summer," you must get it in writing and   entered in court for it to be binding on your spouse and to protect you from contempt.

If you need to change child support or certain types of alimony, you can petition the court for a change. If you show a change of circumstances, then the court may modify those provisions. The change of circumstances that most impresses the court are those changes that are unexpected such as: "I lost my job because the company went bankrupt." The courts are less sympathetic to "I just don't want to work as hard as I used to work."

Sometimes changes that everybody knew were coming are not a change of circumstances: "When my children became teenagers, they were so much more expensive." This should have been anticipated.

RECORDS

It is very important that you keep records of payments you make or receive for alimony and child support. If you are paying, pay by check and keep all canceled checks. If you cannot prove you paid it, you might as well have not paid it. If you are receiving payments, keep a running account in a permanent place. If you cannot prove what you did get, the court might not believe you when you testify about what you did not get. It is easier for both parties, and sometimes required by law, to have payments deducted from the paycheck of the person who is paying.

BANKRUPTCY

Bankruptcy is federal law that gives overburdened debtors certain relief from payment of their debts. Divorce and bankruptcy go together like love and marriage. In our credit-driven society, family budgets are often based on two incomes supporting one household. When the one household becomes two, income can become insufficient resulting in eventual bankruptcy.

Briefly, the person who files bankruptcy is called the *debtor*. The persons or businesses owed money are called creditors. In a Chapter 7 (liquidation) bankruptcy, the debtor gives up his or her non-exempt property and receives a discharge of the obligation to pay his or her dischargeable debts. In theory creditors are paid from the debtor's non-exempt assets but in consumer cases, there is almost never non-exempt assets.

Child and spousal support obligations are not dischargeable in bankruptcy. This means if your spouse owes support and files bankruptcy and receives a discharge, his or her obligation to pay support is not affected. The creditor spouse does not need to take any action in the bankruptcy to preserve support debts. And probably the debtor spouse's ability to pay support will be improved by the discharge of his or her obligation to pay other creditors.

Non-support marital debts are not automatically excepted from the debtor spouse's discharge. Examples are property settlements, payments, and indemnification agreements. In indemnification agreements, your spouse agrees with you that he or she will pay a debt you both owe, then he or she files bankruptcy and receives a discharge of his or her obligation to the joint creditor.

These marital debts are not automatically excepted from the debtor spouse's discharge. The creditor spouse has to file a timely complaint in the bankruptcy case. The bankruptcy court may or may not decide that the marital debt should be excepted from the debtor's discharge. It depends on the relative financial circumstances of the two spouses.

In appropriate cases, the prospect of bankruptcy should be kept in mind when negotiating and drafting *Support and Property Settlement Agreements*. It is not sufficient to simply say Husband (or Wife) agrees not to file bankruptcy or agrees that all debts to the creditor spouse shall be non-dischargeable.

The best protection for creditor spouse is a lien against property of the debtor spouse, if there is substantial equity in the property. Another strategy is for the agreement to state (and perhaps show by means of financial statements) that debts that do not sound like support really are. Perhaps a simpler strategy in cases where the debtor spouse is certain or likely to file bankruptcy, is for the agreement to provide for more support and less or no property settlement.

In a Chapter 13 bankruptcy, the debtor files a plan that provides for payment of the debts, usually from future income. Chapter 13 plans are subject to various rules regarding the treatment of creditors. One such rule is that the plan must provide for full payment of "priority" claims. Debts for child or spousal support are priority claims. In a Chapter 13, the creditor spouse must file a proof of claim in the bankruptcy court to be paid under the Chapter 13 plan.

The filing of a bankruptcy case operates as an *automatic stay* of all other litigation involving the debtor, including divorce. Judgments, decrees, and orders entered in violation of the stay are generally void. If your spouse files bankruptcy during your divorce case, you should take action in the bankruptcy case to have the stay *lifted* or delay action in the divorce case until the bankruptcy case is over.

In those cases where it appears that bankruptcy is inevitable for both spouses, the possibility of a joint bankruptcy should not be overlooked. The spouses must still be husband and wife to be eligible to file a joint bankruptcy case, so the bankruptcy petition would have to be filed before entry of the divorce decree.

POST-DIVORCE CHECKLIST

Your work does not end with the divorce. Check the following list of action items to be sure you have handled the applicable issues.

❏ Complete pension fund transfers and arrange rollovers.

❏ Prepare and record deed for real estate transfer or sell property.

❏ Transfer automobile titles.

❏ Transfer bank accounts and close joint accounts.

❏ Transfer stock and close joint accounts.

❏ Transfer household items.

❏ Cancel joint credit cards or remove ex-spouse's name.

❏ Send letters to creditors and reporting agencies if your spouse has agreed to pay debt.

❏ Notify the IRS and state tax authority if you have changed address. (IRS Form 8822)

❏ Change beneficiaries on insurance policies and pension plans.

❏ Convert health insurance under COBRA by the deadline.

❏ Notify school of addresses of both parents for mailing records.

❏ Revise will.

CONCLUSION 30

Although we are at the end of the book, closing one door opens another. We come full circle again to the subject of marriage. Chances are that you will marry again. Hopefully, you will make a wiser or luckier choice the next time. In any event, you will know that marriage is a complicated and expensive contract, written in the codes, cases, and rules.

PRENUPTIAL AGREEMENTS

If you do marry again, we recommend a *prenuptial agreement* (also called *premarital* or *antenuptial agreement*) highly. This is an agreement with your new spouse to be made before the marriage. Like health insurance, car insurance, or property insurance, it protects you in the event of a calamity. The divorce rate for subsequent marriages is even higher than for first marriages. A prenuptial agreement can help you avoid problems in your next marriage.

FEEDBACK

We would like to hear from you, especially if this book helped you and you were able to use it successfully to obtain your divorce. On the other hand, if you got stuck or stumped while filling out one of the forms, if something we said was confusing or unclear, or if a clerk gives you a hard time, please tell us about your experience. We'll incorporate your feedback into future editions of this book to help others going through a divorce.

Thyden Gross and Callahan
4601 Willard Avenue
Chevy Chase, Maryland 20815
Tel: 301-907-4580
Fax: 301-907-4588
www.divorcenet.com/md/divorce
tgclawyers@smart.net

We hope this book makes your divorce less difficult, less confusing, and less painful. As we said at the outset, things will eventually get better.

GLOSSARY

A

abandonment. A spouse's unjustified departure from the marital home.

absolute divorce. A completed divorce that dissolves the bonds of matrimony and permits the parties to marry again. (Contrast with *limited divorce* and *divorce from bed and board*.)

adultery. Sexual intercourse by a married person with a person other than his or her spouse. This is immediate grounds for divorce in Maryland and Virginia.

alimony. Spousal support paid by one spouse or former spouse to the other.

alimony factors. The factors a court considers in setting the amount of alimony. They are set by statute in Maryland and Virginia and case law in the District of Columbia.

annulment. A legal proceeding whereby a court declares a marriage "never existed" because some impediment prevented a valid marriage. Thus, the marriage is nullified.

alternative dispute resolution (ADR). Any process by which legal adversaries reach a decision other than bringing the matter to trial for a judge's decision; in divorce cases, it usually refers to mediation.

appeal. Procedure by which a trial court decision is brought before a higher court for review.

C

child support. The payment the noncustodial parent pays to the custodial parent for support of the parties' children.

child support guidelines. The charts used to determine the amount of child support to be paid. The guidelines take account of objective economic factors which generally include the custodial parent's income, the noncustodial parent's income, alimony payable between the parties, the cost of health insurance, the cost of day care and usually in some fashion, either parents obligations with respect to other children, those who are not children of both parties.

circuit court. The trial court for divorce case in Maryland and Virginia. There is one in each county in Maryland. There is one in most counties and cities in Virginia, but some circuit courts cover more than one county.

collaborative family law. A settlement process in which the lawyers contract to withdraw if one of the parties decides to litigate the divorce.

commissioners. See *masters*.

conclusions of law. The basis for a court's decision in a case. The result of the judge's application of the law to his or her findings of fact in the case.

constructive desertion. A spouse's withdrawal from spousal duties and the marital relationship without leaving the marital home. Generally, this is grounds for limited divorce immediately and for absolute divorce after a waiting period.

contested divorce. A divorce in which the parties do not agree on one or more issues and bring the case to court for a contested divorce hearing.

contested divorce hearing. The hearing or trial in a divorce case in which the parties do not agree on one or more issues.

corroboration. Additional proof. The law of Maryland and Virginia require corroboration of a party's testimony to the facts entitling him or her to a divorce.

court clerk. The court hires clerks to take care of all that paperwork. There are different clerks for different tasks at the court house. The first clerk you see will be the one that processes your complaint, starts a court file, and assigns your case a number. There is also a file clerk who keeps track of all the files. The judge may also have a courtroom clerk at the hearing, and a law clerk to help research the law. (Clerks are not permitted to give you legal advice, but they can be helpful in moving your case along.)

cruelty. One spouse's mistreatment of the other that is so serious that it is grounds for divorce. Usually cruelty includes physical violence. It is generally grounds for limited divorce immediately and for absolute divorce after a waiting period.

custody. The legal right to act as parent to the children, have the children live with you, make decisions about their welfare and upbringing, etc. In a divorce case, unless the parties reach an agreement, the court decides which parent will have custody of the children.

custody evaluator or assessor. Most courts hire therapists to make an investigation and report to the court on issues of custody. The evaluator will interview you, your spouse, the children, and sometimes third parties like teachers and neighbors. The assessor usually only interviews the children and the parties. The court places great weight on the recommendations of the evaluator or assessor as to custody.

custody mediator. The court has several therapists on staff to try to resolve custody disputes. For example, you may be ordered to have two two-hour sessions with the custody mediator.

custodial parent. The parent who has custody of the children.

D

deposition. A discovery procedure. A party to litigation can compel the other party or other witnesses to submit to oral questions under oath before a court reporter.

decree of divorce. The court's decision concluding a divorce case.

desertion. Abandonment. A spouse's unjustified departure from the marital home. It is generally grounds for limited divorce immediately and for absolute divorce after a waiting period.

direct examination. A party's (or his or her attorney's) questioning of a witness that the party has called as part of his or her case in trial or hearing.

discovery. A variety of pre-trial procedures that can be used to discover facts from the other party. The most common methods are depositions, interrogatories, request for production of documents, and requests for admission.

divorce. Judicial dissolution of the bonds of matrimony between married persons.

divorce from bed and board. Virginia term for limited divorce. Judicial recognition of the separate status of the parties and a divorce for tax and many other purposes but it does not permit the parties to marry again.

divorce hearing. In an uncontested case, the hearing at which the spouse who filed a complaint for divorce presents evidence of the facts constituting grounds for divorce and of facts relevant to any other issue such as the parties' separation and property settlement agreement or the amount of child support to be paid.

domestic violence. Violence against a spouse or a person in another family or romantic relationship. The laws of Maryland, Virginia, and the District of Columbia provide special expedited procedures to meet the security and financial needs of victims of domestic violence.

E

equitable distribution. The process of identifying, valuing, and equitably dividing marital property or ordering compensatory payment from one spouse to the other.

evidence. The proofs presented at trial. A witness's answer under oath or documents or other tangible things presented by a party and accepted as evidence by the court.

exceptions. Procedure by which a master or commissioner's findings and recommendations are brought before the judge for review.

expert witnesses. Expert witnesses can give the court an expert opinion (unlike regular witnesses who can generally only report facts). For example, a therapist can testify about custody and visitation and a real estate appraiser can give values for real estate.

F

family court. The District of Columbia court that hears divorce and other family matters; part of the Superior Court.

family division. In some counties in Maryland there are special divisions of the Circuit Court that hear divorce and other family law matters.

family home. In Maryland if there are minor children, the spouse with custody can be awarded exclusive use and possession of the family home, furniture, and automobile. There is no similar process in Virginia or the District of Columbia.

findings of fact. The judge's (or other judicial officer's) decision about what he or she finds the facts to be after a trial or hearing. The findings of fact state what the judge believed and, sometimes, what he or she did not believe.

findings and recommendations. The title of the Master's report after the hearing in Maryland. In Virginia, the Commissioner's report is titled a report. In the District of Columbia, a Commissioner's report is called Findings of Fact and Conclusions of Law.

G

grounds for divorce. The legal basis for granting a divorce.

guardian ad litem. The court may appoint a lawyer for the children if custody is in dispute. This lawyer can consult with the evaluator or assessor and may also recommend which parent should have custody. In Maryland, the court sometimes appoints a *Nagle v. Hooks attorney*, which is an attorney who can waive the child-therapist privilege. (You will probably have to pay for a portion of this lawyer's fees and usually payment is required in advance.)

I

incorporated but not merged. The term used to mean that the parties' agreement is part of the court's decree, in that failure to perform will be a violation of a court order punishable by contempt. The agreement also remains a private contract that can be enforced by suit for breach of contract. Incorporation does merge the agreement with the decree in D.C. by operation of law, even if the parties agree otherwise.

indefinite alimony. Alimony that is payable until death of either party, remarriage of the payee, or further order of court. The court can modify or terminate indefinite alimony if a party shows that there has been a material change in circumstances since entry of the decree setting alimony and that the change warrants modifying or terminating alimony.

interrogatories. A discovery procedure. A party's written questions to the other party that have to be answered in writing and under oath.

J

judge. The judge will hear your case and decide your divorce.

jurisdiction. The power of a court to hear and decide the matter that is before it and bind the parties by its decision.

L

lawyers. One or both of you may hire a lawyer to represent you. In litigation, the lawyer will be called *Attorney for the Plaintiff* or *Attorney for the Defendant*. Lawyers are also sometimes referred to as *Counsel* or *Counsel of Record*.

legal custody. The right to make long term parenting decisions about the child's upbringing, health, education, religion, etc.

limited divorce. Judicial recognition of the separate status of the parties and a divorce for tax and many other purposes, but it does not permit the parties to marry again.

M

marital property. Marital property is the property that the court will equitably divide between the parties in a divorce, or that it will consider in ordering any compensating payment (monetary award) from one party to the other. Generally, this is property acquired by one or both spouses during the marriage.

masters. Masters are not quite judges, but they are appointed as special assistants to the court to hear uncontested divorces and some contested divorces in order to make recommendations to the judge. The recommendations are usually adopted by the judge.

mediation. A process by which the parties meet to discuss the disputed issues with a skilled neutral person who guides the process and helps the parties reach agreements on the issues in the case.

monetary award. The compensatory payment the court may order one spouse to pay another as an adjustment of their respective equity in marital property.

N

Nagle vs Hooks attorney. In Maryland, the court sometimes appoints an attorney who can waive the child-therapist privilege so that the therapist can testify if that is in the best interest of the child. (*Nagle vs Hooks* is the name of the case in which the court explained this requirement.)

noncustodial parent. The parent who does not have custody of the children, or if custody is shared, the parent with whom the child(ren) does not live on a full-time basis.

non-marital property. Property that was owned by a spouse prior to the marriage; acquired by gift from a third person; or, inheritance or, it is excluded from marital property by a valid agreement.

P

parenting classes. Court-sponsored classes on the negative impact of divorce on children and how to minimize it. The court may order parties to attend in contested custody cases. Maryland, Virginia, and the District of Columbia all have a parenting class program.

party. You and your spouse are the parties to the divorce. In the litigation, the person who files first is called the *Plaintiff* and the other spouse is then the *Defendant*. (In a *Separation Agreement*, you may be referred to as *Husband* and *Wife*.)

pendente lite. During the litigation; temporary, until the trial.

pendente lite alimony. Alimony ordered to be paid until the final hearing; pendent lite alimony is usually only an amount sufficient to pay for necessities.

pendente lite facilitator. Family lawyers with mediation training are available in some courts at the scheduling conference to try to help you settle temporary support and related issues.

pendente lite relief. Court orders regarding support or other matters entered during the litigation to allow the parties to maintain the status quo until the final hearing.

personal jurisdiction. The power of a court to bind a person to its decision. Acquired by proper service of process on the person or his or her voluntary appearance in the case.

physical custody. Refers to the home in which the children primarily reside. The parent who lives in that home has physical custody of the children.

pleadings. Papers filed with the court such as the COMPLAINT, ANSWER and COUNTERCLAIM.

pre-trial conference. Final conference with the court before trial. At or before the conference, the parties have to file a joint statement of marital property and a pre-trial statement regarding such things as identification of witnesses, documents, pending motions, etc.

prayer for relief. The last section of a pleading where the party tells the court what the party wants the court to do.

process servers. Your COMPLAINT can be served by mail, but if your spouse does not sign or does not accept the mail, you can have it hand-delivered by someone other than yourself.

property settlement agreement. An agreement under which the spouses divide marital property.

R

rehabilitative alimony. Alimony for a stated term to permit a party to become self supporting.

requests for production of documents. A discovery procedure. A party's written request to the other party to produce documents for inspection and copying.

S

scheduling conference. First court appearance at which the court schedules various hearings depending on the issues in the case and may schedule mediation or order the parties to attend parenting classes.

separate maintenance. Spousal support paid by one spouse or former spouse to the other.

separate property. Property that is not marital property, generally because it was owned by a spouse prior to the marriage. It may have been acquired by gift from a third party or inheritance, or it was excluded from marital property by a valid agreement.

shared custody. The noncustodial parent has custody a significant amount of time.

separation agreement. Spouses' agreement regarding the terms of their separation. In addition to the agreement that the spouse shall live separately, it will often cover matters such as child custody and support, alimony, division of property, allocation of responsibility for debt, and allocation of tax benefits.

split custody. Each parent has physical custody of one or more of the party's children.

stealth contract. The *author's term* referring to the body of law contained in statutes, rules, and cases, that govern marriage and divorce in the absence of a prenuptial agreement. Although you usually have no knowledge of this "contract" when you get married, you are deemed to have understood and agreed to it, when you get divorced.

suit money. Litigation costs the court can order one spouse to pay to another; comprised of attorney's fees, court costs, and other litigation charges such as expert witness fees.

superior court (Trial court in the District of Columbia). A similar court in Virginia and Maryland is the Circuit Court.

T

timesharing. See *visitation*.

trial. The hearing at which the parties to litigation present witness, documents and other evidence about the facts bearing on the contested issues in a case.

U

uncontested divorce hearing. The hearing at which the spouse who filed a complaint for divorce presents evidence of the facts constituting grounds for divorce and of facts relevant to any other issue such as the parties' separation and property settlement agreement or the amount of child support to be paid.

use and possession. In Maryland a spouse with custody of a minor child or children of the parties can be granted exclusive use and possession of the family home, furniture and automobile.

V

visitation. The noncustodial parent's time with the children. Sometimes referred to in an agreement and orders as *timesharing*.

W

witness. One who sees, knows, or vouches for something. Also, one who gives testimony under oath.

SECTION 8:

MARYLAND

APPENDIX A
SUMMARY OF MARYLAND DIVORCE LAWS

This will summarize the most important laws concerning divorce in Maryland. You can use this summary to find a quick answer to a question or as a starting point for further research.

SUMMARY OF MARYLAND DIVORCE LAWS

1. FILING.
(a) The Complaint is filed in the "Circuit Court of _____ County, Maryland";
(b) it is titled a " Complaint for Divorce" or "Complaint for Limited Divorce";
(c) it is filed by the "Plaintiff";
(d) the other spouse is the "Defendant";
(e) it is filed in a county where either spouse resides; and
(f) the final papers are called the "Judgment of Absolute Divorce". *Maryland Rules.*

2. RESIDENCY.
One of the parties has lived in Maryland for at least one year immediately prior to filing for divorce, or the grounds for divorce occurred in Maryland. If insanity is the grounds for divorce, residency is increased to two years. *Maryland Code; Family Law Article, Title 7, Section 7-103.*

3. GROUNDS FOR ABSOLUTE DIVORCE.
(a) the parties have voluntarily lived under separate roof for one year without interruption or cohabitation and there is no reasonable expectation of reconciliation;
(b) the parties have lived separate and apart without interruption for two years;
(c) adultery;
(d) deliberate desertion for 12 months with no chance for reconciliation;
(e) confinement for incurable insanity of at least 3 years;

(f) conviction of a felony or a misdemeanor with at least a 3-year sentence and after 1 year having been served; and
(g) cruelty and excessively vicious conduct with no reasonable expectation of reconciliation. *Maryland Code; Family Law Article, Title 7, Section 7-103.*

4. GROUNDS FOR LIMITED DIVORCE.
(a) willful desertion;
(b) cruel and excessively vicious conduct;
(b) voluntary separation and living separate and apart without cohabitation. *Maryland Code; Family Law Article, Title 7, Section 7-102.*

5. MEDIATION AND PARENTING CLASSES.
Maryland specifically declares that it is in the best interests of children that there be mediated resolutions of parental disputes regarding custody. In cases where the custody of a child is in dispute, the court may order the parents to attempt to mediate that issue, unless there is a history of physical or sexual abuse of the child. Some courts require the parents to attend parenting classes. Cases may be referred to Alternative Dispute Resolution on the financial issues as well. *Maryland Rules.*

6. UNCONTESTED DIVORCE.
Marital settlement agreements are specifically authorized by statute and may be used for full corroboration of a plaintiff's testimony that a separation was voluntary if
(a) the agreement states that the spouses voluntarily agreed to separate and
(b) the agreement was signed under oath before the application for divorce was filed.
For alimony or child support cases, each party must file

a Financial Statement Affidavit and a Child Support Guideline Worksheet is required. *Maryland Code; Courts and Judicial Procedure Article, Title 3, Section 3-409; and Title 8, Section 8-104.*

7. CHILD CUSTODY. Joint or sole custody may be awarded to either or both parents, based on the best interests of the child. Custody may be denied if the child has been abused by the parent seeking custody. The factors for consideration are established in Maryland case law, not the statute. The court shall attempt to allow the child to live in the environment and community that are familiar to the child and may allow the use and possession of the family home by the person with custody of the children for up to three years from the date of divorce. *Maryland Code; Family Law Article, Title 7, Sections 5-203, 8-208, and 9-101.*

8. CHILD SUPPORT. The court can award child support based on the child support guidelines in the statute. There is a presumption that the amount shown for support in the guidelines is correct. However, the amount may be adjusted up or down if it is shown to be inappropriate or unjust under the circumstances of the case. In determining whether the amount would be unjust, the court may consider:

(a) the terms of any marital settlement agreement between the parents, including any provisions for payments of marital debts, mortgages, college education expenses, the right to occupy the family home, and any other financial terms; and (b) the presence in the household of either parent of other children that the parent has a duty to support. *Maryland Code; Family Law Article, Title 7, Sections 12-101, 12-201, 12-202, 12-203, 12-204 and 8-206.*

9. ALIMONY. The court may award rehabilitative or indefinite alimony based on the following factors:

(a) the time necessary to acquire sufficient education and training to enable the spouse to find appropriate employment, and that spouse's future earning capacity;

(b) the standard of living established during the marriage;

(c) the duration of the marriage;

(d) the ability of the spouse from whom support is sought to meet his or her needs while meeting those of the spouse seeking support;

(e) the financial resources of the spouse seeking alimony, including marital property apportioned to such spouse and such spouse's ability to meet his or her needs independently;

(f) the comparative financial resources of the spouses, including their comparative earning abilities in the labor market;

(g) the contribution of each spouse to the marriage, including services rendered in homemaking, child care, education, and career building of the other spouse;

(h) the age of the spouses;

(i) the physical and emotional conditions of the spouses;

(j) any mutual agreement between the spouses concerning financial or service contributions by one spouse with the expectation of future reciprocation or compensation by the other;

(k) the ability of the spouse seeking alimony to become self-supporting;

(l) the circumstances which lead to the breakdown of the marriage; and

(m) any other factor the court deems just and equitable.

Indefinite alimony may only be awarded if (a) the payee spouse cannot become self-supporting, or (b) after the payee spouse has made all expected progress toward self-sufficiency, there will still be an unconscionable disparity between the spouse's living standards. *Maryland Code; Family Law Article, Title 11, Section 11-106.*

10. EQUITABLE DISTRIBUTION OF PROPERTY: The parties keep their separate property, including

(a) any gifts from third parties and inheritances;

(b) property acquired prior to the marriage (except real property held as tenants by the entireties); and

(c) property which is directly traceable to property listed in (a) or (b). Marital property, including retirement benefits and military pensions, is then divided on an equitable basis. The court may order a division of jointly owned property, a sale of the property and a division of the proceeds, or a monetary award as an adjustment of the values. The court considers the following factors:

(a) the monetary and non-monetary contributions of each spouse to the acquisition of the marital property, including contribution as a homemaker;

(b) the value of each spouse's property;

(c) the economic circumstances of each spouse at the time the division of property is to become effective;

(d) the length of the marriage;

(e) whether the property award is in stead of or in addition to alimony;

(f) how and by whom the property was acquired, including any retirement, profit-sharing, or deferred compensation plans;

(g) the circumstances that contributed to the estrangement of the spouses;

(h) the age, physical and mental condition of the spouses; and

(i) any other factor necessary to do equity and justice between the spouses. A Joint Statement of Marital and Non-Marital Property is required for trial. *Maryland Code; Family Law Article, Title 8, Sections 8-202, 8-203, and 8-205; and Maryland Rules.*

11. NAME CHANGE: A spouse's former or birth name may be restored if it is not for any illegal, fraudulent, or immoral purpose. *Maryland Code; Family Law Article, Title 7, Section 7-105.*

12. PREMARITAL AGREEMENTS. The courts will enforce premarital agreements, but Maryland does not have any specific statutes concerning premarital agreements.

APPENDIX B
CHILD SUPPORT
GUIDELINES IN MARYLAND

The Child Support Guidelines Worksheet is used to calculate the proper amount of child support. The guidelines are presumptively correct and must be followed by the Master, Commissioner or Judge unless there are some special circumstances that would justify deviation from the guidelines.

MARYLAND CHILD SUPPORT GUIDELINES

Combined Adjusted Actual Income *13342	1 Child	2 Children	3 Children	4 Children	5 Children	6 or more Children
100						
200						
300	$20 - $50 Per Month, Based					
400	On Resources And Living					
500	Expenses Of Obligor And Number Of Children Due Support					
600	85	86	87	87	88	89
650	117	118	119	121	122	123
700	149	150	152	154	155	157
750	162	183	185	187	189	191
800	170	215	217	220	222	224
850	178	245	248	251	253	256
900	184	273	276	279	282	285
950	191	296	304	307	311	314
1000	198	307	332	336	340	343
1050	205	318	360	364	368	372
1100	212	329	389	393	397	401
1150	219	339	416	421	425	430
1200	226	350	438	449	454	458
1250	233	360	451	477	482	487
1300	239	371	465	504	510	515
1350	246	382	478	532	538	544
1400	253	392	491	554	566	572
1450	260	403	504	569	594	601
1500	267	413	517	584	623	629
1550	274	424	531	599	651	658
1600	282	436	546	616	672	691
1650	288	447	559	631	688	725
1700	295	457	572	645	704	753
1750	302	467	585	660	720	770
1800	308	477	598	674	735	787
1850	315	488	611	689	751	804
1900	321	498	624	703	767	821
1950	327	506	634	715	780	835
2000	332	515	645	727	793	848
2050	338	523	655	739	806	862
2100	343	531	666	751	819	876
2150	349	540	677	763	832	890
2200	354	548	687	774	845	904
*13343						
2250	359	557	698	786	858	918
2300	365	565	708	798	871	931
2350	370	573	719	810	884	945
2400	376	582	729	822	897	959
2450	381	590	740	833	909	973

2500	386	598	750	845	922	987
2550	392	607	761	857	935	1000
2600	397	615	771	869	948	1014
2650	403	624	782	881	961	1028
2700	408	632	793	893	974	1042
2750	413	640	803	904	987	1056
2800	419	649	814	916	1000	1070
2850	424	657	824	928	1013	1083
2900	429	666	835	940	1026	1097
2950	435	675	846	953	1039	1112
3000	441	684	857	965	1053	1126
3050	446	693	868	978	1067	1141
3100	452	702	879	990	1080	1156
3150	458	710	890	1003	1094	1170
3200	463	719	901	1015	1108	1185
3250	469	728	912	1028	1121	1199
3300	475	737	923	1040	1135	1214
3350	480	746	934	1053	1148	1228
3400	486	755	945	1065	1162	1243
3450	491	764	957	1078	1176	1258
3500	497	773	968	1090	1189	1272
3550	503	782	979	1103	1203	1287
3600	508	790	990	1115	1216	1301
3650	514	799	1001	1128	1230	1316
3700	520	808	1012	1140	1244	1330
3750	525	817	1023	1152	1257	1345
3800	532	827	1035	1166	1273	1361
3850	538	837	1048	1181	1288	1378
3900	544	847	1060	1195	1303	1394
3950	551	857	1073	1209	1319	1411
4000	557	867	1085	1223	1334	1427
★13344						
4050	563	877	1097	1236	1349	1442
4100	569	886	1109	1249	1363	1458
4150	575	895	1120	1262	1377	1473
4200	581	905	1132	1275	1391	1488
4250	587	914	1143	1288	1405	1503
4300	593	923	1155	1301	1420	1518
4350	598	932	1166	1314	1434	1534
4400	604	942	1178	1327	1448	1549
4450	610	951	1189	1340	1462	1564
4500	616	960	1201	1353	1477	1579
4550	622	970	1212	1366	1491	1594
4600	628	979	1224	1379	1505	1610
4650	634	987	1234	1391	1518	1624
4700	639	995	1244	1403	1530	1637
4750	644	1003	1254	1414	1543	1650
4800	649	1011	1264	1425	1555	1663
4850	655	1019	1274	1437	1567	1676
4900	660	1027	1284	1448	1580	1689

4950	665	1035	1294	1459	1592	1703
5000	670	1043	1304	1470	1604	1716
5050	676	1051	1314	1482	1617	1729
5100	681	1059	1324	1493	1629	1742
5150	686	1067	1334	1504	1641	1755
5200	691	1075	1344	1515	1654	1768
5250	696	1083	1354	1527	1666	1781
5300	702	1091	1364	1538	1678	1794
5350	707	1099	1374	1549	1691	1807
5400	712	1107	1384	1561	1703	1821
5450	717	1115	1394	1572	1715	1834
5500	722	1123	1404	1583	1728	1847
5550	728	1131	1414	1594	1740	1860
5600	733	1139	1424	1606	1752	1873
5650	738	1147	1434	1617	1765	1886
5700	743	1155	1444	1628	1777	1899
5750	748	1163	1454	1639	1789	1912
5800	754	1171	1464	1651	1801	1926

*13345

5850	759	1179	1474	1662	1814	1939
5900	764	1187	1484	1673	1826	1952
5950	769	1195	1494	1685	1838	1965
6000	774	1203	1504	1696	1851	1978
6050	780	1211	1513	1707	1863	1991
6100	785	1219	1523	1718	1875	2004
6150	790	1227	1533	1730	1888	2017
6200	795	1235	1543	1741	1900	2030
6250	800	1243	1553	1752	1912	2044
6300	806	1251	1563	1763	1925	2057
6350	811	1259	1573	1775	1937	2070
6400	815	1266	1582	1785	1947	2081
6450	819	1271	1589	1793	1956	2091
6500	823	1277	1597	1801	1965	2100
6550	827	1283	1604	1809	1974	2110
6600	831	1289	1611	1817	1983	2119
6650	834	1294	1618	1826	1992	2129
6700	838	1300	1626	1834	2001	2138
6750	842	1306	1633	1842	2010	2148
6800	846	1311	1640	1850	2019	2157
6850	850	1317	1647	1858	2028	2167
6900	854	1323	1654	1866	2037	2176
6950	857	1329	1662	1874	2045	2186
7000	861	1334	1669	1882	2054	2195
7050	865	1340	1676	1891	2063	2205
7100	869	1346	1683	1899	2072	2214
7150	873	1351	1691	1907	2081	2224
7200	876	1357	1698	1915	2090	2233
7250	880	1363	1705	1923	2099	2243
7300	884	1369	1712	1931	2108	2253
7350	888	1374	1720	1939	2117	2262

7400	892	1380	1727	1947	2126	2272
7450	895	1386	1734	1956	2135	2281
7500	899	1391	1741	1964	2144	2291
7550	903	1397	1748	1972	2153	2300
7600	906	1402	1755	1979	2161	2309
*13346						
7650	909	1407	1761	1986	2168	2317
7700	912	1412	1768	1993	2175	2325
7750	915	1417	1774	1999	2182	2333
7800	918	1422	1780	2006	2190	2340
7850	921	1427	1786	2012	2197	2348
7900	923	1431	1792	2019	2204	2356
7950	926	1436	1798	2026	2211	2364
8000	929	1441	1804	2032	2219	2372
8050	932	1446	1810	2039	2226	2380
8100	935	1451	1817	2045	2233	2388
8150	938	1456	1823	2052	2240	2396
8200	941	1461	1829	2059	2248	2404
8250	944	1465	1835	2065	2255	2412
8300	947	1470	1841	2072	2262	2420
8350	949	1475	1847	2078	2270	2428
8400	952	1480	1853	2085	2277	2436
8450	955	1485	1860	2092	2284	2444
8500	958	1490	1866	2098	2291	2452
8550	961	1494	1872	2105	2299	2460
8600	964	1499	1878	2111	2306	2468
8650	967	1504	1884	2118	2313	2476
8700	970	1509	1890	2125	2320	2484
8750	973	1514	1896	2131	2328	2492
8800	975	1518	1901	2137	2334	2498
8850	978	1521	1906	2142	2340	2504
8900	980	1525	1910	2147	2345	2510
8950	982	1528	1915	2152	2351	2516
9000	989	1539	1928	2168	2367	2534
9050	992	1543	1933	2173	2373	2540
9100	994	1547	1938	2179	2379	2546
9150	997	1551	1943	2184	2385	2552
9200	999	1554	1948	2190	2391	2559
9250	1002	1558	1953	2195	2397	2565
9300	1004	1562	1958	2201	2403	2571
9350	1007	1566	1963	2206	2409	2578
9400	1009	1570	1967	2212	2415	2584
*13347						
9450	1012	1574	1972	2217	2421	2590
9500	1014	1577	1977	2223	2427	2596
9550	1017	1581	1982	2228	2433	2603
9600	1020	1585	1987	2234	2439	2609
9650	1022	1589	1992	2239	2445	2615
9700	1025	1593	1997	2245	2451	2622
9750	1027	1597	2001	2250	2457	2628

APPENDIX C
MARYLAND
LEGAL CLINICS

STATEWIDE PROGRAMS

Family Law Hotline
800-845-8550

House of Ruth Domestic Violence Legal Clinic
301-699-7790

Legal Aid Bureau Central Office
410-539-5340

Legal Aid Bureau, Inc.
800-999-8904

Maryland Volunteer Lawyers Service
800-510-0050

MVLS Family Law Reduced Fee Program
800-300-1009

Pro Se Hotline
800-818-9888

Pro Bono Legal Services Project
410-263-8330

LOCAL PROGRAMS

ALLEGANY/GARRETT COUNTIES

Allegany County
301-777-7474

Allegany County Legal Services Program
301-724-3931

Allegany Law Foundation
301-722-3390

Garrett County
301-334-8832

ANNE ARUNDEL COUNTY

Anne Arundel County Bar Foundation
410-280-6962

Anne Arundel County Lawyer Referral Service
410-280-6961

Legal Aid Bureau
800-666-8330

BALTIMORE CITY

Baltimore Bar Pro Bono Project
410-539-5418

Lawyer Referral and Information Service
410-539-3112

Legal Aid Bureau Cherry Hill Office
410-355-4223

BALTIMORE COUNTY

Legal Aid Bureau
410- 296-6705

Lawyer Referral Service
410- 337-9100

CAROLINE/KENT/TALBOT/ QUEEN ANNE'S COUNTIES

Legal Aid Bureau
410-758-2543

Lawyer Referral Service
Caroline County
410-479-1343

Mid-Shore Council on Family Violence
410- 479-1149

CHARLES/CALVERT/ ST. MARY'S COUNTIES

Calvert County
410- 535-3278

Charles County
301-932-6661

St. Mary's County
301- 884-5935

FREDERICK/CARROLL/ WASHINGTON COUNTIES

Carroll County
800-679-8813

Domestic Violence Program
Family and Children Services
410-857-0077

Heartly House
Domestic Violence Legal Services
301-662-8800

Lawyer Referral Service
Carroll County
800-253-4254

Washington County
800-679-8813

HARFORD/CECIL COUNTIES

Cecil County
800-444-9529

Domestic Violence
Rape Crisis Program
410-996-0444

Harford County
410-836-8202

Harford County Bar Association
410-879-3755

Harford County Lawyer Referral Service
410-836-0123

HOWARD COUNTY

Howard County Sexual Assault Center
410-290-6432

Lawyer Referral Service
Howard County Bar
410-465-2721

The Family Law Center
800-253-4254

MONTGOMERY COUNTY

Abused Persons Program
301-986-5885

Legal Aid Bureau
301-927-6800

Montgomery County Lawyer Referral
301-279-9100

Montgomery County Pro Bono Program
301-424-7651

PRINCE GEORGE'S COUNTY

**Prince George's County
Law Foundation**
301-864-8354

**Prince George's County
Lawyer Referral Service**
301-952-1440

Appendix D
Maryland Domestic Violence Shelters

If your case involves domestic violence, here is a list of shelters you can contact.

ANAPOLIS

YWCA Women's Center
  167 Duke of Gloucester Street
  Annapolis, MD 21401
  HOTLINE: 410-22-7273

ARNOLD

YWCA Domestic Violence Shelter1
  517 Ritchie Highway
  Arnold, MD 21012
  HOTLINE: 410-222-7273

BALTIMORE

Family and Children's Services Central MD
  7131 Liberty Rd.
  Baltimore, MD 21207
  HOTLINE: 410-828-6390

Family Crisis Center of Baltimore County, Inc.
  Baltimore, MD 21224
  410-285-4357

House of Ruth
  2201 Argonne Drive
  Baltimore, MD 21218
  HOTLINE: 410-889-7884

Karis Home
  1228 East Baltimore Street
  Baltimore, MD 21203
  410-342-1323

Marian House I and II
  949 Gorsuch Avenue
  Baltimore, MD 21218
  410-467-4121

Sexual Assault and Domestic Violence Center
  6229 North Charles Street
  Baltimore, MD 21212
  HOTLINE: 410-828-6390

YWCA
  Eleanor D. Corner House
  128 West Franklin Street
  Baltimore, MD 21201
  410-685-1460

BEL AIR

Sexual Assault/Spouse Abuse Resource
21 W. Courtland Street
Bel Air, MD 21014
HOTLINE:410-836-8430

**Sexual Assault/Spouse Abuse
Resource Center, Inc.**
48 E. Gordon St.
Bel Air, MD 21014
HOTLINE: 836-8430

BETHESDA

Abused Persons Program
4905 Del Ray Avenue, #200
Bethesda, MD 20895
HOTLINE: 301-654-1881

BRENTWOOD

**Family Crisis Center of
Prince George's County**
3601 Taylor Street
Brentwood, MD 20722
HOTLINE: 301-731-1203

CALIFORNIA

St. Mary's Women's Center
California, MD 20619
301-862-3636

Walden - Sierra, Inc.
California, MD 20619
HOTLINE: 301-863-6661

COLMAR MANOR

**Family Crisis Center, Inc.
of Prince George's City**
3611 43rd Avenue
Colmar Manor, MD 20722
HOTLINE: 301-864-9191

COLUMBIA

**Domestic Violence Center
of Howard County, Inc.**
8950 Rt. 108
Columbia, MD 21045
HOTLINE: 410-997-2272

CUMBERLAND

Family Crisis Resource Center, Inc.
153 Baltimore Street
Cumberland, MD 21502
HOTLINE: 301-759-9244

DENTON

**Mid-Shore Council on
Family Violence, Inc.**
Denton, MD 21629
HOTLINE: 410-822-5276

ELDERSBURG

The Unity Group, Inc.
Eldersburg, MD 21784
410-795-4849

ELKTON

**Cecil County Domestic Violence/
Rape Crisis Pro.**
Elkton, MD 21922
HOTLINE: 410-996-0444

Wayfarer's House
107 Delaware Avenue
Elkton, MD 21921
410-398-4381

FREDERICK

Heartly House, Inc.
Frederick, MD 21705
HOTLINE: 301-662-8800

Safe Harbor
Frederick, MD 20678
410-535-1121

HAGERSTOWN

**Citizen's Assisting &
Sheltering the Abused CASA**
116 West Baltimore Street
Hagerstown MD 21740
HOTLINE: 301-739-8975

**Citizens Assisting and
Sheltering the Abused**
116 West Baltimore Street
Hagerstown, MD 21740
HOTLINE: 301-739-8975

OAKLAND

**Domestic Violence/Sexual Assault
Resource Center**
Oakland, MD 21550
HOTLINE: 301-334-9000
Toll Free #: 800-894-DVSA

**Domestic Violence/
Sexual Assault Center, Inc.**
12978 Garrett Highway
Oakland, MD 21550
HOTLINE: 800-656-4673

PRINCE FREDERICK

**Abused Persons Program/
Calvert County Health Dept**
Prince Frederick, MD 20678
HOTLINE: 410-535-1121

SALISBURY

**ACTS Ministry Inc. Martha's
Life Crisis Center**
Salisbury, MD 21803
HOTLINE: 410-749-HELP

Life Crisis Center, Inc.
Salisbury, MD 21803
HOTLINE: 410-749-HELP

SILVER SPRING

**Maryland Network Against
Domestic Violence**
11501 Georgia Ave.
Silver Spring, MD 20902
301-942-0900

TOWSON

Place
40 East Burke Ave.
Towson, MD 21204
410-825-8773

WESTMINSTER

**Domestic Violence Program, Family &
Children's Service**
22 North Court St.
Westminster, MD 21157
HOTLINE: 410-857-0077

**Human Services Program
Carroll County, Inc.**
Family, Men's and Women's Shelters
10 Distillery Drive
Westminster, MD 21157
410-857-2999

WHITE PLAINS

Center for Abused Persons
4305 Charles Crossing Dr.
White Plains MD 20695
HOTLINE: 301-645-3336

APPENDIX E
MARYLAND WEBSITES

You will find an abundance of information about divorce in Maryland on the Internet. Here are some of the best websites.

About Divorce in Maryland
divorcesupport.about.com/cs/maryland

ALL LAW Maryland Page
www.alllaw.com/state_resources/maryland

Children's Rights Council of Maryland
www.members.tripod.com/~mdcrc

Divorce Law Info
www.divorcelawinfo.com

Divorcenet Family Law Advisor
www.divorcenet.com/md/divorce

Family Mediation Services
www.familymediator.com/lawlinks.html

Fathers Rights to Custody
www.deltabravo.net/custody/tgbmd.htm

Maryland Child Support Enforcement
www.dhr.state.md.us/csea/index.htm

Maryland Homepage
www.courts.state.md.us

Maryland Legal Aid
www.mdlab.org

Maryland Legal Links
www.lawlib.state.md.us/screens/mdgen.html

Maryland Manual Online
www.mdarchives.state.md.us/msa
/mdmanual/html/mmtoc.html

Montgomery County Circuit Court
www.co.mo.md.us/judicial/circuit/family.html

People's Law Library
www.peoples-law.org

The Divorce Resource Network
www.divorceresourcenetwork.com

The Tao of Divorce
www1.shore.net/g7Etao.contents.html

**The Women's Law Center
of Maryland, Inc.**
www.wlcmd.org

APPENDIX F
MARYLAND BLANK FORMS

TABLE OF FORMS

Circuit Court for_____ **Case No.**_____

City or County

Name _____		Name _____
	VS.	
Street Address _____ Apt. #		Street Address _____ Apt. #
( )		( )

City   State Zip Code   Area   Telephone
                              Code
		City State Zip Code Area Telephone
		                              Code

Plaintiff		*Defendant*

FINANCIAL STATEMENT
(Long)
(DOM REL 31)

Children	Age

MONTHLY EXPENSES

ITEM	SELF	CHILDREN	TOTAL
A. PRIMARY RESIDENCE			
Mortgage			
Insurance (home owners)			
Rent/Ground Rent			
Taxes			
Gas & Electric			
Electric Only			
Heat (Oil)			
Telephone			
Trash Removal			

DR 31 - 13 February 2001

Water Bill			
Cell Phone/Pager			
Repairs			
Lawn & Yard Care (snow removal)			
Replacement Furnishings/Appliances			
Condo Fee (not included elsewhere)			
Painting/ Wallpapering			
Carpet Cleaning			
Domestic Assistance/Housekeeper			
Pool			
Other:			
SUB TOTAL			
B. SECONDARY RESIDENCE (i.e. Summer Home/Rental)			
Mortgage			
Insurance (home owners)			
Rent/Ground Rent			
Gas & Electric			
Electric Only			
Heat (Oil)			
Telephone			
Trash Removal			
Water Bill			
Cell Phone/Pager			
Repairs			
Lawn & Yard Care (snow removal)			

DR 31 - 13 February 2001

Replacement Furnishings/Appliances			
Condo Fee (not included elsewhere)			
Painting/ Wallpapering			
Carpet Cleaning			
Domestic Assistance/Housekeeper			
Pool			
Other:			
SUB TOTAL			
C. OTHER HOUSEHOLD NECESSITIES			
Food			
Drug Store Items			
Household Supplies			
Other:			
SUB TOTAL			
D. MEDICAL/DENTAL			
Health Insurance			
Therapist/Counselor			
Extraordinary Medical			
Dental/Orthodontia			
Ophthalmologist/Glasses			
Other:			
SUB TOTAL			

DR 31 - 13 February 2001

223

E. SCHOOL EXPENSES			
Tuition/Books			
School Lunch			
Extracurricular Activities			
Clothing/Uniforms			
Room & Board			
Daycare/Nursery School			
Other:			
SUB TOTAL			

F. RECREATION & ENTERTAINMENT			
Vacations			
Videos/Theater			
Dining Out			
Cable TV			
Allowance			
Camp			
Memberships			
Dance/Music Lessons etc.			
Horseback Riding			
Other:			
SUB TOTAL			

G. TRANSPORTATION EXPENSE			
Automobile Payment			
Automobile Repairs			
Maintenance/Tags/Tires/etc.			
Oil/Gas			

DR 31 - 13 February 2001

Automobile Insurance			
Other			
Parking fees			
SUB TOTAL			
H. GIFTS			
Christmas/Hanukkah			
Birthdays			
Gifts to others/holidays			
Charities			
SUB TOTAL			
I. MONTHLY CREDIT CARD EXPENSES			
a.			
b.			
c.			
d.			
Other:			
SUB TOTAL			
J. CLOTHING			
Purchasing			
Laundry			
Alterations/Dry Cleaning			
Other:			
SUB TOTAL			

DR 31 - 13 February 2001

K. INCIDENTALS			
Books & Magazines			
Newspapers			
Stamps/Stationary			
Banking Expense			
Other:			
SUB TOTAL			
L. MISCELLANEOUS/OTHER			
Church			
Synagogue			
Hairdresser/Haircuts			
Manicure/Pedicure			
Pets/Boarding			
Life Insurance			
Other:			
SUB TOTAL			
TOTAL MONTHLY EXPENSES:			

Number of Dependent Children _____

DR 31 - 13 February 2001

INCOME STATEMENT

GROSS MONTHLY WAGES:		$
Deductions:		
Federal	$	
State	$	
Medicare	$	
F.I.C.A	$	
Retirement	$	
Total Deductions:	$	
NET WAGES FROM INCOME:		
Other (Gross) Income (alimony, part-time job, etc).	$	
Other Net Income	$	
TOTAL INCOME		$

DR 31 - 13 February 2001

227

ASSETS & LIABILITIES

ASSETS:		
Real Estates/Mortgage	$	
Furniture (in the marital home)	$	
Bank Accounts/Savings	$	
U.S. Bonds	$	
Personal Property	$	
Jewelry	$	
Automobiles	$	
Boats	$	
Other:	$	
TOTAL ASSETS:		$
LIABILITIES:		
Mortgage	$	
Automobiles	$	
Notes payable to relatives	$	
Bank Loans	$	
Accrued Taxes	$	
Balance of Credit Card Accounts	$	
a.		
b.		
c.		
d.		

DR 31 - 13 February 2001

Alimony/Child Support (from a previous order)	$	
Other:		
TOTAL LIABILITIES:		$
TOTAL NET WORTH:		$
SUMMARY:		
TOTAL INCOME:		$
TOTAL EXPENSES:		$
EXCESS OR DEFICIT:		$

I solemnly affirm under the penalties of perjury that the contents of the foregoing Financial Statement, Monthly Expense List and Assets and Liabilities Statement are true to the best of my knowledge, information, and belief.

_____
Date

_____
Signature

DR 31 - 13 February 2001

Circuit Court for _____ Case No. _____
City or County

Name _____		Name _____
Street Address _____ Apt. # ___	VS.	Street Address _____ Apt. # ___
City _____ State _ Zip Code _ Area Telephone		City _____ State _ Zip Code Area Telephone
Code		Code

CHILD SUPPORT GUIDELINES WORKSHEET A
(Primary Physical Custody to One Parent)
(DOM REL 34)

Name of Child	Date of Birth	Name of Child	Date of Birth
Name of Child	Date of Birth	Name of Child	Date of Birth
Name of Child	Date of Birth	Name of Child	Date of Birth

	Mother	Father	Combined
1. MONTHLY ACTUAL INCOME (Before taxes)	$	$	
a. Minus pre-existing child support payment actually paid	-	-	
b. Minus health insurance premium (if child included)	-	-	
c. Minus alimony actually paid	-	-	
d. Plus / minus alimony awarded in this case	+/-	+/-	
2. MONTHLY ADJUSTED ACTUAL INCOME	$	$	$
3. PERCENTAGE SHARE OF INCOME (Divide each parent's income on Line 2 by the combined income on Line 2).	%	%	
4. BASIC CHILD SUPPORT OBLIGATION (Apply Line 2 Combined Income to Child Support Schedule)			$
a. Work-Related Child Care Expenses (Code, FL § 12-204(h))			+
b. Extraordinary Medical Expenses (Code, FL § 12-204(g))			+
c. Additional Expenses (Code, FL § 12-104(i))			+
5. TOTAL CHILD SUPPORT OBLIGATION (Add lines 4, 4a, 4b, and 4c).			$
6. EACH PARENT'S CHILD SUPPORT OBLIGATION (Multiply Line 3 times Line 5 for each parent).	$	$	
7. RECOMMENDED CHILD SUPPORT ORDER (Bring down amount from Line 6 for the non-custodial parent only. Leave custodial parent column blank).	$	$	$
Comments, calculations, or rebuttals to schedule or adjustments if non-custodial parent directly pays extraordinary expenses:			
PREPARED BY:			Date:

Circuit Court for_____ Case No._____

City or County

Name				VS.	Name				

Name _____

Street Address _____ Apt. # _____

City _____ State Zip Code Area Telephone
Code

Name _____

Street Address _____ Apt. # _____

City _____ State Zip Code Area Telephone
Code

CHILD SUPPORT GUIDELINES WORKSHEET B
(Shared Physical Custody)
(DOM REL 35)

Name of Child	Date of Birth	Name of Child	Date of Birth
Name of Child	Date of Birth	Name of Child	Date of Birth
Name of Child	Date of Birth	Name of Child	Date of Birth

	Mother	Father	Combined
1. MONTHLY ACTUAL INCOME (Before taxes)	$	$	
a. Minus pre-existing child support payment actually paid	-	-	
b. Minus health insurance premium (if child included)	-	-	
c. Minus alimony actually paid	-	-	
d. Plus / minus alimony awarded in this case	+/-	+/-	
2. MONTHLY ADJUSTED ACTUAL INCOME	$	$	$
3. PERCENTAGE SHARE OF INCOME (Divide each parent's income on Line 2 by the combined income on Line 2).	%	%	
4. BASIC CHILD SUPPORT OBLIGATION (Apply Line 2 Combined Income to the Child Support Schedule)			$
5. ADJUSTED BASIC CHILD SUPPORT OBLIGATION (Line 4 times 1.5)			$
6. OVERNIGHTS with each parent (must total 365)			365
7. PERCENTAGE WITH EACH PARENT (Line 6 divided by 365)	A %	B %	
STOP HERE IF Line 7 is less than 35% for either parent. Shared physical custody does not apply. Use DOM. REL. 34 instead.			

DR 35 - Revised 6 Apr 2000

231

	Mother	Father	Combined
8. EACH PARENT'S THEORETICAL CHILD SUPPORT OBLIGATION (Multiply Line 3 times Line 5 for each parent)	A$	B$	
9. BASIC CHILD SUPPORT OBLIGATION FOR TIME WITH OTHER PARENT (Multiply Line 7A times Line 8B and put answer on Line 9B. Multiply Line 7B times Line 8A and put answer on Line 9A).	A$	B$	
10. NET BASIC CHILD SUPPORT OBLIGATION (Subtract lesser amount from greater amount in Line 9 and place answer here under column with greater amount in Line 9).			
11. EXPENSES			
a. Work-Related Child Care Expenses (Code, FL § 12-204(g))			+
b. Extraordinary Medical Expenses (Code, FL § 12-204(h))			+
c. Additional Expenses (Code, FL § 12-104(i))			+
12. NET ADJUSTMENT from ADJUSTMENT WORKSHEET, below, if applicable. If not, continue to Line 13.	$	$	
13. NET BASIC CHILD SUPPORT OBLIGATION (From Line 10 of this worksheet, above.)	$	$	
14. RECOMMENDED CHILD SUPPORT ORDER (If the same parent owes money under Lines 12 and Line 13, add these two figures to obtain amount owed by that parent. If one parent owes money under Line 12 and the other owes money under Line 13, subtract the lesser amount from the greater to obtain the difference. The parent owing the greater of the two amounts on Lines 12 and 13 will owe that difference as the child support obligation. <u>NOTE</u>: The amount owed in a shared custody arrangement may not exceed the amount that would be owed if the obligor parent were a non-custodial parent. See DOM. REL. _____).	$	$	

Comments, calculations, or rebuttals including in-kind responsibility because of sharing or special adjustments because of direct payments:

PREPARED BY: Date:

DR 35 - Revised 6 Apr 2000

ADJUSTMENT WORKSHEET
(For Calculating Line 12 of Shared Physical Custody Worksheet, above)

INSTRUCTIONS FOR ADJUSTMENT WORKSHEET: *Use this Worksheet ONLY if any of the Expenses listed in Lines 11a, 11b, or 11c, is directly paid out or received by the parents in a different proportion than the percentage share of income entered on Line 3 of the Shared Physical Custody Worksheet, above. Example: If the mother pays all of the daycare, or parents split education/medical costs 50/50 and Line 3 is other than 50/50. If there is more than one 11c expenses, the calculations on Lines e and f below must be made for each expense.*

		Mother	Father
a.	Total amount of direct payments made for Line 11a expenses times each parent's percentage of income (Line 3, Shared Physical Custody Worksheet) (Proportionate share)	$	$
b.	The excess amount of direct payments made by the parent who pays more than the amount calculated in Line a, above. (The difference between amount paid and proportionate share).	$	$
c.	Total amount of direct payments made for Line 11b expenses times each parent's percentage of income (Line 3, Shared Physical Custody Worksheet).	$	$
d.	The excess amount of direct payments made by the parent who pays more than the amount calculated on Line c, above.	$	$
e.	Total amount of direct payments made for Line 11c expenses times each parent's percentage of income (Line 3, Shared Physical Custody Worksheet).	$	$
f.	The excess amount of direct payments made by the parent who pays more than the amount calculated in Line e, above.	$	$
g.	For each parent, add lines b, d and f.	$	$
h.	Subtract lesser amount from greater amount in Line g, above. Place the answer on this line under the lesser amount in Line g. Also enter this answer on Line 12 of the Shared Physical Custody Worksheet, in the same parent's column.	$	$

DR 35 - Revised 6 Apr 2000

Circuit Court for _____ Case No._____

Name _____		**Name** _____
_____	**VS.**	_____
Street Address _____ **Apt. #** ___		**Street Address** _____ **Apt. #** ___
( )		( )
City **State** **Zip Code** **Area Code** **Telephone**		**City** **State** **Zip Code** **Area Code** **Telephone**
Plaintiff		*Defendant*

COMPLAINT FOR ABSOLUTE DIVORCE
(DOM REL 20)

I, _____ , representing myself, state that:
My name

1. The Defendant and I were married on _____
Month   Day   Year
    in _____ in a civil/religious ceremony.
City/County/State where Married   (Circle One)

2. *Check all that apply:*

    ☐ I have lived in Maryland since: _____
    Month/Year

    ☐ My spouse has lived in Maryland since:_____
    Month/Year

    ☐ The grounds for divorce occurred in the State of Maryland.

3. *Check one:*

    ☐ We have no children together (skip paragraphs 5 and 6) or

    ☐ My spouse and I are the parents of the following child(ren):

Name	Date of Birth	Name	Date of Birth
Name	Date of Birth	Name	Date of Birth
Name	Date of Birth	Name	Date of Birth

4. I know of the following related cases concerning the child(ren) or parties (such as domestic violence, paternity, divorce, custody, visitation or juvenile court cases):

Court	Case No.	Kind of Case	Year Filed	Results or Status (if you know)

5. The child(ren) are currently living with :_____
    Name

6. It is in the best interests of the child(ren) that I have (*check all that apply*):

    ☐ joint / sole (*circle one*) physical custody of _____.
    Name of Children

    ☐ joint / sole (*circle one*) legal custody of _____.
    Name of Children

    ☐ visitation with _____.
    Name of Children

7.	I am / am not *(circle one)* seeking alimony because _____.

8.	*(You do not have to complete paragraph 8 if you are not asking the court to make decisions about your property.)* My spouse and/or I have the following property and debts (check all that apply):

☐ House(s)	☐ Furniture
☐ Pension(s)	☐ Bank account(s) and investment(s)
☐ Motor Vehicle(s)	☐ Other: _____
☐ Debts (attach list)	_____

9.	My grounds for an absolute divorce are: (Check all that apply)

☐ **Two-Year Separation** - From on or about _____ , my spouse and I have lived
	Month/Day/Year
separate and apart from each other in separate residences, without interruptions, without sexual intercourse, for more than two years and there is no reasonable expectation that we will reconcile.

☐ **Voluntary Separation** - From on or about _____ , my spouse and I by mutual
	Month/Day/Year
and voluntary agreement have lived separate and apart from one another in separate residences, without interruption, without sexual intercourse, for more than 12 months with the express purpose and intent of ending our marriage, and there is no reasonable expectation that we will reconcile.

☐ **Adultery** - My spouse committed adultery.

☐ **Actual Desertion** - On or about _____ , my spouse, without just cause or reason,
	Month/Day/Year
abandoned and deserted me, with the intention of ending our marriage. This abandonment has continued without interruption for more than 12 months and there is no reasonable expectation that we will reconcile.

☐ **Constructive Desertion** - I left my spouse because his/her cruel and vicious conduct made the continuation of our marriage impossible, if I were to preserve my health, safety, and self-respect. This conduct was the final and deliberate act of my spouse and our separation has continued without interruption for more than 12 months and there is no reasonable expectation that we will reconcile.

☐ **Criminal Conviction of a Felony or Misdemeanor** - On or about _____ , my
	Month/Day/Year
spouse was sentenced to serve at least three years or an indeterminate sentence in a penal institution and has served 12 or more months of the sentence.

☐ **Cruelty/Excessively Vicious Conduct Against Me** - My spouse has persistently treated me cruelly and has engaged in excessively vicious conduct rendering continuation of the marital relationship impossible if I am to preserve my health, safety, and self-respect, and there is no reasonable expectation that we will reconcile.

☐ **Insanity** - On or about _____ , my spouse was confined to a mental institution,
	Month/Day/Year
hospital, or other similar institution and has been confined for 3 or more years. Two doctors competent in psychiatry will testify that the insanity is incurable and there is no hope of recovery. My spouse or I have been a resident of Maryland for at least two years before the filing of this complaint.

DR 20 - Revised 21 Nov 2000

235

FOR THESE REASONS, I request (check all that apply):

☒ An Absolute Divorce

☐ A change back to my former name: _____
Full Former Name

☐ Sole/Joint physical custody of the minor child(ren).
(Circle One)

☐ Sole/Joint legal custody of the minor child(ren).
(Circle One)

☐ Visitation with the minor child(ren).

☐ Use and possession of the family home for up to three years from the date of the divorce.

☐ Use and possession of the family use personal property for up to three years from the date of the divorce.

☐ Child support (Attach Form DOM REL 30 or DOM REL 31).

☐ Health insurance for the child(ren).

☐ Health insurance for me.

☐ My share of the property or its value.

☐ A monetary award (money) based on marital property.

☐ Alimony (Attach Form DOM REL 31).

☒ Any other appropriate relief.

_____   _____
Date   **Signature**

Circuit Court for _____

CIVIL–DOMESTIC CASE INFORMATION REPORT

Directions:

    Plaintiff: *This Information Report must be completed and attached to the complaint filed with the Clerk of Court unless your case is exempted from the requirement by the Chief Judge of the Court of Appeals pursuant to Rule 2-111. A copy must be included for each defendant to be served.*

    Defendant: *You must file an Information Report as required by Rule 2-323(h).*

    THIS INFORMATION REPORT CANNOT BE ACCEPTED AS AN ANSWER OR RESPONSE.

FORM FILED BY: ❏ PLAINTIFF ❏ DEFENDANT   CASE NUMBER:_____

                                                   (Clerk to insert)

CASE NAME: _____ v _____

                      Plaintiff   Defendant

PARTY'S NAME:_____ PHONE: (___)_____

                                                  (Daytime phone)

ADDRESS: _____

PARTY'S ATTORNEY'S NAME: _____ PHONE: (___)_____

ATTORNEY'S ADDRESS:_____

     ❏ I am not represented by an attorney

RELATED CASE PENDING? ❏ Yes   ❏ No   If yes, Court and Case #(s), if known:_____

Special Requirements?   ❏   Interpreter/communication impairment
                             ❏   Other ADA accommodation:_____

Has Alternative Dispute Resolution (ADR):   been tried? ❏ Yes   ❏ No
                                        requested? ❏ Yes   ❏ No

If yes, specify: _____

IS THIS CASE CONTESTED?   ❏ Yes   ❏ No   If yes, which issues appear to be contested?

    ❏ Ground for divorce
    ❏ Child Custody   ❏ Visitation
    ❏ Child Support
    ❏ Alimony   ❏ Permanent   ❏ Rehabilitative
    ❏ Use and possession of family home and property
    ❏ Marital property issues involving:
        ❏ Valuation of business   ❏ Pensions   ❏ Bank accounts/IRA's   ❏ Real Property
        ❏ Other: _____
    ❏ Paternity
    ❏ Adoption/termination of parental rights
    ❏ Other: _____

Request is made for: ❏ Initial order ❏ Modification ❏ Contempt ❏ Absolute Divorce ❏ Limited Divorce

For non-custody/visitation issues, do you intend to request:
    ❏ Court-appointed expert (name field)_____   ❏ Mediation by a Court-sponsored settlement program
    ❏ Initial conference with the Court   ❏ Other: _____

For custody/visitation issues, do you intend to request:
    ❏ Mediation by a private mediator   ❏ Appointment of counsel to represent child (not just to
    ❏ Evaluation by mental health professional   waive psychiatric privilege)
    ❏ Other Evaluation _____   ❏ A conference with the Court

Is there an allegation of physical or sexual abuse of party or child?   ❏ Yes   ❏ No

CASE NAME: _____ V _____ CASE NUMBER: _____
                        Plaintiff   Defendant   (Clerk to insert)

TIME ESTIMATE FOR A MERITS HEARING: _____ hours _____ days

TIME ESTIMATE FOR HEARING OTHER THAN A MERITS HEARING: _____ hours _____ days

_____
Signature of Counsel/Party

_____
Print Name

_____
Street Address

_____
City/State/ZIP

_____
Date

Circuit Court for_____ **Case No.**_____

City or County

Name_____   Name_____

_____ **VS.**   _____
Street Address   Apt. #   Street Address   Apt. #

( )   ( )
_____   _____
City   State   Zip Code   Area   Telephone   City   State   Zip Code   Area   Telephone
                         Code   Code

Plaintiff   *Defendant*

AFFIDAVIT OF SERVICE
(Certified Mail)
(DOM REL 56)

I certify that I served a copy of the _____
Name of ALL pleadings/documents served

(which were previously filed with this Court) upon _____
Name of person served

on _____ , _____ , at _____
Date   Street Address   City   State   Zip Code

by certified mail, restricted delivery, return receipt requested. The **original** return receipt signed

by _____ is attached. Also attached is a copy of any
Name of person served

summons ("process") issued by the Court, the original of which I included in the certified mail

service upon the person served. I certify that I am over eighteen (18) years of age and I am not

the Plaintiff or the Defendant.

I SOLEMNLY AFFIRM under the penalties of perjury that the contents of the foregoing paper
are true to the best of my knowledge, information, and belief.

_____
Date

_____
Name of person certifying service (signature)

_____
Name of person certifying service (printed or typed)

_____
Street Address   City   State   Zip Code
of person certifying service

( )
_____
Area Code   Telephone Number of person certifying service

Circuit Court for_____ **Case No.**_____

City or County

Name_____   Name_____

_____ VS. _____
Street Address   Apt. #   Street Address   Apt. #

                                          (   )   (   )
City   State   Zip Code   Area   Telephone   City   State   Zip Code   Area   Telephone
                                     Code   Code

Plaintiff   *Defendant*

AFFIDAVIT OF SERVICE
(Private Process)
(DOM REL 55)

I certify that I served _____ at _____ a.m.   p.m.

Name of person served   Time   Check One

on _____ , _____ , at _____ ,

Date   Street Address   City   State   Zip Code

a copy of the _____

Name of ALL pleadings/documents served

which were previously filed with this Court. Attached is a copy of any summons ("process")

issued by the Court, the original of which I served upon the person served. I certify that I am over

eighteen (18) years of age and I am not the Plaintiff or the Defendant.

I SOLEMNLY AFFIRM under the penalties of perjury that the contents of the foregoing paper are
true to the best of my knowledge, information, and belief.

_____   _____
Date   Name of Server (signature)

                                                            _____
                                                            Name of Server (printed or typed)

                                                            _____
                                                            Street Address   City   State   Zip
                                                            of Server   Code
                                                            (   )
                                                            Area Code   Telephone Number of Server

DR 55 - Revised 8 Nov 2000

Circuit Court for_____ **Case No.**_____

_____
Name

_____ **VS.**
Street Address   Apt. #

_____
City   State Zip Code   Area   Telephone
                              Code

~~Plaintiff~~

_____
Name

_____
Street Address   Apt. #

_____
City   State Zip Code   Area   Telephone
                              Code

~~Defendant~~

MOTION FOR ALTERNATE SERVICE
(DOM REL 70)

I,_____ , representing myself state that:

My name

1. I filed the following document(s): _____

    Name of Document(s)

    with the Circuit Court for _____ on _____ ,_____ .

    County or City   Date document(s) filed

2. Since that time I have made reasonable efforts to locate the Defendant to effect service of

    process, but have been unable to do so as more fully set forth in the Affidavit below.

    FOR THESE REASONS, I request that the Court order service by posting, or in the

alternative by publication, or any other means of notice that the court may deem appropriate,

pursuant to Maryland Rule 2-121 or 2-122.

_____   _____
Date   Signature

AFFIDAVIT IN COMPLIANCE WITH

MARYLAND RULE 2-121 OR 2-122

STATE OF MARYLAND, COUNTY OF _____ :

I HEREBY CERTIFY that before me, the subscriber, a Notary Public in and for the State
and County aforesaid, personally appeared _____ , Plaintiff,

My Name

in the above-entitled case, and made oath, in due form of law as follows:

1. I filed the following document(s): _____

    Name of Document(s)

    with the Circuit Court for _____ on _____ ,_____ .

    County or City   Date document(s) filed

DR 70 - Revised 9 March 2001

2. Since that time I have attempted to serve the opposing party with that document and any related court summons in the following manner *(Check all that apply and attach appropriate documents.)*:

❐ I have attempted to serve the opposing party at _____
                                                               Address

but the opposing party has avoided service by _____ .

❐ I have tried to serve the opposing party by **certified mail** at their last known address _____ times, as shown by the attached Affidavit(s) of Service.

❐ I have tried to get the opposing party's current address by **sending letter(s) to the following relative(s) or friend(s),** as indicated by the attached copies of letters, mail return receipts, Affidavit(s) of Service and responses, if received:

Name of Person to Whom Letter Was Sent	Date Sent	Indicate whether you received a reply.
Name of Person to Whom Letter Was Sent	Date Sent	Indicate whether you received a reply.
Name of Person to Whom Letter Was Sent	Date Sent	Indicate whether you received a reply.

❐ I have tried to get the opposing party's current address by sending a letter to his/her last known employer, _____ , as shown by the attached copy of my letter, mail return receipts, Affidavit(s) of Service and response, if received:

Name of Employer	Date Sent	Indicate whether you received a reply.

❐ I have hired a private investigator or attorney who was unable to locate the opposing party as shown on the attached affidavit.

❐ I looked in the telephone directory and/or called directory assistance in the following areas:

_____ .

❐ I have contacted the Motor Vehicle Administration of Maryland and have learned the following: _____ .

❐ I have contacted the Military Worldwide Locator for Defendant's branch of the armed services and have learned the following: _____ .

❐ I asked the following former neighbors of the opposing party at his/her last known address, as indicated on the attached affidavits signed by those neighbors:

Name of Neighbor	Their Address	Date You Spoke With Them
Name of Neighbor	Their Address	Date You Spoke With Them
Name of Neighbor	Their Address	Date You Spoke With Them

❏ I tried to get the opposing party's current address by contacting the local child support enforcement agency. They reported that they have been unable to locate the opposing party.

❏ I have tried the following additional means to obtain the opposing party's current address:

3. I have not seen the opposing party since _____ , _____ and (*Check all that apply below and attach Financial Statement if required*):

       ❏ I do not know his/her current address.
       ❏ I do not know where he/she is working.
       ❏ I have no current address for any close relatives.
       ❏ I have no money to hire a private investigator or attorney to find him/her, as indicated in the attached Financial Statement.
       ❏ I have no money to do service by publication, as indicated in the attached Financial Statement.

I have made reasonable efforts to locate the Defendant, but have been unable to do so. I am over eighteen years old and am competent to testify.

_____
Signature

SUBSCRIBED AND SWORN to before me, this _____ day of _____ , _____ .

_____
Notary Public
MY COMMISSION EXPIRES: _____

DR 70 - Revised 9 March 2001

MILITARY SERVICE LOCATORS

To contact the Military Services, you will need the following information about they defendant: Name, Social Security Number, assigned base (if relevant). If you do not have any of the above information, include whatever you do have.

United States Army:	Commander U.S. Army Enlisted Records & Evaluation Center ATTN: Locator Fort Benjamin Harrison, IN 46249-5301
United States Navy:	Navy World Wide Locator Navy Personnel Command PERS 312F 5720 Integrity Drive Millington, TN 38055-3120 877-414-5359
United States Marine Corps:	Commandant of the Marine Corps Headquarters, USMC Code MMSB-10 Quantico, VA 22134-5030 703-640-3942/43
United States Air Force:	HQ AFMPC/RMIQL 550 C Street, West, Suite 50 Randolph AFB, TX 78150-4752 210-652-5774 210-652-5775

Circuit Court for_____ Case No._____
City or County

Name_____   Name_____

_____   VS.   _____
Street Address   Apt. #   Street Address   Apt. #
                                 ( )   ( )
_____   _____
City   State   Zip Code   Area   Telephone   City   State   Zip Code   Area   Telephone
                        Code   Code

Plaintiff   *Defendant*

REQUEST FOR ORDER OF DEFAULT

I, _____ , representing myself, request an Order of Default against
        My name

_____ for failure to file a responsive pleading to:
        Opposing Party

_____
        Indicate the name of the petition, complaint or motion you originally filed.

as provided by the Maryland Rules. The last known address of the opposing party is

_____   _____
            Date   Signature

NON-MILITARY AFFIDAVIT

_____ :
    Opposing Party

1.   is not in the military service of the United States;
2.   is not in the military service of any nation allied with the United States;
3.   has not been ordered to report for induction under the Selective Training and Service Act; and
4.   is not a member of the Enlisted Reserve Corps who has been ordered to report for military service.

I solemnly affirm under the penalties of perjury that the contents of the foregoing paper are true to the best of my knowledge, information, and belief.

_____   _____
            Date   Signature

Circuit Court for_____ **Case No.**_____

City or County

_____   _____

Name of Plaintiff   Name of Defendant

ORDER OF DEFAULT
(Order to be Completed by Court)

This court enters an Order of Default against _____ for

Opposing Party

failure to file a responsive pleading to: _____,

Name of Complaint/Petition/Motion

and orders that testimony to support the allegations of the Complaint be taken before

❏ one of the Judges or ❏ a Standing Examiner/Master of this Court.

_____

Judge

_____

Date

IMPORTANT: Person obtaining Order of Default must contact the Clerk's Office at

_____ for further instructions to schedule a hearing.

Telephone Number

Circuit Court for_____ Case No._____

<table>
<tr><td>City or County</td><td></td><td></td></tr>
</table>

_____
Name

                 VS.
_____
Street Address   Apt. #

(   )
_____
City   State Zip Code Area   Telephone
                      Code

_____
Name

_____
Street Address   Apt. #

(   )
_____
City   State Zip Code Area   Telephone
                      Code

       Plaintiff   *Defendant*

ANSWER TO ❏ COMPLAINT ❏ PETITION ❏ MOTION
(DOM REL 50)

I, _____ representing myself, answering the

_____
Name of Complaint, Petition, or Motion that you are answering

filed against me, state:

1. Answering Paragraph No. 1 (check one):
   - ❏ I admit all of the statement(s) in Paragraph No. 1.
   - ❏ I deny all of the statements(s) in Paragraph No. 1, except I admit that _____
   _____
   State the facts that you admit or write "none"
   - ❏ I do not have enough information to know whether or not the statement(s) in Paragraph 1 are true.

2. Answering Paragraph No. 2 (check one):
   - ❏ I admit all of the statements(s) in Paragraph No. 2.
   - ❏ I deny all of the statement(s) in Paragraph No. 2, except I admit that _____
   _____
   State the facts that you admit or write "none"
   - ❏ I do not have enough information to know whether or not the statement(s) in Paragraph 2 are true.
   - ❏ There is no Paragraph No. 2

3. Answering Paragraph No. 3 (check one):
   - ❏ I admit all of the statement(s) in Paragraph No. 3.
   - ❏ I deny all of the statement(s) in Paragraph No. 3, except I admit that _____
   _____
   State the facts that you admit or write "none"
   - ❏ I do not have enough information to know whether or not the statement(s) in Paragraph 3 are true.
   - ❏ There is no Paragraph No. 3

4. Answering Paragraph No. 4 (check one):
   - ❏ I admit all of the statement(s) in Paragraph No. 4.
   - ❏ I deny all of the statement(s) in Paragraph No. 4, except I admit that _____
   _____
   State the facts that you admit or write "none"
   - ❏ I do not have enough information to know whether or not the statement(s) in Paragraph 4 are true.
   - ❏ There is no Paragraph No. 4.

5. Answering Paragraph No. 5 (check one):
   - ❏ I admit all of the statement(s) in Paragraph No. 5.
   - ❏ I deny all of the statement(s) in Paragraph No. 5, except I admit that _____
   _____
   State the facts that you admit or write "none"
   - ❏ I do not have enough information to know whether or not the statement(s) in Paragraph 5 are true.
   - ❏ There is no Paragraph No. 5.

DR 50 - Revised 9 April 2001

6. Answering Paragraph No. 6 (check one):
   ☐ I admit all of the statement(s) in Paragraph No. 6.
   ☐ I deny all of the statement(s) in Paragraph No. 6, except I admit that _____
   _____
   State the facts that you admit or write "none"
   ☐ I do not have enough information to know whether or not the statement(s) in Paragraph 6 are true.
   ☐ There is no Paragraph No. 6.
7. Answering Paragraph No. 7 (check one):
   ☐ I admit all of the statement(s) in Paragraph No. 7.
   ☐ I deny all of the statement(s) in Paragraph No. 7, except I admit that _____
   _____
   State the facts that you admit or write "none"
   ☐ I do not have enough information to know whether or not the statement(s) in Paragraph 7 are true.
   ☐ There is no Paragraph No. 7.
8. Answering Paragraph No. 8 (check one):
   ☐ I admit all of the statement(s) in Paragraph No. 8.
   ☐ I deny all of the statement(s) in Paragraph No. 8, except I admit that _____
   _____
   State the facts that you admit or write "none"
   ☐ I do not have enough information to know whether or not the statement(s) in Paragraph 8 are true.
   ☐ There is no Paragraph No. 8.
9. Answering Paragraph No. 9 (check one):
   ☐ I admit all of the statement(s) in Paragraph No. 9.
   ☐ I deny all of the statement(s) in Paragraph No.9, except I admit that _____
   _____
   State the facts that you admit or write "none"
   ☐ I do not have enough information to know whether or not the statement(s) in Paragraph 9 are true.
   ☐ There is no Paragraph No. 9.
10. In my defense, I also want the Court to consider the following facts (A copy of any court order relating to my defense is attached, if available):

FOR THESE REASONS, I request the Court (*check all that apply*):
   ☐ Dismiss/deny the Complaint/ Petition/ Motion.
   ☐ Grant the relief requested in the Complaint/Petition/Motion.
   ☐ Grant the relief requested in the Complaint/Petition/Motion except

_____
State the relief you do NOT want the Court to grant.

Order any other appropriate relief.

_____   _____
Date   Signature

CERTIFICATE OF SERVICE
I HEREBY CERTIFY that on this _____ day of _____ , _____ , a copy of the foregoing Answer was mailed, postage prepaid, to _____
Opposing Party or His/Her Attorney

_____
Opposing Party or His/Her Attorney's Address including City / State / Zip

_____   _____
Date   Signature

DR 50 - Revised 9 April 2001

IMPORTANT (TIME FOR FILING YOUR ANSWER IF YOU WISH TO CONTEST THIS MATTER): You must file your Answer with the Court within the time stated in the summons. If you were served with a "Motion" but no summons, you must file your Answer within 15 days after being served.

IMPORTANT (ADDITIONAL PAPERS YOU MUST FILE): If the Opposing Party is seeking child support, alimony, or both, you must complete and attach to your Answer the appropriate financial statement(s) (child support - use Form DOM REL 30 or DOM REL 31; alimony - use Form DOM REL 31). If you want the Court to grant relief to you, you must complete page 3 of this form and file the appropriate additional form(s).

Instructions: If you want something different from what the other side wants, check below and fill out the appropriate DOM REL Form(s). See General Instructions and Forms DOM REL 1 through 21.

COUNTERCLAIM

I, _____ representing myself, state that:

1.   I want (check all that apply):

☐ child support

☐ custody

☐ visitation

☐ modification of child support

☐ modification of custody/visitation

☐ absolute divorce

☐ limited divorce

2.   I have attached Form(s) DOM REL _____

_____
List form numbers of the DOM REL forms you completed

to this Answer and I request that the form(s) I have attached be considered as my counterclaim against the other side.

_____   _____
Date   Signature

CERTIFICATE OF SERVICE

I HEREBY CERTIFY that on this _____ day of _____ , _____ , a copy of this Counterclaim and a copy of the forms listed in Paragraph 2, above, were mailed, postage prepaid, to

_____
Opposing Party or His/Her Attorney

_____
Opposing Party's or His/Her Attorney's Address including City/State/Zip

_____   _____
Date   Signature

DR 50 - Revised 9 April 2001

IN THE CIRCUIT COURT FOR MONTGOMERY COUNTY, MARYLAND

Plaintiff

          :

v.   :   Case No.

Defendant   :

JOINT REQUEST TO SCHEDULE AN UNCONTESTED DIVORCE HEARING

The parties agree that this matter is uncontested as to all issues and request that this matter be scheduled for a ten-minute divorce hearing. They further agree that they have read the statements below and have checked all appropriate lines that apply to their case.

Grounds for divorce_____ **Separation date (if appropriate)**_____
(Grounds and separation date (if appropriate) must be entered or request will have no effect.)

1a._____   There are no minor children of the marriage who are subject to this Court's jurisdiction.

  OR

1b._____   Custody and visitation have been agreed to or have been previously determined by the Court.

2._____   Child support has been established in compliance with the Child Support Guidelines. <u>IF THIS LINE IS CHECKED, THIS JOINT REQUEST MAY NOT BE FILED UNLESS A COMPLETED CHILD SUPPORT GUIDELINES WORKSHEET IS ATTACHED.</u>

3._____   All parties/witnesses speak and understand English, and there is no need for a translator. The court will provide an interpreter only in cases where a party/witness is hearing impaired. **NOTE: You must provide your own language interpreter.**

4._____   There are no pension rights <u>or</u> any pension rights have been waived <u>or</u> pension rights shall be addressed by a consent qualified domestic relations order to be submitted at the divorce hearing.

5._____   There are no support or property rights to be adjudicated by the Court and/or there is a written agreement disposing of all such rights.

_____
Plaintiff or Plaintiff's
Attorney (signature)

_____
Defendant or Defendant's
Attorney (signature)

_____

_____

_____
Address

_____
Address

_____
Daytime Telephone

_____
Daytime Telephone

THIS JOINT REQUEST IS NOT AN ANSWER AND SHOULD NOT BE FILED **UNTIL** AN **ANSWER** HAS BEEN FILED.

MARYLAND STATE DEPARTMENT OF HEALTH AND MENTAL HYGIENE
Division of Vital Records   4201 Patterson Avenue, Baltimore, MD 21215-2290
REPORT OF ABSOLUTE DIVORCE OR ANNULMENT OF MARRIAGE

	COURT FILE NUMBER	STATE FILE NUMBER	

Authority for This Report is Article Health-General, Title 4, Subtitle 2, Section 4-206, Annotated Code of Maryland

HUSBAND

1a. HUSBAND'S NAME (First, Middle, Last) — 1b. AGE

2a. RESIDENCE - CITY, TOWN, OR LOCATION — 2b. COUNTY

2c. STATE — 3. BIRTHPLACE (State or Foreign Country) — 4. DATE OF BIRTH (Month, Day, Year)

WIFE

5a. WIFE'S NAME (First, Middle, Last) — MAIDEN SURNAME — 5b. AGE

6a. RESIDENCE - CITY, TOWN, OR LOCATION — 6b. COUNTY

6c. STATE — 7. BIRTHPLACE (State or Foreign Country) — 8. DATE OF BIRTH (Month, Day, Year)

MARRIAGE

9a. PLACE OF THIS MARRIAGE - CITY OR LOCATION — 9b. COUNTY — 9c. STATE OR FOREIGN COUNTRY — 10. DATE OF THIS MARRIAGE (Month, Day, Year)

11. DATE COUPLE LAST RESIDED IN SAME HOUSEHOLD (Month, Day, Year) — 12. NUMBER OF CHILDREN UNDER 18 IN THE HOUSEHOLD AS OF THE DATE IN ITEM 11. Number ____ Non ____ — 13. PLAINTIFF ☐ Husband ☐ Wife ☐ Both   ☐ Other (specify) _____

ATTORNEY

14a. NAME OF PLAINTIFF'S ATTORNEY (Type/Print) — 14b. ADDRESS (Street and Number or Rural Route Number, City or Town, State, Zip Code)

DECREE

15. NUMBER OF CHILDREN UNDER 18 WHOSE PHYSICAL CUSTODY WAS AWARDED TO

Husband _____   Wife _____

Joint (Husband/Wife) _____ Other _____

☐ No children

16. LEGAL GROUND FOR DECREE — 17a. TYPE OF COURT

17b. COUNTY OF DECREE

CLERK OF COURT

18. I CERTIFY THAT THE MARRIAGE OF THE ABOVE NAMED PERSONS WAS DISSOLVED ON (Month, Day, Year) — 19. TYPE OF DECREE - Divorce, Dissolution, or Annulment (specify) — 20. DATE RECORDED (Month, Day, Year)

21. SIGNATURE OF CERTIFYING OFFICIAL — 22. TITLE OF CERTIFYING OFFICIAL — 23. DATE SIGNED (Month, Day, Year)

	24. NUMBER OF THIS MARRIAGE - First, Second, etc. (Specify below)	25 IF PREVIOUSLY MARRIED, LAST MARRIAGE ENDED — By Death, Divorce, Dissolution or Annulment (Specify below) — Date (Month, Day, Year)	26. RACE - American Indian, Black, White, etc. (Specify below)	27. EDUCATION (Specify only highest grade completed) Elementary/Secondary (0 - 12) — College (1 - 4 or 5+)
HUSBAND	24a.	25a.	25b.	26a.
WIFE	24b.	25c.	25d.	26b.

CLERK OF THE COURT: When a petition for absolute divorce or annulment is filed, please give a copy of this form to the attorney for completion of Items 1-20 and 24-27b. When the decree is signed, check completeness of these items, execute the bottom section, and mail it to the Maryland Department of Health and Mental Hygiene, Division of Vital Records, 4201 Patterson Avenue, Baltimore, Maryland 21215-2299 on or before the 10th of the month succeeding the divorce.

ATTORNEY: Please complete items 1-20 and 24-27b of this form and ask your client to verify the information. RETURN THIS FORM TO THE CLERK OF THE COURT FOR CERTIFICATION.

Entries should be typewritten or printed in indelible black ink.

VR A24   3/94

(An original of this document must be obtained directly from the court.)

IN THE CIRCUIT COURT FOR MONTGOMERY COUNTY, MARYLAND

_____

Plaintiff

vs.   Case No. _____

_____

Defendant

SUBMISSION FOR JUDGMENT OF DIVORCE

TO THE HONORABLE, THE JUDGES OF SAID COURT:

The above case is respectfully submitted for judgment and Rule S74Ad is hereby waived.

_____
Attorney for Plaintiff

_____
Attorney for Defendant

Circuit Court for_____ Case No._____

City or County

Name_____		Name_____	
	VS.		
Street Address_____ Apt. #		Street Address_____ Apt. #	
( )		( )	
City State Zip Code Area Telephone		City State Zip Code Area Telephone	
Code		Code	

Plaintiff   *Defendant*

JOINT STATEMENT OF PARTIES CONCERNING MARITAL AND NON-MARITAL PROPERTY

(DOM REL 33)

1.   The parties agree that the following property is "**marital property**" as defined by MD. FAM. LAW CODE ANN. § 8-201(1999):

Description of Property	How Titled		Fair Market Value		Liens, Encumbrances or Debt Directly Attributable	
	Husband's Assertion	Wife's Assertion	Husband's Assertion	Wife's Assertion	Husband's Assertion	Wife's Assertion

2. The parties agree that the following property is **not marital property** because the property (a) was acquired by one party before marriage, (b) was acquired by one party by inheritance or gift from a third person, (c) has been excluded by valid agreement, or (d) is directly traceable to any of these sources:

Description of Property	Reason Why Non-Marital	How Titled		Fair Market Value		Liens/Debts	
		Husband's Assertion	Wife's Assertion	Husband's Assertion	Wife's Assertion	Husband's Assertion	Wife's Assertion

3. The parties are **not in agreement** as to whether the following property is marital or non-marital:

Description of Property	Marital ?		How Titled		Fair Market Value		Liens/Debts	
	Husband's Assertion	Wife's Assertion	Husband's Assertion	Wife's Assertion	Husband's Assertion	Wife's Assertion	Husband's Assertion	Wife's Assertion

_____
Date

_____
Signature of Plaintiff or Attorney

_____
Date

_____
Signature of Defendant or Attorney

SECTION 9:
VIRGINIA

APPENDIX G

SUMMARY OF VIRGINIA DIVORCE LAWS

This will summarize the most important laws concerning divorce in Virginia. You can use this summary to find a quick answer to a question or as a starting point for further research.

1. FILING.
(a) The Complaint is filed in "Virginia: In the Circuit Court of _____";
(b) it is titled a "Bill of Complaint for Divorce" or "Bill of Complaint for Limited Divorce";
(c) it is filed by the "Complainant";
(d) the other spouse is the "Defendant";
(e) The divorce may be filed for in
  (i) the county or city in which the spouses last lived together; or at the option of the plaintiff;
  (ii) the county or city where the defendant resides, if the defendant is a resident of Virginia; or
  (iii) if the defendant is a non-resident of Virginia, the county or city where the plaintiff resides; and
(f) the final papers are called the "Final Decree of Divorce". *Code of Virginia; Title 20, Sections 20-96 and 20-97.*

2. RESIDENCY.
One of the spouses must have been a resident of Virginia for at least six months prior to filing for divorce. *Code of Virginia; Title 20, Section 20-97.*

3. GROUNDS FOR ABSOLUTE DIVORCE.
(a) living separate and apart without cohabitation for one year; or
(b) living separate and apart without cohabitation for six months if there are no minor children and the spouses have entered into a separation agreemen;
(c) adultery (including homosexual acts);

(d) conviction of a felony and imprisonment for one year;
(e) cruelty, one year of the act complained of; and
(f) willful desertion or abandonment continuing for one year. *Code of Virginia; Title 20, Section 20-91.*

4. GROUNDS FOR LIMITED DIVORCE.
(a) cruelty;
(b) willful desertion or abandonment; and
(c) reasonable apprehension of bodily injury. *Code of Virginia; Title 20, Section 20-95.*

5. MEDIATION AND PARENTING CLASSES.
The courts can order mediation of child custody disputes and parenting classes. *Code of Virginia; Title 20, Section 20-124.4.*

6. UNCONTESTED DIVORCE.
Written separation agreements are specifically authorized by statute. A party may waive service of process, but the waiver of service of process form must be signed in front of the clerk of the court or a notary. The testimony of either spouse must be corroborated by a witness. *Code of Virginia; Title 20, Sections 20-99(1), 20-99.1:1, and 20-109.1.*

7. CHILD CUSTODY. Joint or sole child custody will be awarded based on the best interests of the child, taking into account the following factors:

(a) the age and physical and mental condition of the child;

(b) the age and physical and mental condition of the parents;

(c) the relationship between the child and each parent;

(d) the needs of the child;

(e) the role each parent has played in the upbringing and care of the child;

(f) the propensity of each parent to support contact of the child with the other parent;

(g) the willingness of the parents to maintain a relationship with the child and cooperate in parenting;

(h) the preference of the child;

(i) any history of family abuse; and

(j) any other factors the court deems necessary and proper. No preference is to be given to either parent. *Code of Virginia; Title 20, Sections 20-124.2 and 20-124.3.*

8. CHILD SUPPORT. Child support is determined based on guidelines are provided in the statute, which are presumed to be correct unless there is a showing that the amount would be unjust or inappropriate and the following:

(a) support provided for other children or family members;

(b) custody arrangements;

(c) voluntary unemployment or under-employment, unless it is the custodial parent and the child is not in school and child care services are not available and the cost of child care services are not included in the computations for child support;

(d) debts incurred during the marriage for the benefit of the child;

(e) debts incurred for the purpose of producing income;

(f) direct court-ordered payments for health insurance or educational expenses of the child; and

(g) any extraordinary capital gains, such as gains from the sale of the marital home. *Code of Virginia; Title 20, Sections 20-107.2, 20-108.1, and 20-108.2.*

9. ALIMONY. Either spouse may be awarded maintenance, to be paid in either a lump sum, periodic payments, or both. The factors for consideration are:

(a) the obligations, needs and financial resources of the parties;

(b) the standard of living established during the marriage;

(c) the age and physical and mental condition of the parties and any special circumstances of the family;

(d) the duration of the marriage;

(e) circumstances involving a child that make it appropriate that a parent not work outside the home;

(f) the contributions, monetary and nonmonetary, to the wellbeing of the family;

(g) property of the parties;

(h) provisions made regarding marital property;

(i) earning capacity of each party;

(j) the ability and time necessary to acquire sufficient education and training to enable the spouse to find appropriate employment, and that spouse's future earning capacity;

(k) decisions about employment made during the marriage;

(l) contributions by either party to the education or career of the other spouse;

(m) any other factor, including tax consequences, that the court deems necessary and equitable. However, permanent maintenance will not be awarded to a spouse who was at fault in a divorce granted on the grounds of adultery, unless such a denial of support would be unjust. *Code of Virginia; Title 20, Sections 20-95, 20-107.1 and 20-108.1.*

10. EQUITABLE DISTRIBUTION OF PROPERTY: Each party will keep his or her separate property consisting of property

(a) acquired prior to the marriage;

(b) any gifts from third parties and inheritances;

(c) any increase in the value of separate property, unless marital property or significant personal efforts contributed to such increases; and

(d) any property acquired in exchange for separate property.

The court will equitably divide marital property, consisting of

(a) all property acquired during the marriage that is not separate property;

(b) all property titled in the names of both spouses, whether as joint tenants or tenants-by-the entireties;

(c) income from or increase in value of separate property during the marriage if the income or increase arose from significant personal efforts;

(d) any separate property which is commingled with marital property and can not be clearly traced. The court may also order a payment from one spouse's retirement benefits, profit-sharing benefits, personal injury award, or worker's compensation award, to the other spouse. The court may order the division or transfer of jointly owned marital property or permit one party to purchase the other's interest. The court may also grant a monetary award payable by one spouse to the other.

In distributing property or granting a monetary award, the court considers the following factors:
(a) the contribution of each spouse to the acquisition, care, and maintenance of the marital property;
(b) the liquid or non-liquid character of the property;
(c) the length of the marriage;
(d) the age and health of the spouses;
(e) the tax consequences;
(f) any debts and liabilities of the spouses, the basis for such debts and liabilities, and the property which serves as security for such debts and liabilities;
(g) how and when the property was acquired;
(h) the circumstances that contributed to the divorce;
(i) the contributions, monetary and non-monetary of each spouse to the well-being of the family; and
(j) any other factor necessary to do equity and justice between the spouses. *Code of Virginia; Title 20, Section 20-107.3.*

11. NAME CHANGE: Upon request, a spouse may have his or her former name restored. *Code of Virginia; Title 20, Section 20-121.4.*

12. PREMARITAL AGREEMENTS. The agreement shall be in writing and signed by both parties and is enforceable without consideration. The agreement is not enforceable if it is proven that
(1) the agreement was not executed voluntarily;
(2) the agreement was unconscionable when executed and before execution the party was not provided a fair and reasonable disclosure of the property or financial obligations of the other party and did not waive the right to the disclosure of this information.

If the marriage is determined to be void, the agreement is enforceable only to the extent necessary to avoid an inequitable result. *Code of Virginia; Title 20, Sections 20-149 and 20-151.*

APPENDIX H
CHILD SUPPORT
GUIDELINES IN VIRGINIA

The Child Support Guidelines Worksheet is used to calculate the proper amount of child support. The guidelines are presumptively correct and must be followed by the Master, Commissioner or Judge unless there are some special circumstances that would justify deviation from the guidelines.

MONTHLY BASIC CHILD SUPPORT OBLIGATIONS

COMBINED MONTHLY GROSS INCOME	ONE CHILD	TWO CHILDREN	THREE CHILDREN	FOUR CHILDREN	FIVE CHILDREN	SIX CHILDREN
0-599	65	65	65	65	65	65
600	110	111	113	114	115	116
650	138	140	142	143	145	146
700	153	169	170	172	174	176
750	160	197	199	202	204	206
800	168	226	228	231	233	236
850	175	254	257	260	263	266
900	182	281	286	289	292	295
950	189	292	315	318	322	325
1000	196	304	344	348	351	355
1050	203	315	373	377	381	385
1100	210	326	402	406	410	415
1150	217	337	422	435	440	445
1200	225	348	436	465	470	475
1250	232	360	451	497	502	507
1300	241	373	467	526	536	542
1350	249	386	483	545	570	576
1400	257	398	499	563	605	611
1450	265	411	515	581	633	645
1500	274	426	533	602	656	680
1550	282	436	547	617	672	714
1600	289	447	560	632	689	737
1650	295	458	573	647	705	754
1700	302	468	587	662	721	772
1750	309	479	600	676	738	789
1800	315	488	612	690	752	805
1850	321	497	623	702	766	819
1900	326	506	634	714	779	834
1950	332	514	645	727	793	848
2000	338	523	655	739	806	862
2050	343	532	666	751	819	877
2100	349	540	677	763	833	891
2150	355	549	688	776	846	905
2200	360	558	699	788	860	920
2250	366	567	710	800	873	934
2300	371	575	721	812	886	948
2350	377	584	732	825	900	963
2400	383	593	743	837	913	977
2450	388	601	754	849	927	991
2500	394	610	765	862	940	1006
2550	399	619	776	874	954	1020
2600	405	627	787	886	967	1034
2650	410	635	797	897	979	1048
2700	415	643	806	908	991	1060
2750	420	651	816	919	1003	1073
2800	425	658	826	930	1015	1085
2850	430	667	836	941	1027	1098
2900	435	675	846	953	1039	1112

COMBINED MONTHLY GROSS INCOME	ONE CHILD	TWO CHILDREN	THREE CHILDREN	FOUR CHILDREN	FIVE CHILDREN	SIX CHILDREN
2950	440	683	856	964	1052	1125
3000	445	691	866	975	1064	1138
3050	450	699	876	987	1076	1152
3100	456	707	886	998	1089	1165
3150	461	715	896	1010	1101	1178
3200	466	723	906	1021	1114	1191
3250	471	732	917	1032	1126	1205
3300	476	740	927	1044	1139	1218
3350	481	748	937	1055	1151	1231
3400	486	756	947	1067	1164	1245
3450	492	764	957	1078	1176	1258
3500	497	772	967	1089	1189	1271
3550	502	780	977	1101	1201	1285
3600	507	788	987	1112	1213	1298
3650	512	797	997	1124	1226	1311
3700	518	806	1009	1137	1240	1326
3750	524	815	1020	1150	1254	1342
3800	530	824	1032	1163	1268	1357
3850	536	834	1043	1176	1283	1372
3900	542	843	1055	1189	1297	1387
3950	547	852	1066	1202	1311	1402
4000	553	861	1078	1214	1325	1417
4050	559	871	1089	1227	1339	1432
4100	565	880	1101	1240	1353	1448
4150	571	889	1112	1253	1367	1463
4200	577	898	1124	1266	1382	1478
4250	583	907	1135	1279	1396	1493
4300	589	917	1147	1292	1410	1508
4350	594	926	1158	1305	1424	1523
4400	600	935	1170	1318	1438	1538
4450	606	944	1181	1331	1452	1553
4500	612	954	1193	1344	1467	1569
4550	618	963	1204	1357	1481	1584
4600	624	972	1216	1370	1495	1599
4650	630	981	1227	1383	1509	1614
4700	635	989	1237	1395	1522	1627
4750	641	997	1247	1406	1534	1641
4800	646	1005	1257	1417	1546	1654
4850	651	1013	1267	1428	1558	1667
4900	656	1021	1277	1439	1570	1679
4950	661	1028	1286	1450	1582	1692
5000	666	1036	1295	1460	1593	1704
5050	671	1043	1305	1471	1605	1716
5100	675	1051	1314	1481	1616	1728
5150	680	1058	1323	1492	1628	1741
5200	685	1066	1333	1502	1640	1753
5250	690	1073	1342	1513	1651	1765
5300	695	1081	1351	1524	1663	1778
5350	700	1088	1361	1534	1674	1790
5400	705	1096	1370	1545	1686	1802
5450	710	1103	1379	1555	1697	1815
5500	714	1111	1389	1566	1709	1827
5550	719	1118	1398	1576	1720	1839
5600	724	1126	1407	1587	1732	1851
5650	729	1133	1417	1598	1743	1864
5700	734	1141	1426	1608	1755	1876
5750	739	1148	1435	1619	1766	1888
5800	744	1156	1445	1629	1778	1901

COMBINED MONTHLY GROSS INCOME	ONE CHILD	TWO CHILDREN	THREE CHILDREN	FOUR CHILDREN	FIVE CHILDREN	SIX CHILDREN
5850	749	1163	1454	1640	1790	1913
5900	753	1171	1463	1650	1801	1925
5950	758	1178	1473	1661	1813	1937
6000	763	1186	1482	1672	1824	1950
6050	768	1193	1491	1682	1836	1962
6100	773	1201	1501	1693	1847	1974
6150	778	1208	1510	1703	1859	1987
6200	783	1216	1519	1714	1870	1999
6250	788	1223	1529	1724	1882	2011
6300	792	1231	1538	1735	1893	2023
6350	797	1238	1547	1745	1905	2036
6400	802	1246	1557	1756	1916	2048
6450	807	1253	1566	1767	1928	2060
6500	812	1261	1575	1777	1940	2073
6550	816	1267	1583	1786	1949	2083
6600	820	1272	1590	1794	1957	2092
6650	823	1277	1597	1801	1965	2100
6700	827	1283	1604	1809	1974	2109
6750	830	1288	1610	1817	1982	2118
6800	834	1293	1617	1824	1990	2127
6850	837	1299	1624	1832	1999	2136
6900	841	1304	1631	1839	2007	2145
6950	845	1309	1637	1847	2016	2154
7000	848	1315	1644	1855	2024	2163
7050	852	1320	1651	1862	2032	2172
7100	855	1325	1658	1870	2041	2181
7150	859	1331	1665	1878	2049	2190
7200	862	1336	1671	1885	2057	2199
7250	866	1341	1678	1893	2066	2207
7300	870	1347	1685	1900	2074	2216
7350	873	1352	1692	1908	2082	2225
7400	877	1358	1698	1916	2091	2234
7450	880	1363	1705	1923	2099	2243
7500	884	1368	1712	1931	2108	2252
7550	887	1374	1719	1938	2116	2261
7600	891	1379	1725	1946	2124	2270
7650	895	1384	1732	1954	2133	2279
7700	898	1390	1739	1961	2141	2288
7750	902	1395	1746	1969	2149	2297
7800	905	1400	1753	1977	2158	2305
7850	908	1405	1758	1983	2164	2313
7900	910	1409	1764	1989	2171	2320
7950	913	1414	1770	1995	2178	2328
8000	916	1418	1776	2001	2185	2335
8050	918	1423	1781	2007	2192	2343
8100	921	1428	1787	2014	2198	2350
8150	924	1432	1793	2020	2205	2357
8200	927	1437	1799	2026	2212	2365
8250	929	1441	1804	2032	2219	2372
8300	932	1446	1810	2038	2226	2380
8350	935	1450	1816	2045	2232	2387
8400	937	1455	1822	2051	2239	2395
8450	940	1459	1827	2057	2246	2402
8500	943	1464	1833	2063	2253	2410
8550	945	1468	1839	2069	2260	2417
8600	948	1473	1845	2076	2266	2425
8650	951	1478	1850	2082	2273	2432
8700	954	1482	1856	2088	2280	2440

COMBINED MONTHLY GROSS INCOME	ONE CHILD	TWO CHILDREN	THREE CHILDREN	FOUR CHILDREN	FIVE CHILDREN	SIX CHILDREN
8750	956	1487	1862	2094	2287	2447
8800	959	1491	1868	2100	2294	2455
8850	962	1496	1873	2107	2300	2462
8900	964	1500	1879	2113	2307	2470
8950	967	1505	1885	2119	2314	2477
9000	970	1509	1891	2125	2321	2484
9050	973	1514	1896	2131	2328	2492
9100	975	1517	1901	2137	2334	2498
9150	977	1521	1905	2141	2339	2503
9200	979	1524	1909	2146	2344	2509
9250	982	1527	1914	2151	2349	2514
9300	984	1531	1918	2156	2354	2520
9350	986	1534	1922	2160	2359	2525
9400	988	1537	1926	2165	2365	2531
9450	990	1541	1930	2170	2370	2536
9500	993	1544	1935	2175	2375	2541
9550	995	1547	1939	2179	2380	2547
9600	997	1551	1943	2184	2385	2552
9650	999	1554	1947	2189	2390	2558
9700	1001	1557	1951	2194	2396	2563
9750	1003	1561	1956	2198	2401	2569
9800	1006	1564	1960	2203	2406	2574
9850	1008	1567	1964	2208	2411	2580
9900	1010	1571	1968	2213	2416	2585
9950	1012	1574	1972	2218	2421	2590
10000	1014	1577	1977	2222	2427	2596

The following is a list of legal clinics that may offer services to persons meeting the clinic's criteria. (They are alphabetized by city.)

Legal Services of Northern Virginia
110 N. Royal Street
Alexandria, VA 22314
703-684-5566

Client Centered Legal Services of Southwest Virginia
Castlewood, VA 24224
540-762-5501

Charlottesville-Albemarle Legal Aid Society
Suite A
105 Fourth Street, SE,
Charlottesville, VA 22902
800-763-7323

Piedmont Legal Services
Suite 201
416 E. Main Street
Charlottesville, VA 22902
804-296-8851

Legal Aid Society of New River Valley
155 Arrowhead Trail
Christiansburg, VA 24073
540-382-6157

Rappahannock Legal Services
314 N. West Street
Culpepper, VA
800-989-3758

Virginia Legal Aid Society
Masonic Temple
Suite 517
Danville, VA
804-799-3550

Virginia Legal Aid Society
412 S. Main Street
Emporia, VA
804-634-5172

Legal Services of Northern Virginia
4080 Chain Bridge Road
Fairfax, VA 22030
703-246-4500

Legal Services of Northern Virginia
6400 Arlington Blvd., Suite 630
Falls Church, VA 22042
703-534-4343

Virginia Legal Aid Society
104 High Street
Farmville, VA
804-392-8108

Rappahannock Legal Services
2nd Floor
910 Princess Anne Street
Fredericksburg, VA 22401
540-371-1105

Virginia Legal Aid Society
129 S. Main Street
Halifax, VA
804-476-2136

Peninsula Legal Aid Center
Suite 336
2013 Cunningham Drive
Hampton, VA 23666
757-827-5078

Blue Ridge Legal Services, Inc.
204 North High Street
Harrisonburg, VA 22801
540-433-1830

Legal Services of Northern Virginia
3 Royal Street, S.E.
Leesburg, VA 20175
703-777-7450

Virginia Legal Aid Society
513 Church Street
Lynchburg, VA
804-528-4722

Legal Services of Northern Virginia
9240 Center St.
Manassas, VA 22110
540-368-5711

Southwest Virginia Legal Aid Society
227 West Cherry Street
Marion, VA 24354
540-783-8300

Tidewater Legal Aid Society
125 St. Paul's Boulevard, #400
Norfolk, VA
757-627-5423

Southside Virginia Legal Services
10-A Bollingbrook Street
Petersburg, VA 23803
804-862-1100

Central Virginia Legal Aid Society
Suite 101
101 West Broad Street
Richmond, VA 23220
804-648-1012

Legal Aid Society of Roanoke Valley
416 Campbell Avenue, SW
Roanoke, VA 24016
540-344-2088

Virginia Legal Aid Society
140 W. Washington Street
Suffolk, VA
757-539-3441

The following is a list of Virginia domestic violence shelters. Contact your local Virginia Department of Social Services office for additional information on shelters.

REGIONAL OFFICES

Central Regional Office
1604 Santa Rosa Road
Wythe Building
Richmond, VA 23229
804-662-7653

Eastern Regional Office
Pembroke Office Park
Virginia Beach, VA 23462
757-491-3990

Northern Regional Office
170 West Shirley Avenue
Warrenton, VA 20186
540-347-6300

Piedmont Regional Office
210 Church Avenue, S.W.
Roanoke, VA 24011
540-857-7920

Western Regional Office
190 Patton Street
Abingdon, VA 24210
540-676-5490

CITY PROGRAMS

Accomack Department of Social Services
Onancock, VA 23417-0299
757-787-1530

**Albemarle County
Department of Social Services**
1023 Millmont Street
Charlottesville, VA 22903-4866
434-972-4010

Alexandria Department of Social Services
2525 Mt Vernon Avenue
Alexandria, VA 22301
703-838-0700

**Alleghany-Covington
Department of Social Services**
110 Rosedale Avenue
Covington, VA 24426-1244
540-965-1780

Amelia Department of Social Services
Court Street
Amelia, VA 23002-0136
804-561-2681

Amherst Department of Social Services
224 Second Street
Amherst, VA 24521-0414
434-946-9330

Appomattox
Department of Social Services
Court Street
Appomattox, VA 24552-0549
434-352-7125

Arlington County
Department of Human Services
3033 Wilson Blvd.
Arlington, VA 22201
703-228-1550

Bath County
Department of Social Services
Warm Springs, VA 24484
540-839-7271

Bedford Department of Social Services
119 East Main Street
Bedford, VA 24523-7750
540-586-7750

Bland County
Department of Social Services
Old Bank Building
Bland, VA 24315-0055
276--688-4111

Botetourt County
Department of Social Services
20 South Roanoke Street
Fincastle, VA 24090-0160
540-473-8210

Bristol City Department of Social Services
621 Washington Street
Bristol, VA 24201-4644
276--645-7450

Brunswick County
Department of Social Services
228 North Main Street
Lawrenceville, VA 23868-0089
434-848-2142

Buchanan County
Department of Social Services
Grundy, VA 24614-0674
276--935-8106

Buckingham County Department of Social Services
Buckingham, VA 23921-0170
434-969-4246

Campbell County
Department of Social Services
69 Kabler Lane
Rustburg, VA 24588-0006
434-332-9585

Caroline Department of Social Services
Bowling Green, VA 22427-0430
804-633-5071

Carroll County
Department of Social Services
605-8 Pine Street
Hillsville, VA 24343
276--728-9186

Charles City
Department of Social Services
Charles City, VA 23030-0098
804-829-9207

Charlotte County
Department of Social Services
Highway 147
Charlotte Court House, VA 23923-0040
434-542-5164

Charlottesville
Department of Social Services
120 7th Street N.E.
Charlottesville, VA 22902-0911
804-970-3400

Chesapeake Bureau of Social Services
100 Outlaw Street
Chesapeake, VA 23320
757-382-2000

Chesterfield/Colonial Heights
Department of Social Services
9501 Lucy Corr Drive
Chesterfield, VA 23832-0430
804-748-1100

Clarke County
Department of Social Services
311 East Main Street
Berryville, VA 22611
540-955-3700

Craig Department of Social Services
Mains and Ocurt Streets
New Castle, VA 24127-0330
540-864-5117

Culpeper County
Department of Social Services
219 East Davis Street
Culpeper, VA 22701
540-727-0372

Cumberland County
Department of Social Services
Cumberland, VA 23040-9803
804-492-4915

Danville Division of Social Services
510 Patton Street
Danville, VA 24543
804-799-6543

Dickenson County
Department of Social Services
Brush Creek Road
Clintwood, VA 24228-0417
276--926-1661/1664

Dinwiddie Department of Social Services
Dinwiddie, VA 23841
804-469-4524

Essex Department of Social Services
Tappahannock, VA 22560-1004
804-443-3561

Fairfax County
Department of Family Services
12011 Government Center Parkway
Fairfax, VA 22035
703-324-7500

Fauquier County
Department of Social Services
320 Hospital Drive, Suite 11
Warrenton, VA 20188-0300
540-347-2316

Floyd County
Department of Social Services
Courthouse Building
Floyd, VA 24091-0314
540--745-9316

Fluvanna County
Department of Social Services
Fork Union, VA 23055
434-842-8221

Franklin County
Department of Social Services
11161 Virgil H. Goode Highway
Rocky Mount, VA 24151
540-483-9247

Franklin Department of Social Services
207 W. Second Ave.
Franklin, VA 23851
757-562-8520

Frederick County
Department of Social Services
107 N. Kent Street
Winchester, VA 22601
540-665-5688

Fredericksburg
Department of Social Services
608 Jackson Street
Fredericksburg, VA 22404-0510
540-372-1032

Galax City Department of Social Services
105 E Center St
Galax, VA 24333-0166
276-236-8111

Giles County
Department of Social Services
6012 Virginia Avenue
Pembroke, VA 24136-0529
540-626-7291

Gloucester
Department of Social Services
Gloucester, VA 23061-0186
804-693-2671

Goochland Department of Social Services
Administration Annex Building
Goochland, VA 23063-0034
804-556-5332
804-784-5510

Grayson County
Department of Social Services
129 Davis Street
Independence, VA 24348-0434
276-773-2452

Greene County
Department of Social Services
Stanardsville, VA 22973-0117
804-985-5246

Greensville/Emporia
Department of Social Services
1748 East Atlantic Street
Emporia, VA 23847-1136
434-634-6576

Halifax County
Department of Social Services
Mary Bethune Complex
Halifax, VA 24558-0666
434-476-6594

Hampton
Department of Social Services
1320 LaSalle Avenue
Hampton, VA 23669
757-727-1800

Hanover Department of Social Services
12304 Washington Highway
Ashland, VA 23005
800-770-0837

Harrisonburg / Rockingham County
Department of Social Services
110 North Mason Street
Harrisonburg, VA 22801
540-574-5100

Henrico County
Department of Social Services
8600 Dixon Powers Drive
Richmond, VA 23273
804-501-4001

Henry County/Martinsville
Department of Social Services
20 East Church Street
Martinsville, VA 24114
540-656-4300

Highland County
Department of Social Services
Courthouse Annex
Monterey, VA 24465-0247
540-468-2199

Hopewell Department of Social Services
256 East Cawson Street
Hopewell, VA 23860
804-541-2330

Isle of Wight
Department of Social Services
17100 Monument Circle
Isle of Wight, VA 23397-0110
757-365-0880

James City County
Department of Social Services
5249 Old Towne Road
Williamsburg, VA 23188
757-259-3100

King & Queen
Department of Social Services
Courthouse Annex
King & Queen Courthouse, VA
23095-9999
804-785-5977

King George
Department of Social Services
King George, VA 22484-0130
540-775-3544

King William
Department of Social Services
172 Courthouse Lane
King William, VA 23086-0187
804-769-4905

Lancaster Department of Social Services
Lancaster, VA 22503
804-462-5141

Lee County Department of Social Services
Main Street
Jonesville, VA 24263-0346
276--346-1010

Loudoun County
Department of Social Services
102 Heritage Way, NE
Leesburg, VA 20176
703-777-0353

Louisa County
Department of Social Services
McDonald Street
Louisa, VA 23093-0425
540-967-1320

Lunenburg County
Department of Social Services
Courthouse Square
Lunenburg, VA 23952-9999
434-696-2134

Lynchburg Division of Social Services
2210 Langhorne Road
Lynchburg, VA 24501
804-847-1531

Madison County
Department of Social Services
101 S. Main Street
Madison, VA 22727-0176
540-948-5521

Manassas City
Department of Social Services
8955 Center Street
Manassas, VA 20110
703-361-8277

Manassas Park
Department of Social Services
1 Park Center Court
Manassas Park, VA 20111
703-335-8680

Mathews Department of Social Services
Mathews, VA 23109-0925
804-725-7192

Mecklenburg County
Department of Social Services
132-133 Washington Street
Boydton, VA 23917-0400
434-738-6138

Middlesex Department of Social Services
Urbanna, VA 23175-0216
804-758-2348

Montgomery County
Department of Social Services
210 S. Pepper Street
Christiansburg, VA 24073
540--382-6990

Nelson County
Department of Social Services
Court St.
Lovingston, VA 22949
434-263-8334

New Kent Department of Social Services
Providence Forge, VA 23140
804-966-1853

Newport News
Department of Social Services
6060 Jefferson Avenue
Newport News, VA 23605
757-926-6300

Norfolk Division of Social Services
220 W. Brambleton Avenue
Norfolk, VA 23510-1506
757-664-6000

Northhampton County
Department of Social Services
Eastville, VA 23347-0568
757-678-5153

Northumberland County
Department of Social Services
Heathsville, VA 22473-0399
804-580-3477

Norton City
Department of Social Services
644 Park Avenue
Norton, VA 24273-0378
276--679-4393/2701

Nottoway County
Department of Social Services
Nottoway, VA 23955-0026
434-645-8494

Orange County
Department of Social Services
146 Madison Road
Orange, VA 22960
540-672-1155

Page County
Department of Social Services
Luray, VA 22835
540-743-6568

Patrick County
Department of Social Services
106 Rucker Street
Stuart, VA 24171-0498
540-694-3328

Petersburg
Department of Social Services
400 Farmer Street
Petersburg, VA 23804
804-748-8426

Pittsylvania County
Department of Social Services
220 H. G. McGhee Drive
Chatham, VA 24531
434-432-7281

Portsmouth Department of Social Services
1701 High Street
Portsmouth, VA 23701
757-405-1800

Powhatan Department of Social Services
3908 Old Buckingham Road
Powhatan, VA 23139-0099
804-598-5630

Prince Edward
Department of Social Services
111 South Street
Farmville, VA 23901-0628
434-392-3113

Prince George
Department of Social Services
   Prince George, VA 23875-0068
   804-733-2650

Prince William County
Department of Social Services
   7987 Ashton Ave., Suite 200
   Manassas, VA 20109
   703-792-7500

Pulaski County
Department of Social Services
   143 Third Street, NW
   Pulaski, VA 24301-0110
   540-980-7995

Radford City
Department of Social Services
   928 W. Main Street
   Radford, VA 24141
   540-731-3663

Rappahannock County
Department of Social Services
   Washington, VA 22747-0087
   540-675-3313

Richmond City
Department of Social Services
   Richmond, VA 23240
   804-646-7212

Richmond County
Department of Social Services
   5579 Richmond Road
   Warsaw, VA 22572-0035
   804-333-4088

Roanoke City
Department of Social Services
   215 West Church Avenue
   Roanoke, VA 24006
   540-853-2894

Roanoke County
Department of Social Services
   220 East Main Street
   Salem, VA 24153-1127
   540-387-6087

Rockbridge / Buena Vista /Lexington Area
Social Services
   20 East Preston Street
   Lexington, VA 24450
   540-463-7143

Russell County
Department of Social Services
   155 Combs Street
   Lebanon, VA 24266-1207
   276-889-2679/3031

Scott County
Department of Social Services
   Gate City, VA 24251-0637
   276-386-3631/6031

Shenandoah County
Department of Social Services
   600 North Main Street
   Woodstock, VA 22664
   540-459-6226

Smyth County
Department of Social Services
   121 Bagley Circle
   Marion, VA 24354
   276-783-8148

Southampton Co.
Department of Social Services
   26022 Administration Center Drive
   Courtland, VA 23837-0550
   757-653-3080

Spotsylvania
Department of Social Services
   9104 Courthouse Road
   Spotsylvania, VA 22553-0249
   540-582-7065

Stafford County
Department of Social Services
1300 Courthouse Road
Stafford, VA 22555-0007
540-658-8720

Staunton / Augusta County
Department of Social Services
68 Dick Huff Lane
Verona, VA 24482
540-245-5800

Suffolk Department of Social Services
440 Market Street
Suffolk, VA 23434-1818
757-923-3000

Surry Department of Social Services
Surry, VA 23883-0263
757-294-5240

Sussex Department of Social Services
20103 Princeton Road
Sussex, VA 23884-1336
804-246-7020

Tazewell County
Department of Social Services
Tazwell, VA 24651
276--988-2521

Virginia Beach
Department of Social Services
3432 Virginia Beach Blvd.
Virginia Beach, VA 23452-4420
757-437-3313

Warren County
Department of Social Services
912 Warren Avenue
Front Royal, VA 22630-0506
540-635-3430

Washington County
Department of Social Services
15068 Lee Highway
Bristol, VA 24201
276-623-2661

Waynesboro
Department of Social Services
1200 Shenandoah Avenue
Waynesboro, VA 22980
540-942-6646

Westmoreland
Department of Social Services
Peach Grove Lane
Montross, VA 22520-0302
804-493-9305

Williamsburg Social Service Bureau
401 Lafayette St.
Williamsburg, VA 23185
757-220-6161

Winchester Department of Social Services
33 East Boscawen Street
Winchester, VA 22601
540-662-3807

Wise County
Department of Social Services
Coeburn Mountain Road
Wise, VA 24293-0888
276-329-8056-8057

Wythe County
Department of Social Services
275 South 4th Street
Wytheville, VA 24383-2597
276-228-5493/5912

York - Poquoson Social Services
301 Goodwin Neck Road
Yorktown, VA 23692-0917
757-890-3930

Appendix K
Virginia Websites

These websites contain information regarding divorce and Virginia procedures. You will find references and links to many other useful sites as well.

Virginia Divorce Laws
www.divorcenet.com/va/va-div.html

Virginia Divorce Bulletin Board
www.divorcenet.com/va/divorce

Virginia Divorce Bulletin Board
www.divorcenet.com:3336/?forum
=va-board

Virginia Child Support Guidlines Statute
http://leg1.state.va.us
/cgi-bin/legp504.exe?000+cod+20-108.2

Virginia Courts and Cases
www.courts.state.va.us/opin.htm

Virginia Family Law Forms at Findlaw
http://forms.lp.findlaw.com/states
/vaf_1.html

Virginia Child Support Calculator
http://alllaw.com/calculators/childsupport
/virginia

Virginia Law Resource Center
www.us-law.com/links

Family Law Information
http://patriot.net/%7Ecrouch/fln.html

Fairfax County Divorce
www.co.fairfax.va.us/courts/circuit
/divorce.htm

Arlington County Divorce
http://adams.patriot.net/%7Ecrouch
/acbalnx.html

Divorce Law Info
www.divorcelawinfo.com/VA/flc.htm

DivorceInfo.Com
www.divorceinfo.com/vahelps.htm

About.Com
http://divorcesupport.about.com/cs/virginia

APPENDIX L
VIRGINIA
BLANK FORMS

TABLE OF FORMS

Monthly Income and Expenses of _____

Date: _____

Chancery No. _____

Employed By	
City & State	
Occupation	
Pay Period	
Next Payday	
Salary/Wage	
# Exemptions	

Children in Household

Name	Age

Average Gross Pay per Month [ ]

LESS:

Federal Taxes	
State Taxes	
FICA	
Health Insurance	
Life Insurance	
Required Retirement	
Average Monthly Net Pay	
Other Income	
MONTHLY NET INCOME	

Household
- Mortgage (PITI) or Rent
- Real Estate Property Taxes
- Homeowner's Insurance
- Repairs/Maintenance
- Furniture/Furnishings

Utilities
- Electricity
- Gas/Heating Oil
- Water/Sewer
- Telephone
- Trash
- Cable TV

Food
- Groceries
- Lunches

Automobile
- Payment/Depreciation
- Gasoline
- Repair/Tags/Inspection, etc.
- Auto Insurance
- Parking/Other Transportation
- Personal Property Tax

Children's Expenses
- Child Care
- School Tuition
- Lunch Money
- School Supplies
- Lessons, Sports
- New Clothing
- _____

Clothing
- New (Excluding Children)
- Cleaning/Laundry
- Uniforms

Health Expenses
- Doctor
- Dentist
- Therapist
- Eyeglases
- Hospital
- Medicines
- Other

Dues
- Professional Associations
- Social Associations
- Homeowner's Association

Miscellaneous
- Gifts (Xmas, Birthday)
- Church/Charity
- Entertainment
- Vacations
- Hobbies
- Personal Grooming
- Newspaper/Magazines
- Disability Insurance
- Life Insurance
- Legal Expenses

Totals Per Month
Subtotal Expenses	
Subtotal Debt Payments	
TOTAL EXPENSES	
TOTAL NET INCOME	
BALANCE (+)	
BALANCE (-)	

Fixed Debts with Payments

	Balance	Mo. Pmt.

Charge Account Debt

Liquid Assets on Hand
Cash/Checking/Savings	
Other Liquid Assets	
TOTAL LIQUID ASSETS	

Submitted By: _____

form 2

CHILD SUPPORT GUIDELINES WORKSHEET

Case No.: ....

Commonwealth of Virginia   VA. CODE § 20-108.2

.... v. ....

DATE

		MOTHER	FATHER
1.	Monthly Gross Income (see instructions on reverse)	$	$ ....
2.	Adjustments for spousal support payments (see instructions on reverse)	$	$ ....
3.	Adjustments for support of child(ren) (see instructions on reverse)	$	$ ....
4.	Deductions from Monthly Gross Income (see instructions on reverse)	-$	-$ ....
5.	a. Available monthly income	$	$ ....

b. Combined monthly available income

(combine both available monthly income figures from line 5.a.) $ [   ]

6. Number of children in the present case for whom support is sought: [   ]

7. a. Monthly basic child support obligation
   (from schedule — see instructions on reverse)   a. $..........................

   b. Monthly amount allowable for extraordinary medical and dental expense
   (see instructions on reverse)   b. $..........................

   c. Monthly amount allowable for health care coverage
   (see instructions on reverse)   c. $..........................

   d. Monthly amount allowable for employment-related child care expenses
   (see instructions on reverse)   d. $..........................

8. Total monthly child support obligation (add lines 7.a., 7.b., 7.c. and 7.d.) $ [   ]

		MOTHER	FATHER
9.	Percent obligation of each party (divide "available monthly income" on line 5.a. by line 5.b.)	.... %	.... %
10.	Monthly child support obligation of each party (multiply line 8 by line 9)	$ [ ]	$ [ ]
11.	Deduction by non-custodial parent for health care coverage when paid directly by non-custodial parent (from line 7.c.)	$	$ ....

		MOTHER	FATHER
12.	Adjustments (if any) to Child Support Guidelines Calculation (see instructions on reverse)	$..........................	$..........................
	a. Credit for benefits received by or for the child derived from the parent's entitlement to disability insurance benefits to the extent that such derivative benefits are included in a parent's gross income	-$..........................	-$..........................
	b.	....	....
	c.	....	....
	d. Each party's adjusted share	$ [ ]	$ [ ]

CHILD SUPPORT GUIDELINES WORKSHEET INSTRUCTIONS

General — Use monthly financial information rounded to the nearest dollar in making these calculations. To convert data to monthly figures,

- multiply weekly financial data by 4.33
- multiply bi-weekly financial data by 2.167
- multiply semi-monthly financial data by 2
- divide annual financial data by 12

Amounts of $.50 or more should be rounded up to the nearest dollar; amounts less than $.50 should be rounded down to the nearest dollar.

Line 1 — Gross income is defined by Virginia Code § 20-108.2(C).

   a. Gross income "shall mean all income from all sources, and shall include, but not be limited to, income from salaries, wages, commissions, royalties, bonuses, dividends, severance pay, pensions, interest, trust income, annuities, capital gains, social security benefits, worker's compensation benefits, disability insurance benefits, veterans' benefits, spousal support, rental income, gifts, prizes or awards. If a parent's gross income includes disability insurance benefits, it shall also include any amounts paid to or for the child who is the subject of the order and derived by the child from the parent's entitlement to disability insurance benefits."

   b. Gross income "shall not include benefits from public assistance programs as defined in Virginia Code § 63.1-87 [aid to dependent children, auxiliary grants to the aged, blind and disabled, medical assistance, food stamps, general relief, fuel assistance and social services] or child support received."

Line 2 — If spousal support is being paid by a party pursuant to an existing court or administrative order or written agreement, regardless of whether it is being paid to the other party or to a person not a party to this proceeding, subtract that amount under the payee's column. If spousal support is being received by a party pursuant to an existing court or administrative order or written agreement, regardless of whether it is being paid by the other party to this proceeding, add the amount under the payee's column. Use plus and minus signs appropriately. If a party is not paying or receiving spousal support, insert "none" in the appropriate column(s).

Line 3 — When a party is paying child support payments pursuant to an existing court or administrative order or written agreement for a child or children who are not the subject of the proceeding, subtract this amount from gross income. When a party has a child or children who are not the subject of the proceeding in their household or primary physical custody, subtract the amount as shown on the schedule of Monthly Basic Child Support Obligations that represents that party's support obligation for that child or children based solely on the party's income as the total income available. If these provisions are inapplicable, insert "none" in the appropriate column(s). There is only a presumption that these amounts will be deducted from gross income.

Line 4 (Virginia Code § 20-108.2(C)) — If either parent has income from self-employment, a partnership or a closely-held business, subtract reasonable business expenses under the column of the party with such income. If none, insert "none."

Line 5.a. — As applicable, add to and subtract from line 1 the figures in lines 2, 3 and 4 and enter the total for each column.

NOTE: Any adjustments to gross income shall not create or reduce a support obligation to an amount which seriously impairs the custodial parent's ability to maintain minimal adequate housing and provide other basic necessities for the child.

Line 7.a. — Using § 20-108.2(B) SCHEDULE OF MONTHLY BASE CHILD SUPPORT OBLIGATIONS, use line 5.b. (combined monthly available income) to find the applicable income level under COMBINED GROSS INCOME, then use line 6 (number of children) to determine the base child support obligation under the appropriate column at the applicable income level.

Line 7.b. (Virginia Code § 20-108.2(D)) — Insert uninsured medical or dental expenses in excess of $100 for a single illness or condition, which shall include but not be limited to eyeglasses, prescription medication, prostheses, and mental health services whether provided by a social worker, psychologist, psychiatrist or counselor. For past events, allocate an amount to be recouped monthly. For ongoing events, enter the amount to be paid monthly to the health care provider or the amount allocated monthly to be applied toward the bill of the health care provider.

Line 76.c. (Virginia Code §§ 20-108.2(E) and 63.1-250) — Insert costs for "health care coverage" when actually being paid by a parent, to the extent such costs are directly allocable to the child or children, and which are the extra costs of covering the child or children beyond whatever coverage the parent providing the coverage would otherwise have. "Health care coverage" means any plan providing hospital, medical or surgical care coverage for dependent children provided such coverage is available and can be obtained by a person obligated under Virginia law for support of a dependent child or the child's caretaker at a reasonable cost (such as through employers, unions or other groups without regard to service delivery mechanism). This item should also include the cost of any dental care coverage for the child or children paid by a parent.

Lines 7.d. (Virginia Code § 20-108.2(F)) — Insert actual cost or the amount required to provide quality child care, whichever is less. If applicable, allocate ratably between employment-related child care and other child care based on custodian's activities while child care is being provided.

Line 12(a) — If amounts paid to or for the child who is the subject of the order and derived by the child from the parent's entitlement to disability insurance benefits have been included in a parent's gross income, that amount should be subtracted from that parent's child support obligation.

Line 12 (b-c) (Virginia Code § 20-108.1(B)) — If applicable, describe adjustment to child support for factors not addressed in guidelines calculation, then show amount to be added to or subtracted from each party-parent's child support obligation (use plus and minus signs appropriately).

Line 12 (d) — If additional items are entered in lines 12 (a-c), add and subtract such items from line 10 and enter the totals on this line. In cases involving split custody, the amount of child support to be calculated using these guidelines shall be the difference between the amounts owed by each parent as a noncustodial parent, computed in accordance with these guidelines, with the noncustodial parent owing the larger amount paying the difference to the other parent.

For the purpose of applying this provisions, split custody shall be limited to those situations where each parent has physical custody of a child or children born of the parents, born of either parent and adopted by the other parent or adopted by both parents. For the purposes of calculating a child support obligation where split custody exists, a separate family unit exists for each parent, and child support for that family unit shall be calculated upon the number of children in that family unit who are born of the parents, born of either parent and adopted by the other parent or adopted by both parents. Where split custody exists, a parent is a custodial parent to the children in that parent's family unit and is a noncustodial parent to the children in the other parent's family unit.

form 3

CHILD SUPPORT GUIDELINES WORKSHEET —
SHARED CUSTODY   VA. CODE § 20-108.2
Commonwealth of Virginia

Case No.: ....

. . . . v. . . . .

DATE

I. GUIDELINE CALCULATION
A. INCOME

	Mother	Father	Combined

Monthly Gross Income (see instructions on back) (1) $ .... (2) $ ....

Adjustments for spousal support payments (3) $ .... (4) $ ....
  (see instructions on back)

Adjustments for support of child(ren) (5) $ .... (6) $ ....
  (see instructions on back)

Deductions from Monthly Gross Income (7) -$ .... (8) -$ ....
  allowable by law (see instructions on back)

Available Gross Income (9) $ .... (10) $ .... = (11) $ ....

Percentage of Combined Gross Income (12) $ ....% (13) $ ....% = 100%

B. CHILD SUPPORT NEEDS

Number of children for whom support is sought (14) ....

Child support from guideline table — apply lines (11) and (14) to table (15) $ ....

Total shared support — line (15) x 1.40 (16) $ ....

	Mother	Father	

Total days in year each parent has custody (17) .... (18) .... = 365

Each parent's custody share (19) ....% (20) ....% = 100%

C. EACH PARENT'S SUPPORT OBLIGATION TO OTHER PARENT

	Mother	Father

1. Father's obligation to Mother

Basic support to Mother — lines (19) x (16) (21) $ ....

Health care coverage PAID by Mother (if any) (22) $ ....

Work-related child care of Mother (if any) (23) $ ....

Total — lines (21) + (22) + (23) (24) $ ....

Father's obligation — lines (24) x (13) = (25) $ ....

2. Mother's obligation to Father

Basic support to Father — lines (20) x (16) (26) $ ....

Health care coverage PAID by Father (if any) (27) $ ....

Work-related child care of Father (if any) (28) $ ....

Total — lines (26) + (27) + (28) (29) $ ....

Mother's obligation — lines (29) x (12) = (30) $ ....

D. NET MONTHLY CHILD SUPPORT PAYABLE FROM ONE PARENT TO THE OTHER PARENT

Shared custody child support guideline amount — difference between lines (25) and (30) = (31) $ ....

(32) Payable to ☐ Mother ☐ Father (see instructions on back)

II. ADJUSTMENTS (IF ANY) TO SHARED CUSTODY CHILD SUPPORT GUIDELINE AMOUNT

	Mother	Father

A. ADJUSTMENT ITEMS

a. Credit for benefits received by or for the child derived from the parent's entitlement to disability insurance benefits to the extent that such derivative benefits are included in a parent's gross income (33) $ .... (34) $ ....

b. .... $ .... $ ....

c. .... $ .... $ ....

Total adjustments (35) $ .... (36) $ ....

Net adjustment (difference between lines (35) and (36)) (37) $ ....

(38) Owed to ☐ Mother ☐ Father (see instructions on back)

C. TOTAL ADJUSTED SUPPORT (see instructions on back) (39) $ ....

(40) Payable to ☐ Mother ☐ Father

CHILD SUPPORT GUIDELINES WORKSHEET INSTRUCTIONS

General — Use monthly financial information rounded to the nearest dollar in making these calculations. To convert data to monthly figures,

- multiply weekly financial data by 4.33
- multiply bi-weekly financial data by 2.167
- multiply semi-monthly financial data by 2
- divide annual financial data by 12

Amounts of $.50 or more should be rounded *up* to the nearest dollar; amounts less than $.50 should be rounded *down* to the nearest dollar.

Lines 1 and 2 — Gross income is defined by Virginia Code § 20-108.2(C).

    a. Gross income "shall mean all income from all sources, and shall include, but not be limited to, income from salaries, wages, commissions, royalties, bonuses, dividends, severance pay, pensions, interest, trust income, annuities, capital gains, social security benefits, worker's compensation benefits, disability insurance benefits, veterans' benefits, spousal support, rental income, gifts, prizes or awards. If a parent's gross income includes disability insurance benefits, it shall also include any amounts paid to or for the child who is the subject of the order and derived by the child from the parent's entitlement to disability insurance benefits."

    b. Gross income "shall not include benefits from public assistance programs as defined in Virginia Code § 63.1-87 [aid to dependent children, auxiliary grants to the aged, blind and disabled, medical assistance, food stamps, general relief, fuel assistance and social services] or child support received."

Lines 3 and 4 — If spousal support is paid by a party pursuant to an existing court or administrative order or written agreement, regardless of whether it is being paid to the other party or to a person not a party to this proceeding, subtract that amount under the payor's column. If spousal support is being received by a party pursuant to an existing court or administrative order or written agreement, regardless of whether it is being paid by the other party to this proceeding, add the amount under the payee's column. Use plus and minus signs appropriately. If a party is not paying or receiving spousal support, insert "none" in the appropriate column(s).

Lines 5 and 6 - When a party is paying child support payments pursuant to an existing court or administrative order or written agreement for a child or children who are not the subject of the proceeding, subtract this amount from gross income. When a party has a child or children who are not the subject of the proceeding in their household or primary physical custody, subtract the amount as shown on the Schedule of Monthly Basic Child Support Obligations that represents that party's support obligation for that child or children based solely on that party's income as the total income available. If these provisions are inapplicable, insert "none" in the appropriate column(s). **There is only a presumption that these amounts will be deducted from gross income.**

Line 7 and 8 (Virginia Code § 20-108.2(C)) — If either parent has income from self-employment, a partnership or a closely-held business, subtract reasonable business expenses under the column of the party with such income. If none, insert "none."

NOTE: Any adjustments to gross income shall not create or reduce a support obligation to an amount which seriously impairs the custodial parent's ability to maintain minimal adequate housing and provide other basic necessities for the child.

Line 15 — Using Virginia Code § 20-108.2(B) SCHEDULE OF MONTHLY BASE CHILD SUPPORT OBLIGATIONS, use line (11) (combined monthly available income) to find the applicable income level under COMBINED GROSS INCOME, then use line (14) (number of children) to determine the base child support obligation under the appropriate column at the applicable income level.

Line 22 and 27 (Virginia Code §§ 20-108.2(E) and 63.1-250) — Insert costs for "health care coverage" when actually paid by a parent, to the extent such costs are directly allocable to the child or children, and which are the extra costs of covering the child or children beyond whatever coverage the parent providing the coverage would otherwise have. "Health care coverage" means any plan providing hospital, medical or surgical care coverage for dependent children provided such coverage is available and can be obtained by a person obligated under Virginia law for support of a dependent child or the child's caretaker at a reasonable cost (such as through employers, unions or other groups without regard to service delivery mechanism). This item should also include the cost of any dental care coverage for the child or children paid by a parent.

Lines 23 and 28 (Virginia Code § 20-108.2(F)) — Any child-care costs incurred on behalf of the child or children due to employment of the custodial parent shall be added to the basic child support obligation. Child-care costs shall not exceed the amount required to provide quality care from a licensed source.

Line 32 — If Line (25) is larger than Line (30), check Mother on Line (32). If Line (25) is smaller than Line (30), check Father on Line (32).

Lines 33 and 34 — If amounts paid to or for the child who is the subject of the order and derived by the child from the parent's entitlement to disability insurance benefits have been included in a parent's gross income, that amount should be subtracted from that parent's child support obligation.

Line 38 — If Line (35) is larger than Line (36), check Mother on Line (38). If Line (35) is smaller than Line (36), check Father on Line (38).

Lines 39 and 40 — If Lines (31) and (37) are owed to the same party, put the sum of the amounts in these lines on Line (39) and, in Line (40), check the party checked on line (32). If Lines (31) and (37) are owed to different parties, put the difference between the amounts in these amounts in these lines on Line (39) and, in Line (40), check the party to whom the larger of the amounts in Lines (31) and (37) are owed.

FEDERAL POVERTY GUIDELINES (Notice Date: February 6, 2001)						
Household Size	1	2	3	4	5	6
Guideline plus 50%	$ 12,885	$ 17,415	$ 21,945	$ 26,475	$31,005	$35,535
(Add $4,530 for each additional member in households of more than six.)						

form 4

WORKSHEET — SPLIT CUSTODY
Commonwealth of Virginia   VA. CODE § 20-108.2

.... v. ....

DATE

	MOTHER	FATHER
1. Monthly Gross Income (see instructions on Page Two)	$	$ ....
2. Adjustments for spousal support payments (see instructions on Page Two)	$	$ ....
3. Adjustments for support of child(ren) (see instructions on Page Two)	$	$ ....
4. Allowable business expenses (see instructions on Page Two)	-$	-$ ....
5. a. Available monthly income	$	$ ....

5. b. Combined monthly available income
   (combine both available monthly income figures from line 5.a.) $ [   ]

6. Percent obligation of each party (divide "available monthly income" on line
   Line 5.a. by line 5.b.)   % ....   % ....

7. Number of children for which that person is the <u>noncustodial</u> parent.   [   ]   [   ]

	MOTHER	FATHER
8. a. Monthly basic child support obligation for number of children listed above (from schedule — see instructions on Page Two)	$	$ ....
b. Monthly amount allowable for extraordinary medical and dental expense paid by <u>other</u> parent (see instructions on Page Two)	$	$ ....
c. Monthly amount allowable for health care coverage paid by <u>other</u> parent (see instructions on Page Two)	$	$ ....
d. Monthly amount allowable for employment-related child care expense paid by <u>other</u> parent (see instructions on Page Two)	$	$ ....

9. Total monthly child support obligation of each parent (add lines 8.a.,
   8.b., 8.c. and 8.d. for each parent)   [   ]   [   ]

10. Total monthly child support obligation of each party (multiply line 6 by line 9) $ [   ] $ [   ]

	MOTHER	FATHER
11. Adjustments (if any) to Child Support Guidelines Calculation (see instructions on Page Two)	$	$ ....
12. a. Credit for benefits received by or for the child derived from the parent's entitlement to disability insurance benefits to the extent that such derivative benefits are included in a parent's gross income	-$	-$ ....
b.	....	....
c.	....	....

d. Each party's adjusted obligation to other party $ [   ] $ [   ]

e. Net payment $ [   ] $ [   ]

...LD SUPPORT GUIDELINES WORKSHEET INSTRUCTIONS

...e purpose of applying this provision, split custody shall be limited to those situations where each parent has physical custody of a child or children born of the parents, born ...er parent and adopted by the other parent or adopted by both parents. For the purposes of calculating a child support obligation where split custody exists, a separate ...unit exists for each parent, and child support for that family unit shall be calculated upon the number of children in that family unit who are born of the parents, born of ...parent and adopted by the other parent or adopted by both parents. Where split custody exists, a parent is a custodial parent to the children in that parent's family unit and ...oncustodial parent to the children in the other parent's family unit.

...ral — Use monthly financial information rounded to the nearest dollar in making these calculations. To convert data to monthly figures,

- multiply weekly financial data by 4.33
- multiply bi-weekly financial data by 2.167
- multiply semi-monthly financial data by 2
- divide annual financial data by 12

...nts of $.50 or more should be rounded up to the nearest dollar; amounts less than $.50 should be rounded down to the nearest dollar.

...1 — Gross income is defined by Virginia Code § 20-108.2(C).

Gross income "shall mean all income from all sources, and shall include, but not be limited to, income from salaries, wages, commissions, royalties, bonuses, dividends, severance pay, pensions, interest, trust income, annuities, capital gains, social security benefits, worker's compensation benefits, disability insurance benefits, veterans' benefits, spousal support, rental income, gifts, prizes or awards. If a parent's gross income includes disability insurance benefits, it shall also include any amounts paid to or for the child who is the subject of the order and derived by the child from the parent's entitlement to disability insurance benefits."

Gross income "shall not include benefits from public assistance programs as defined in Virginia Code § 63.1-87 [aid to dependent children, auxiliary grants to the aged, blind and disabled, medical assistance, food stamps, general relief, fuel assistance and social services] or child support received."

...2 —If spousal support is being paid by a party pursuant to an existing court or administrative order or written agreement, regardless of whether it is being paid to the other ...or to a person not a party to this proceeding, subtract that amount under the payor's column. If spousal support is being received by a party pursuant to an existing court or ...nistrative order or written agreement, regardless of whether it is being paid by the other party to this proceeding, add the amount under the payee's column. Use plus and ...s signs appropriately. If a party is not paying or receiving spousal support, insert "none" in the appropriate column(s).

...3 —When a party is paying child support payments pursuant to an existing court or adminitrative order or written agreement for a child or children who are not the subject ...s proceeding, subtract this amount from gross income. When a party has a child or children who are not the subject of the proceeding in their household or primary physical ...dy, subtract the amount as shown on the Schedule of Monthly Basic Child Support Obligations that represents that party's support obligation for that child or children based ...y on that party's income as the total income available. If these provisions are inapplicable, insert "none" in the appropriate column(s). **There is only a presumption that ...amounts will be deducted from gross income.**

...4 (Virginia Code § 20-108.2(C)) — If either parent has income from self-employment, a partnership or a closely-held business, subtract reasonable business expenses ...r the column of the party with such income. If none, insert "none."

...5.a. — As applicable, add to and subtract from line 1 the figures in lines 2, 3 and 4 and enter the total for each column.

...E: Any adjustments to gross income shall not create or reduce a support obligation to an amount which seriously impairs the custodial parent's ability to ...tain minimal adequate housing and provide other basic necessities for the child.

...8.a. — Using Virginia Code § 20-108.2(B) SCHEDULE OF MONTHLY BASE CHILD SUPPORT OBLIGATIONS, use line 5.b. (combined monthly available income) ...d the applicable income level under COMBINED GROSS INCOME, then use line 7 (number of children) to determine the base child support obligation under the ...opriate column at the applicable income level.

...8.b. (Virginia Code § 20-108.2(D)) — Insert uninsured medical or dental expenses in excess of $100 for a single illness or condition, which shall include but not be ...ed to eyeglasses, prescription medication, prostheses, and mental health services whether provided by a social worker, psychologist, psychiatrist or counselor. For past ...ts, allocate an amount to be recouped monthly. For ongoing events, enter the amount to be paid monthly to the health care provider or the amount allocated monthly to be ...ed toward the bill of the health care provider.

...8.c. (Virginia Code §§ 20-108.2(E) and 63.1-250) — Insert costs for "health care coverage" when actually being paid by a parent, to the extent such costs are directly ...able to the child or children, and which are the extra costs of covering the child or children beyond whatever coverage the parent providing the coverage would otherwise ... "Health care coverage" means any plan providing hospital, medical or surgical care coverage for dependent children provided such coverage is available and can be ...ned by a person obligated under Virginia law for support of a dependent child or the child's caretaker at a reasonable cost (such as through employers, unions or other ...ps without regard to service delivery mechanism). This item should also include the cost of any dental coverage for the child or children paid by a parent.

...s 8.d. (Virginia Code § 20-108.2(F)) — Insert actual cost or the amount required to provide quality child care, whichever is less. If applicable, allocate ratably between ...oyment-related child care and other child care based on custodian's activities while child care is being provided.

...12(a) — If amounts paid to or for the child who is the subject of the order and derived by the child from the parent's entitlement to disability insurance benefits have been ...ded in a parent's gross income, that amount should be subtracted from that parent's child support obligation.

...12 (b-c) (Virginia Code § 20-108.1(B)) — If applicable, describe adjustment to child support for factors not addressed in guidelines calculation, then show amount to be ...d to or subtracted from each party-parent's child support obligation (use plus and minus signs appropriately).

...12 (d) — If additional items are entered in lines 11 (a-c), add and subtract such items from line 10 and enter the totals on this line. In cases involving split custody, the ...unt of child support to be calculated using these guidelines shall be the difference between the amounts owed by each parent as a noncustodial parent, computed in ...rdance with these guidelines, with the noncustodial parent owing the larger amount paying the difference to the other parent.

VIRGINIA:
IN THE CIRCUIT COURT FOR _____ COUNTY

_____	*	
Complainant,	*	
	*	
vs.	*	IN CHANCERY NO. _____
	*	
_____	*	
Defendant.	*	

BILL OF COMPLAINT FOR DIVORCE

COMES NOW the Complainant, by counsel, and as and for his Bill of Complaint for Divorce, respectfully states as follows:

1. The parties hereto were lawfully married on _____ in _____ ;

2. There were no children born or adopted of the marriage.

3. Both parties hereto are over the age of eighteen (18) years. Neither party is an active duty member of the Armed Forces of the United States.

4. The Complainant and Defendant are both domiciliaries and residents of the Commonwealth of Virginia and have been for more than six (6) months prior to the filing of this suit. The parties last cohabited as husband and wife in _____ .

5. The parties did separate and cease cohabiting together as husband and wife on _____, with the intent to terminate the marriage. The parties have remained separate and apart without any cohabitation and without interruption since the aforesaid date, constituting a period now in excess of one year.

6. The parties have entered into a written Property Settlement Agreement dated _____ which Agreement resolves all matters of property and support between them.

DIVORCE Case Cover Sheet

To be filed with the Bill of Complaint and any Cross-Bill of Complaint in ALL divorce cases

Date Filed: _____   Case Number: _____

PLEASE COMPLETE ALL SHADED AREAS

PARTIES

COMPLAINANT	DEFENDANT	SERVICE DATE/TYPE

ATTORNEYS

COMPLAINANT ATTORNEY	DEFENSE ATTORNEY:
BAR ID:	BAR ID:
	ANSWER DATE:
	CROSS-BILL DATE:
FIRM:	FIRM:
Name:	Name:
Street:	Street:
City: State: Zip	City: State: Zip
Phone Number: ( )	Phone Number: ( )

(Check all that apply):

❐	TOTALLY UNCONTESTED (custody, support and property issues resolved OR no custody, property or support issues)	❐	CONTESTED PROPERTY OR SUPPORT ISSUES	❐	CONTESTED CUSTODY ISSUES
❐	ORE TENUS (planning to file a Request for Ore Tenus hearing)				

REQUESTED SERVICE:
❐ SHERIFF   ❐ SPECIAL PROCESS SERVER   ❐ ACCEPTANCE
❐ PUBLICATION   ❐ WAIVER   ❐ NO SERVICE AT THIS TIME

VIRGINIA:
IN THE CIRCUIT COURT FOR THE COUNTY OF _____

_____,)
           Complainant,)
)
v.   )   **IN CHANCERY NO. _____**
)
_____)
           Defendant.)

ACCEPTANCE OF SERVICE

COMES NOW the Defendant, _____, who hereby accepts Service of Process of the Bill of Complaint with attached Subpoena in Chancery in this matter.

_____
                    Defendant

COMMONWEALTH OF VIRGINIA:
COUNTY OF _____ to-wit:

ACKNOWLEDGED, SUBSCRIBED and **SWORN** to before me by _____

_____, this ____ day of _____, 200__.

My Commission Expires: _____

_____
                 Notary Public

**ACCEPTANCE/WAIVER OF SERVICE OF PROCESS AND
WAIVER OF FUTURE SERVICE OF PROCESS
AND NOTICE**
COMMONWEALTH OF VIRGINIA

Case No.: .... (1) ....

(2) .... Circuit Court

(3)   (4)
.... V. ....
PLAINTIFF   DEFENDANT

(5) I, the undersigned party named below, swear under oath/affirm the following:

1.   I am a party ☐ plaintiff ☐ defendant in the above-styled suit.

2.   I have received a copy of the following documents on this date:

(6)
☐ Subpoena in Chancery (Process)
☐ Bill of Complaint
☐ Other – Describe: ....

(7)   I understand that my receipt of these copies and my signature below constitute
☐ the acceptance of service of process of these copies, or
☐ a waiver of service of process and notice which may be prescribed by law.

3.   I agree to voluntarily and freely waive any future service of process and notice as checked below in this case:
☐ a.   any further service of process.
☐ b.   notice of the appointment of a commissioner in chancery and hearings held by such commissioner in chancery, if a
(8) commissioner in chancery is appointed.
☐ c.   notice of the taking of depositions.
☐ d.   notice of the filing of any reports by a commissioner in chancery or of the filing of depositions.
☐ e.   notice of entry of any order or decree, including the final decree of divorce.
        I understand that, by waiving service of process, I am giving up my right to be notified of the events described
        immediately above.

(9)   (10)
....   _____
DATE   ☐ DEFENDANT   ☐ PLAINTIFF

TO DEFENDANT: Notify the Court in writing of any changes of your address while this case is pending.
State of .... (11) .... , ☐ City ☐ County of ....
Subscribed and sworn to/affirmed before me this day by the above-named party.

(12)   (13)
....   _____
DATE   ☐ CLERK   ☐ DEPUTY CLERK

(14)
_____   My commission expires: .... (15) ....
NOTARY PUBLIC

FORM CC-1406 (w) MASTER 5/98 PC
VA. CODE §§ 8.01-327; 20-99.1:1
Rule 2:7

DATA ELEMENTS

1.   Court case number. (If not known, inquire with the clerk of court.)

2.   Name of court.

3.   Name of plaintiff.

4.   Name of defendant.

5.   Check appropriate box to identify person accepting/waiving process.

6.   Check appropriate box for applicable service. If document is not a Subpoena in Chancery or Bill of Complaint, check box below Bill of Complaint and enter description of document received. See Using This Form, 2(a).

7.   Check appropriate box to indicate acceptance or waiver of process.

8.   Check appropriate box for which the defendant has waived future service of process.

9.   Date defendant is accepting process and/or waiving process.

10. Signature of person accepting process or counsel in proceeding. Check appropriate title box. See Using This Form, 2(c).

11. Enter name of state, check applicable box and enter the city or county name where affirmation is taken. Not filled out online.

12. Date of defendant/plaintiff affirmation. Not filled out online

13. Signature of person taking affirmation, if clerk or deputy clerk. Check the appropriate title box. Not filled out online.

14. Notary public. Not filled out online.

15. Date Notary Public's commission expires. Not filled out online.

VIRGINIA:

IN THE CIRCUIT COURT OF THE [CITY] _____ [COUNTY] OF _____

_____,

Plaintiff,

Chancery No.: _____

_____,

Defendant.

AFFIDAVIT

I, the undersigned, swear/affirm as follows:

1. I am [name], [address], [telephone number]. I am a private process server in this suit.
2. I am not a party to or otherwise interested in the subject matter in controversy in this case.
3. I am 18 years of age or older.
4. I served [name of person served with papers], upon whom service of process was to be made, with copies of the Bill of Complaint, filed on _____, _____, with Subpoena in Chancery attached, and the [here, identify other papers served, for example, "Notice to Take Depositions, filed on _____, _____"], as shown below:
   a. Date of Service: _____
   b. Place of Service (address): _____
   c. Method of Service: (Check one)
      (1) _____ By personal service;
      (2) _____ Being unable to make personal service, a copy was delivered to a family member (not a temporary sojourner or guest) age 16 or older at the usual place of abode of the person to be served after giving information of its purport. The name, age of recipient, and relation of recipient to party served are:

      _____

      (3) _____ Being unable to make personal service, a copy was posted on front door or such other door as appears to be the main entrance of the usual place of abode (other authorized recipient not found).

_____   _____

Date   [Name of process server]

COMMONWEALTH OF VIRGINIA
[CITY] [COUNTY] of _____

Subscribed and sworn to/affirmed before me this _____ day of _____, _____, by [name of process server].

_____   _____

Date   Notary Public
                                        My commission expires: _____

VIRGINIA:

    IN THE CIRCUIT COURT OF THE [CITY] [COUNTY] OF _____

_____,

                    Plaintiff,

v.   Chancery No.: ____

_____,

                    Defendant.

REQUEST FOR ORDER OF PUBLICATION

    The clerk will please enter an order of publication in this matter. Plaintiff's Affidavit in Support of Order of Publication is filed herewith.

_____
Plaintiff's name
Address
Address
Telephone

VIRGINIA:

      IN THE CIRCUIT COURT OF THE [CITY] [COUNTY] OF _____

_____,

                Plaintiff,

v.   Chancery No.: ____

_____,

                Defendant.

AFFIDAVIT IN SUPPORT OF ORDER OF PUBLICATION

Name of plaintiff], being duly sworn, deposes and says:
  1. [Name of plaintiff] is the Plaintiff in the above-styled divorce suit.
  2. The above-named Defendant's last known address [was [address]] [is not known].
  3. The Defendant's present whereabouts are unknown.
  4. The Plaintiff has used due diligence to attempt to locate the Defendant without effect.

                        _____

                              [Name of Plaintiff]

COMMONWEALTH OF VIRGINIA

[CITY] [COUNTY] of _____, to-wit:

Subscribed and sworn to/affirmed before me this _____ day of _____, _____, by [name of plaintiff].

                        _____

                        Notary Public
                        My commission expires: _____

VIRGINIA:

IN THE CIRCUIT COURT OF THE [CITY] [COUNTY] OF _____

_____,

Plaintiff,

v.   Chancery No.: _____

_____,

Defendant.

AFFIDAVIT IN SUPPORT OF ORDER OF PUBLICATION

Name of plaintiff], being duly sworn, deposes and says:
1.   [Name of plaintiff] is the Plaintiff in the above-styled divorce suit.
2.   The Defendant is not a resident of the Commonwealth of Virginia.
3.   The above-named Defendant's last known address was [address outside of Virginia].

_____
[Name of Plaintiff]

COMMONWEALTH OF VIRGINIA

[CITY] [COUNTY] of _____, to-wit:

Subscribed and sworn to/affirmed before me this _____ day of _____, _____, by [name of plaintiff].

_____
Notary Public
My commission expires: _____

VIRGINIA:

IN THE CIRCUIT COURT OF THE [CITY] [COUNTY] OF _____

_____,

Plaintiff,

v.

Chancery No.: ____

_____,

Defendant.

AFFIDAVIT IN SUPPORT OF ORDER OF PUBLICATION

Name of plaintiff], being duly sworn, deposes and says:
1. [Name of plaintiff] is the Plaintiff in the above-styled divorce suit.
2. The above-named Defendant's last known address was [address], which is located within the [City] [County] of _____, Virginia.
3. Plaintiff sought service of process on the Defendant at [his] [her] last known residence, and the Sheriff of _____, Virginia has filed a return of service stating that the process has been in [his] [her] hands for 21 days and that [he] [she] has been unable to make service of process.
4. The Defendant's present whereabouts are unknown.

_____

[Name of Plaintiff]

COMMONWEALTH OF VIRGINIA

[CITY] [COUNTY] of _____, to-wit:

Subscribed and sworn to/affirmed before me this _____ day of _____, _____, by [name of plaintiff].

_____
Notary Public
My commission expires: _____

IN THE CIRCUIT COURT OF _____ COUNTY

_____
Complainant

VS

CHANCERY NO.

_____
Defendant

AFFIDAVIT FOR SERVICE BY PUBLICATION

Comes now _____, *Complainant herein, seeking service on* _____ , *the defendant by ORDER OF PUBLICATION, AND who under oath deposes and states under oath that the Defendant in this cause,*

☐　　*Is a non-resident individual, other than a non-resident individual fiduciary who has appointed a statutory agent;*

OR

☐　　*Cannot be found, and that diligence has been used without effect to ascertain the location of the party to be served;*

OR

☐　　*Cannot be served with court process, and that a return has been filed by the Sheriff which shows that the process has been in his or her hands for twenty-one (21) days and the Sheriff has been unable to make service;*

OR

☐　　*OTHER:*

and the last known mailing address of the Defendant is as follows:

Name: _____
Address: _____
_____

OTHER INFORMATION:

_____
Signature of Complainant

_____
Counsel for Complainant

VIRGINIA
IN THE CIRCUIT COURT OF _____ COUNTY

_____
Complainant

VS

_____
Defendant

CHANCERY NO.

ORDER OF PUBLICATION

The reason for this cause is ___to obtain a divorce___

An affidavit having been made and filed showing that the Defendant in the above-entitled cause is

☐   *Is a non-resident individual, other than a non-resident individual fiduciary who has appointed a statutory agent;*

OR

☐   *Cannot be found, and that diligence has been used without effect to ascertain the location of the party to be served;*

OR

☐   *Cannot be served with court process, and that a return has been filed by the Sheriff which shows that the process has been in his or her hands for twenty-one (21) days and the Sheriff has been unable to make service;*

OR

☐   *OTHER: _____*

and last known mailing address of the Defendant is as follows:

     Name   _____

     Address _____

TO BE COMPLETED BY CLERK'S OFFICE

Upon consideration, this Order of Publication is granted and it is ORDERED that the above named Defendant shall appear here on or before _____ day of _____, _____ after proper publication of this Order, to protect his/her interest in this cause.

Entered: _____

TESTE: _____

BY: _____

         DEPUTY CLERK

Signature of Complainant or Counsel for Complainant
Address: _____

Phone Number: _____

VIRGINIA:

IN THE CIRCUIT COURT OF _____ COUNTY

)
)
Complainant,   )
)
v.   )   IN CHANCERY NO. _____
)
)
)
Defendant.   )

ANSWER TO BILL OF COMPLAINT

I admit the allegations of the Bill of Complaint filed in this matter and do not object to the granting of the relief requested.

_____

_____

_____

VIRGINIA:
IN THE CIRCUIT COURT OF _____ COUNTY

_____   )
            Complainant   )
)   IN CHANCERY NO. _____
VS   )
)
_____   )
            Defendant

REQUEST FOR ORE TENUS HEARING

I, _____, [ ]Complainant, [ ]Defendant, [ ]Counsel for Complainant, [ ] Counsel for Defendant (Check one), hereby request that this matter be set for an *Ore Tenus* hearing as all issues in this case are totally uncontested. I have received and read the Fairfax Circuit Court's *Ore Tenus* Hearing Instructions and agree to fully comply with them.

_____
NAME

Attachments:

1. Property Settlement Agreement: [ ]
2. Final Decree: [ ]
3. Other: [ ] _____

Address:

_____
_____
_____

Daytime Phone No: (____) _____

VSB# (If Attorney): _____

CERTIFICATE OF SERVICE

I hereby certify that if notice is required by either Rule 1:12 of the Rules of the Supreme Court Virginia of Virginia Code Section 20-99 or 20-99.1:1, a true copy of this pleading and all attachments have been served on opposing counsel of record.

_____
(Print name and sign)

(request.ot)

H-41

COMMONWEALTH OF VIRGINIA – REPORT OF DIVORCE OR ANNULMENT
Department of Health – Division of Vital Records – Richmond

1. CIRCUIT COURT FOR CITY OR COUNTY OF

STATE FILE NUMBER

2. FULL NAME

2A. SOCIAL SECURITY #

HUSBAND

3. PLACE OF BIRTH (state or foreign country)

4. DATE OF BIRTH

5. RACE

6. NUMBER OF THIS MARRIAGE (first, second, etc.)

7. EDUCATION Elementary or Secondary (Specify only highest grade completed) (0-12) College (1-4 or 5+)

8. USUAL RESIDENCE (street no. or rural route no.) (city or town) (county-if not independent city) (state)

9. FULL MAIDEN NAME

9A. SOCIAL SECURITY #

WIFE

10. PLACE OF BIRTH (state or foreign country)

11. DATE OF BIRTH

12. RACE

13. NUMBER OF THIS MARRIAGE (first, second, etc.)

14. EDUCATION Elementary or Secondary (Specify only highest grade completed) (0-12) College (1-4 or 5+)

15. USUAL RESIDENCE (street no. or rural route no.) (city or town) (county-if not independent city) (state)

16. PLACE OF MARRIAGE (city or town) (state or foreign country)

17. DATE OF MARRIAGE

18. NUMBER OF CHILDREN UNDER 18 IN THIS FAMILY

19. NUMBER OF CHILDREN UNDER 18 WHOSE PHYSICAL CUSTODY WAS AWARDED TO:

20. DATE OF SEPARATION

21. PLAINTIFF
☐ HUSBAND ☐ WIFE ☐ BOTH

Husband _____ Wife _____
Joint (Husband/Wife) _____ Other _____ ☐ No children

22. DIVORCE GRANTED TO
☐ HUSBAND ☐ WIFE ☐ BOTH

23. LEGAL GROUNDS OR CAUSE OF DIVORCE (if annulment - so state)

24. INFORMANT'S SIGNATURE ▶

☐ PETITIONER
☐ ATTORNEY FOR PETITIONER

NAME OF INFORMANT (Type or Print)

ADDRESS OF INFORMANT

I CERTIFY THAT A FINAL DECREE OF _____ (divorce or annulment) WAS ENTERED _____ (date of divorce or annulment) CONCERNING THE ABOVE

MARRIAGE AND WAS NUMBERED _____ (court file number)

▶ SIGNATURE OF CLERK OF COURT OR DEPUTY

(SEAL)

NAME OF CLERK OR DEPUTY (Type or Print) _____

SAMPLE

(An original of this document must be obtained directly from the court.)

302

I-20

VIRGINIA:

IN THE CIRCUIT COURT OF _____ COUNTY

_____)

Complainant,)

v.)

) CHANCERY NO. _____

_____)

Defendant)

DECREE OF REFERENCE

THIS CAUSE came on upon the Bill of Complaint for Divorce filed duly herein; upon process service of the Bill of Complaint for Divorce upon the Defendant; upon this cause having matured for a hearing; and upon motion of the Complainant for referral of this cause to a Commissioner in Chancery; and

IT APPEARING TO THE COURT that this cause has matured for the appointment of and reference to a Commissioner in Chancery; it is, accordingly

ADJUDGED, ORDERED and DECREED that this cause hereby is referred to _____, a Commissioner in Chancery for this Court, for the purpose of taking evidence of the parties and their witnesses, and reporting to this Court findings, conclusions of law recommendations in regard to the allegations contained in the pleadings.

The Commissioner and parties are governed by the General Order for Commissioners of March 11, 1996.

ENTERED this _____ day of _____, 20____.

_____
JUDGE

WE ASK FOR THIS:
Counsel

[Certificate of Service]

VIRGINIA:

IN THE CIRCUIT COURT OF _____ COUNTY

_____)

Complainant,)

v.)   CHANCERY NO. _____

_____)

Defendant)

AGREED DECREE OF REFERENCE

The parties, by their respective counsel, request this Court to appoint _____ to be the Commissioner in Chancery in this cause.

Further, the undersigned represent that:

1. They have familiarized themselves with the General Order for Commissioners Hearings in Divorce Cases, dated March 11, 1996.

2. The above named person is a Commissioner in Chancery for this Court.

3. This Commissioner does not have a conflict with either party or counsel.

4. This Commissioner has agreed to serve in this matter.

5. A copy of this Decree of Reference will be transmitted to the Commissioner.

6. The cause will be set for the Commissioner's Hearing no closer to the trial date than Sixty days, to allow for the Report to be filed and any Exceptions taken.

WHEREFORE, it appearing that this cause should be referred to a Commissioner in Chancery in accordance with the stipulations set forth above, it is:

ADJUDGED, ORDERED and DECREED that _____ is hereby appointed the Commissioner in Chancery in this matter. The Commissioner and parties are governed by the General Order for Commissioners of March 11, 1996.

ENTERED this ___ day of _____, 20____.

_____

                                                    JUDGE

SEEN & AGREED   SEEN & AGREED

_____   _____
Counsel for Complainant   Counsel for Defendant

VIRGINIA:
       IN THE CIRCUIT COURT OF _____ **COUNTY**

_____,)
            Complainant,   )
)
vs.   )   IN CHANCERY NO _____
)
_____,   )
            Defendant.   )

FINAL DECREE OF DIVORCE

THIS MATTER CAME ON upon the Bill of Complaint filed by the Complainant; upon the filing of an Answer by the Defendant; upon the signing of an Acceptance of Service; upon the taking of depositions of the Complainant and his witness before a Notary Public; and the filing of a transcript of said depositions herein; and

IT APPEARING unto the Court

1. That the parties herein were married on _____, in _____;

2. That there were no children born or adopted of the marriage;

3. That the Complainant and Defendant last cohabited as husband and wife in _____;

4. That both parties are *bona fide* residents and domiciliaries of the Commonwealth of Virginia and have been so for more than six months prior to the institution of this suit;

5. That both parties are over the age of eighteen years and neither party is an active duty member of the Armed Forces of the United States;

6. That the parties have lived separate and apart, without any cohabitation and without interruption, for a period of more than one year, with the intent to permanently terminate the marital relationship;

7. That the parties entered into a Property Settlement Agreement dated _____, which Agreement settles all issues of property and support;

8. That there is no child or spousal support payable by one party to the other, nor are there any health insurance obligations in this Decree, hence the provisions of Virginia Code §20-60.3 do not apply.

WHEREFORE, your Complainant prays:

a. That he be granted a divorce *a vinculo matrimonii* on the grounds that the parties have lived separate and apart from each other, without any cohabitation, pursuant to Virginia Code §20-91 (9);

b. That the parties' Property Settlement Agreement of _____ be ratified, affirmed and incorporated, but not merged, into the Final Decree of Divorce entered in this matter pursuant to Virginia Code §20-109.1;

Respectfully submitted,

_____,
By Counsel

Counsel for Complainant

VIRGINIA:
    IN THE CIRCUIT COURT OF FAIRFAX COUNTY

_____,) Complainant,)) vs.)) _____,) Defendant.)	IN CHANCERY NO _____

FINAL DECREE OF DIVORCE WITH CHILD/SPOUSAL SUPPORT

THIS MATTER CAME ON upon the Bill of Complaint filed by the Complainant; upon the filing of an Answer by the Defendant; upon the signing of an Acceptance of Service; upon the taking of depositions of the Complainant and his witness before a Notary Public; and the filing of a transcript of said depositions herein; and

WHEREUPON, pursuant to Virginia Code §20-60.3, the parties are hereby notified of the following provisions of Virginia law and the parties hereby represent to this Court that the information provided below is true information:

NOTICES and INFORMATION:

1. Support payments may be withheld as they become due pursuant to §20-79.1 or §20-79.2, from income as defined in §63.1-250, without further amendments of this Order or having to file an application for services with the Department of Social Services.

2. Support payments may be withheld pursuant to Chapter 13 (§63.1-249, et seq.) of Title 63.1 without further amendments to the order upon application for services with the Department of Social Services.

3. A duty of support is owed for the following children of the parties:

Name	Date of Birth	Resides With
_____	_____	_____
_____	_____	_____

4. The following is true information regarding the parties subject of this Order:
Person responsible for paying child support is the _____.

MOTHER: _____
  Date of Birth:_____
  SSN: _____ ___ _____
  Driver's License #:_____
  State of Issuance: _____
  Resid. Address: _____
  Home Phone #:_____
  Employment: _____
  Work Address: _____
  Work Phone #: _____

FATHER: _____
  Date of Birth:_____
  SSN: _____ ___ _____
  Driver's License #:_____
  State of Issuance: _____
  Resid. Address: _____
  Home Phone #:_____
  Employment: _____
  Work Address: _____
  Work Phone #: _____

5. A petition may be filed for the suspension of any license, certificate, registration or other authorization to engage in a profession, trade, business or occupation issued by the Commonwealth of Virginia to a person responsible for support as provided in §63.1-263.1, upon a delinquency for a period of ninety days or more or in an amount of $5,000 or more.

Neither party holds any such license, certificate, registration or authorization. [OR put in who holds what license]

6. The Order of this Court as to the amount and terms of the child support and spousal support are as set forth in the support provisions of this Decree.

7.a. The Order of this Court as to health care coverage for spouse and children and any policy information are set forth in the health care provision of this Order.

b. This Order does not contain any provision for extraordinary medical expenses to be paid by or reimbursed to a party pursuant to subsection D and G3 of §20-108.2.

8. There are no support arrearages as of the date of entry of this Decree.

9. If child support payments have been ordered, then, unless the Court orders otherwise for good cause shown, the parties shall give each other and this Court at least thirty days' advance written notice of any change in address, and shall give notice of any change of telephone number within thirty days after the change. The parties shall give these notices to each other and, when payments are to be made through the Department of Social Services (DSS), to the DSS.

10. If child support payments are ordered to be paid through the (DSS), the obligor shall keep the DSS informed of his or her current employer's name, address and telephone number. If payments are made directly to the obligee then the obligor shall keep this Court informed of his or her current employer's name, address and telephone number.

11. The separate amounts due to each person under this Order for child support or the affirmation of a separation agreement, are set forth in the support provision of this Order.

12. In determination of a support obligation, the support obligation as it becomes due and unpaid creates a judgment by operation of law.

13. The Department of Social Services may, pursuant to Chapter 13 (§63.1-249, et seq.) of Title 63.1 and in accordance with §20-108.2 and §63.1-252.2, initiate a review of the amount of support ordered by any court.

WHEREUPON, it appearing to this Court:

1. That the parties herein were married on _____, in _____;

2. That there were two children born of the marriage;

3. That the Complainant and Defendant last cohabited as husband and wife in _____;

4. That both parties are *bona fide* residents and domiciliaries of the Commonwealth of Virginia and have been so for more than six months prior to the institution of this suit;

5. That both parties are over the age of eighteen years and neither party is an active member of the Armed Forces of the United States;

6. That the parties have lived separate and apart, without any cohabitation and without interruption since _____, constituting a period of more than one year, with the intent to permanently terminate the marital relationship;

7. That the parties entered into a Property Settlement Agreement dated_____, which Agreement settles all issues of property and support;

8. That the Complainant is entitled to a divorce *a vinculo matrimonii* pursuant to Virginia Code §20-91(9), therefore, it is:

ADJUDGED, ORDERED and DECREED as follows:

1. Divorce: That the Complainant is hereby granted a Final Decree of Divorce, *a vinculo matrimonii*, from the Defendant pursuant to Virginia Code §20-91(9), based on the fact that the parties have lived separate and apart, without any cohabitation and without interruption, for a period in excess of one year; and

2. Agreement: That the Property Settlement Agreement of the parties dated _____, is hereby ratified and affirmed and is incorporated into, but is not merged into, this Final Decree of Divorce pursuant to Virginia Code §20-109.1 and the parties are ordered to comply with all provisions thereof.

3. Custody: [Specify the basic custody/visitation provisions of the PSA]

Pursuant to Virginia Code §20-124.5, either party who intends to relocate his or her residence shall give a thirty-day advance written notice of any such intended relocation and of any intended change of address, said notice being given to both the other party and to this Court

4. Child Support: _____ shall pay to _____, as child support, the sum of $_____ per _____, beginning _____ 200__ and to be paid _____, until further order of this Court.

(1) This support amount set forth above [ ]Does [ ]Does Not include any payment for extraordinary medical expenses to be paid by or reimbursed to a party pursuant to subsection D and G 3 of § 20-108.2.   OR

In addition to the support amount set forth above, _____ shall pay or reimburse to _____, for the extraordinary medical expenses of _____, as follows: _____ .

(2) Support shall be paid for any child until the child reaches the age of eighteen, and shall continue to be paid for a child who is: (i) a full-time high school student, (ii) not self-supporting, and (iii) living in the home of the parent seeking or receiving child support, until the child reaches the age of nineteen or graduates from high school, whichever occurs first.

(3) That said support shall be payable directly by the _____ to the _____ and shall NOT be by Income Deduction Order.

5. Spousal Support: [Specify any spousal support provisions of the PSA]

6. Health Care: That the _____ shall provide health insurance for the minor children so long as such insurance coverage is available under the terms of his employer-provided health insurance policy. The health insurance carrier is _____, and said insurance is provided as a benefit of the Defendant's employment with _____.

Health insurance [is] [is not] required by this Order for a spouse or former spouse.

7. Arrearages: There are no support arrearages of as the date of this Order.

THIS CAUSE IS FINAL.

ENTERED this _____ day of _____, 20 ____

_____
JUDGE

WE ASK FOR THIS: **SEEN and AGREED:**

Counsel for Complainant   Counsel for Defendant

Section 10:
District of Columbia

APPENDIX M

SUMMARY OF DIVORCE LAWS FOR THE DISTRICT OF COLUMBIA

This appendix summarizes the most important laws concerning divorce in the District of Columbia. You can use this summary to find a quick answer to a question or as a starting point for future research.

1. **FILING**.
   (a) The Complaint is filed in the "Superior Court of the District of Columbia, Family Division";
   (b) it is titled a "Complaint for Divorce" or "Complaint for Legal Separation";
   (c) it is filed by the "Plaintiff";
   (d) the other spouse is the "Defendant";
   (e) it is filed at 500 Indiana Avenue, NW, 5th Floor; and
   (f) the final papers are called the "Findings of Fact, Conclusions of Law, and Judgment of Absolute Divorce". District of Columbia Rules.

2. **RESIDENCY**. One party must have been a resident for six months immediately prior to filing for divorce. Military personnel are considered residents if they have been stationed in DC for six months. District of Columbia Code; Title 16, Chapter 9, Section 902.

3. **GROUNDS FOR ABSOLUTE DIVORCE**.
   (a) Mutual and voluntary separation for six months;
   (b) involuntary separation for one year. District of Columbia Code; Title 16, Chapter 9, Sections 904(a), 905, and 906.

4. **GROUNDS FOR LEGAL SEPARATION.**
   (a) Mutual and voluntary separation (no minimum duration);
   (b) involuntary separation for one year;
   (c) adultery; and

   (d) cruelty. District of Columbia Code; Title 16, Chapter 9, Section 904(b).

5. **MEDIATION AND PARENTING CLASSES**. The court has started a pilot program of sending cases to a mediator. In child custody cases, the court may order either or both spouses to attend parenting classes. District of Columbia Code; Title 16, Chapter 9, Sections 911(2)d.

6. **UNCONTESTED DIVORCE**. Upon written request, the Court will schedule a brief hearing before a Commissioner, where at least one party testifies, to obtain a divorce. District of Columbia Rules.

7. **CHILD CUSTODY**. The court may award sole or joint custody based on the best interests of the child, without regard to spouse's sex or sexual orientation, race, color, national origin, or political affiliations. The following factors shall also be considered:
   (a) the preference of the child, if the child is of sufficient age and capacity;
   (b) the wishes of the parents;
   (c) the child's adjustment to his or her home, school, and community;
   (d) the mental and physical health of all individuals involved;
   (e) the relationship of the child with parents, siblings, and other significant family members;
   (f) the willingness of the parents to share custody and make shared decisions;

(g) the prior involvement of the parent in the child's life;

(h) the geographical proximity of the parents;

(i) the sincerity of the parent's request;

(j) the age and number of children;

(k) the demands of parental employment;

(l) the impact on any welfare benefits;

(m) any evidence of spousal or child abuse;

(n) financial capability of providing custody; and

(o) the benefit to the parties. There is a rebuttable presumption that joint custody is in the best interests of the child; unless child abuse, neglect, parental kidnapping or other intrafamily violence has occurred. The court may order the parents to submit a written parenting plan for custody. District of Columbia Code; Title 16, Chapter 9, Sections 911 and 914.

8. **CHILD SUPPORT.** Either parent may be ordered to pay reasonable child support in accordance with the child support guidelines in Title 16, Chapter 9, Section 916.1 and 916.2 of the DC Code. The guidelines provide that the judge may exercise discretion and increase or decrease the recommended child support by 3% based on the facts of the case. Greater variations from the child support guidelines are based on the following factors:

(a) the child's needs are exceptional;

(b) the non-custodial parent's income is substantially less than the custodial parent's income;

(c) a property settlement between the parents provides resources for the child above the minimum support requirements;

(d) the non-custodial parent provides support for other dependents and the guideline amounts would cause hardship;

(f) the non-custodial parent needs a temporary reduction (of no longer than 12 months) in support payments to repay a substantial debt;

(g) the custodial parent provides medical insurance coverage;

(h) the custodial parent receives child support payments for other children and the custodial parent's household income is substantially greater than that of the non-custodial parent; and

(i) any other extraordinary factors. Child support may be ordered to be paid through the Clerk of the Superior Court. District of Columbia Code; Title 16, Chapter 9, Sections 911 and 916.

9. **ALIMONY**. Either party may be awarded alimony, during the divorce proceeding or after, if it is just or proper. There are no specific factors listed in the statute. However, martial fault may be considered. Alimony in the District of Columbia is either a lump sum or indefinite. There is no rehabilitative alimony in D.C. District of Columbia Code; Title 16, Chapter 9, Sections 911, 912 and 913.

10. **EQUITABLE DISTRIBUTION OF PROPERTY**: If there is no Separation Agreement, each party keeps his or her non-marital property (acquired before the marriage or acquired during the marriage by gift from a third party or inheritance) and any increase in such separate property and any property acquired in exchange for such separate property. All other property, regardless of how title is held, is marital property. The court will distribute it based on:

(a) the contribution of each spouse to the acquisition of the marital property, including the contribution of each spouse as homemaker;

(b) the length of the marriage;

(c) the occupation of the spouses;

(d) the vocational skills of the spouses;

(e) the employability of the spouses;

(f) the estate, liabilities, and needs of each spouse and the opportunity of each for further acquisition of capital assets and income;

(g) the assets and debts of the spouses;

(h) any prior marriage of each spouse;

(i) whether the property award is in stead of or in addition to alimony;

(j) any custodial provisions for the children;

(k) the age and health of the spouses;

(l) the amount and sources of income of the spouses; and

(m) any other factor the court wants to consider. District of Columbia Code; Title 16, Chapter 9, Section 910.

11. **NAME CHANGE**: Upon request, the birth name or previous name may be restored. District of Columbia Code; Title 16, Chapter 9, Section 915.

12. **PREMARITAL AGREEMENTS**. The agreement must be in writing and signed by both parties and is enforceable without consideration. An agreement is not enforceable if the party can prove that

(a) the agreement was not voluntarily executed;

(b) the agreement was unconscionable when executed and before the execution the party was not provided a fair and reasonable disclosure of the property or financial obligations of the other party, the party did not voluntarily waive any right to the disclosure of these obligations, and the party did not have adequate knowledge regarding these obligations. If a provision of the agreement modifies or eliminates spousal support and that causes the party to be eligible for public assistance, the court may require the party to provide support to the extent to avoid that eligibility. If the marriage is determined to be void, the agreement is enforceable only to the extent necessary to avoid an inequitable result, unless the agreement expressly provides that it shall be enforceable in the event the marriage is determined to be void. District of Columbia Code, Title 16, Chapter 30, Sections 142, 146, and 147.

APPENDIX N
CHILD SUPPORT GUIDELINES IN THE DISTRICT OF COLUMBIA

The Child Support Guidelines Worksheet is used to calculate the proper amount of child support. The guidelines are presumptively correct and must be followed by the Master, Commissioner or Judge unless there are some special circumstances that would justify deviation from the guidelines.

CHART 1
CHILD SUPPORT ORDER FORMULA
FOR THE SUPERIOR COURT
ONE CHILD
AGES 0-6

ANNUAL GROSS INCOME OF NONCUSTODIAL PARENT	CHILD SUPPORT ORDER
0 -- $7,500	Discretion--Minimum $50/month
$7,501 -- 15,000	20% of Gross Income
15,001 -- 25,000	21% of Gross Income
25,001 -- 50,000	22% of Gross Income
50,001 -- 75,000	23% of Gross Income

AGES 7-12

ANNUAL GROSS INCOME OF NONCUSTODIAL PARENT	CHILD SUPPORT ORDER
0 -- $7,500	Discretion--Minimum $50/month
$7,501 -- 15,000	20% of Gross Income + 10% of Basic Order (22%)
15,001 -- 25,000	21% of Gross Income + 10% of Basic Order (23.1%)
25,001 -- 50,000	22% of Gross Income + 10% of Basic Order (24.2%)
50,001 -- 75,000	23% of Gross Income + 10% of Basic Order (25.3%)

AGES 13-21

ANNUAL GROSS INCOME OF NONCUSTODIAL PARENT	CHILD SUPPORT ORDER
0 -- $7,500	Discretion--Minimum $50/month
$7,501 -- 15,000	20% of Gross Income + 15% of Basic Order (23%)
15,001 -- 25,000	21% of Gross Income + 15% of Basic Order (24.15%)
25,001 -- 50,000	22% of Gross Income + 15% of Basic Order (25.3%)
50,001 -- 75,000	23% of Gross Income + 15% of Basic Order (26.45%)

CHART 2
CHILD SUPPORT ORDER FORMULA
FOR THE SUPERIOR COURT
TWO CHILDREN
AGES 0-6 (oldest child)

ANNUAL GROSS INCOME OF NONCUSTODIAL PARENT	CHILD SUPPORT ORDER
0 -- $7,500	Discretion--Minimum $50/month
$7,501 -- 15,000	26% of Gross Income
15,001 -- 25,000	27% of Gross Income
25,001 -- 50,000	28% of Gross Income
50,001 -- 75,000	29% of Gross Income

AGES 7-12 (oldest child)

ANNUAL GROSS INCOME OF NONCUSTODIAL PARENT	CHILD SUPPORT ORDER
0 -- $7,500	Discretion--Minimum $50/month
$7,501 -- 15,000	26% of Gross Income + 10% of Basic Order (28.6%)
15,001 -- 25,000	27% of Gross Income + 10% of Basic Order (29.7%)
25,001 -- 50,000	28% of Gross Income + 10% of Basic Order (30.8%)
50,001 -- 75,000	29% of Gross Income + 10% of Basic Order (31.9%)

AGES 13-21 (oldest child)

ANNUAL GROSS INCOME OF NONCUSTODIAL PARENT	CHILD SUPPORT ORDER
0 -- $7,500	Discretion--Minimum $50/month
$7,501 -- 15,000	26% of Gross Income + 15% of Basic Order (29.9%)
15,001 -- 25,000	27% of Gross Income + 15% of Basic Order (31.05%)
25,001 -- 50,000	28% of Gross Income + 15% of Basic Order (32.2%)
50,001 -- 75,000	29% of Gross Income + 15% of Basic Order (33.35%)

CHART 3
CHILD SUPPORT ORDER FORMULA
FOR THE SUPERIOR COURT
THREE CHILDREN
AGES 0-6 (oldest child)

ANNUAL GROSS INCOME OF NONCUSTODIAL PARENT	CHILD SUPPORT ORDER
0 -- $7,500	Discretion--Minimum $50/month
$7,501 -- 15,000	30% of Gross Income
15,001 -- 25,000	31% of Gross Income
25,001 -- 50,000	32% of Gross Income
50,001 -- 75,000	33% of Gross Income

AGES 7-12 (oldest child)

ANNUAL GROSS INCOME OF NONCUSTODIAL PARENT	CHILD SUPPORT ORDER
0 -- $7,500	Discretion--Minimum $50/month
$7,501 -- 15,000	30% of Gross Income + 10% of Basic Order (33.0%)
15,001 -- 25,000	31% of Gross Income + 10% of Basic Order (34.1%)
25,001 -- 50,000	32% of Gross Income + 10% of Basic Order (35.2%)
50,001 -- 75,000	33% of Gross Income + 10% of Basic Order (36.3%)

AGES 13-21 (oldest child)

ANNUAL GROSS INCOME OF NONCUSTODIAL PARENT	CHILD SUPPORT ORDER
0 -- $7,500	Discretion--Minimum $50/month
$7,501 -- 15,000	30% of Gross Income + 15% of Basic Order (34.5%)
15,001 -- 25,000	31% of Gross Income + 15% of Basic Order (35.65%)
25,001 -- 50,000	32% of Gross Income + 15% of Basic Order (36.8%)
50,001 -- 75,000	33% of Gross Income + 15% of Basic Order (37.95%)

CHART 4
CHILD SUPPORT ORDER FORMULA
FOR THE SUPERIOR COURT
FOUR OR MORE CHILDREN
AGES 0-6 (oldest child)

ANNUAL GROSS INCOME OF NONCUSTODIAL PARENT	CHILD SUPPORT ORDER
0 -- $7,500	Discretion--Minimum $50/month
$7,501 -- 15,000	32% of Gross Income
15,001 -- 25,000	33% of Gross Income
25,001 -- 50,000	34% of Gross Income
50,001 -- 75,000	35% of Gross Income

AGES 7-12 (oldest child)

ANNUAL GROSS INCOME OF NONCUSTODIAL PARENT	CHILD SUPPORT ORDER
0 -- $7,500	Discretion--Minimum $50/month
$7,501 -- 15,000	32% of Gross Income + 10% of Basic Order (35.2%)
15,001 -- 25,000	33% of Gross Income + 10% of Basic Order (36.3%)
25,001 -- 50,000	34% of Gross Income + 10% of Basic Order (37.4%)
50,001 -- 75,000	35% of Gross Income + 10% of Basic Order (38.5%)

AGES 13-21 (oldest child)

ANNUAL GROSS INCOME OF NONCUSTODIAL PARENT	CHILD SUPPORT ORDER
0 -- $7,500	Discretion--Minimum $50/month
$7,501 -- 15,000	32% of Gross Income + 15% of Basic Order (36.8%)
15,001 -- 25,000	33% of Gross Income + 15% of Basic Order (37.95%)
25,001 -- 50,000	34% of Gross Income + 15% of Basic Order (39.1%)
50,001 -- 75,000	35% of Gross Income + 15% of Basic Order (40.25%)

APPENDIX O
DISTRICT OF COLUMBIA
LEGAL CLINICS

If you qualify, you may be eligible for free legal assistance at one of the following legal clinics.

American University Law Clinic
American University
Washington College of Law
4801 Massachusetts Avenue NW
Washington, DC 20016
202-274-4140

Archdiocesan Legal Network (ALN)
Catholic Charities
1221 Massachusetts Ave., NW
Washington, DC 20005
202-628-4263

Ayuda, Inc.
1736 Columbia Road, NW
Washington, DC 20005
202-387-4848

Bread for the City
1525 7th Street NW
Washington, D.C. 20001
202-265-2400

Catholic University of America Families and the Law Clinic
3600 John McCormick Road, N.E.
Washington, DC 20064
202-319-6788

Columbus Community Legal Services
Catholic University
Columbus School of Law
3602 John McCormack Road NE
Washington, DC 20064
202-319-6788

D.C. Bar Pro Bono Program's Legal Information Helpline
202-626-3499

Family Advocacy Clinic
Georgetown University Law Center
600 New Jersey Avenue, NW
Washington, DC 20001
202-662-9535

Jacob Burns Community Legal Clinics
George Washington University Law School
2000 G Street, NW
Washington, DC 20052
202-994-7463

Legal Aid Society of the District of Columbia
666 11th Street, NW
Suite 800
Washington, DC 20001
202-628-1161

So Others Might Eat (S.O.M.E.)
71 'O' Street, NW
Washington, D.C. 20001
202-797-8806

**University of the District of Columbia
Law Clinic**
David A. Clarke
School of Law
4200 Connecticut Avenue
NWWashington, DC 20008
202-274-7323

**Washington Legal Clinic
for the Homeless**
1800 Massachusetts Avenue, NW
Washington, D.C. 20036
202-872-1494

Women Empowered Against Violence
1111 16th Street, NW
Suite 410
Washington, DC 20036
202-452-8253

Appendix P
District of Columbia
Domestic Violence
Shelters

If you need assistance or housing in a case of domestic violence, contact one of the following shelters in the District of Columbia.

D.C. Hotline
P.O. Box 57194
Washington DC 20037
202-223-2255

House of Imagene
214 P St. NW
Washington, DC 20001
Hotline: 202-797-7460

House of Ruth - "Herspace"
651 10th Street NE
Washington, DC 20002
Hotline: 202-347-2777

My Sister's Place
5 Thomas Circle, 4th Floor
Washington, DC 20005
Hotline: 202-529-5991

Mary House
4303 13th St. NE,
Washington, DC 20017
Hotline: 202-635- 0534

APPENDIX Q
DISTRICT OF COLUMBIA
WEBSITES

You can find more information about divorce in the District of Columbia on the Internet at the following websites.

District of Columbia Divorce Laws
http://divorcenet.com/dc/dcart-01.html

District of Columbia Links
http://divorcenet.com/dc/divorce/

District of Columbia Divorce Bulletin Board
http://www.divorcenet.com:3336/?forum=dc-board

District of Columbia Child Support Guidelines Statute
http://www.supportguidelines.com/glines/dc_cs.html

District of Columbia Cases
http://www.divorcesource.com/research/edj/states/dc.shtml

District of Columbia Family Law Court
http://www.dcbar.org/for_lawyers/courts/superior_court/family_court/index.cfm

District of Columbia Legal Crier
http://www.paralegal-concierge.com/LegalCrier/familylaw.html

District of Columbia Child Support Calculator
http://alllaw.com/calculators/childsupport/dc/

Divorce Law Info
http://www.divorcelawinfo.com/DC/flc.htm

About.Com
http://divorcesupport.about.com/cs/washingtondc/

APPENDIX R
DISTRICT OF COLUMBIA BLANK FORMS

TABLE OF FORMS

SUPERIOR COURT OF THE DISTRICT OF COLUMBIA
FAMILY DIVISION

Jacket No. _____

FINANCIAL STATEMENT

Date _____

_____ V. _____

NAME:	SOCIAL SECURITY NO.:	OCCUPATION:

NAME AND ADDRESS OF CURRENT EMPLOYER:

I claim _____ exemptions for withholding tax purposes.

INCOME INFORMATION*	AVERAGE MONTHLY EXPENSES

	Wife/Husband	Children

INCOME INFORMATION*

1. Monthly gross wages .... $_____

2. Less Mandatory Monthly Deductions:

   Federal Income Tax............ $_____

   State Income Tax .... _____

   Retirement:

    FICA .... _____

    Social Security .... _____

   Medical Insurance............. _____

   Other .... $_____

   TOTAL........................ $_____

3. Monthly Net Wages .... $_____
(Subtract Line 2 form line 1)

4. Monthly income from all other sources (e.g., part-time or overtime wages, fees rents, dividends, commissions, unemployment compensation, disability, social security, retirement, interest, bonuses, etc.) .... $_____

5. Less Other Mandatory Monthly Deductions:

   Federal Income Tax............ $_____

   State Income Tax .... _____

   Retirement:

   FICA .... _____

   Social Security .... _____

   Medical Insurance............ _____

   Other........................ _____

   TOTAL .... $_____

6. Monthly Net Income from all other sources .... $_____
(Subtract Line 5 form Line 4)

7. Total Monthly Net Disposable Income .... $_____
(Add Lines 3 and 6)

8. Total Monthly Gross Income .... $_____
(Add Lines 1 and 4)

SUMMARY

9. Total Monthly Net Disposable Income .... $_____

10. Less Total Monthly Expenses .... $_____

11. Difference: .... $_____

AVERAGE MONTHLY EXPENSES

Housing, etc.

	Wife/Husband	Children
Rent/Mortages	$_____	$_____
Utilities	_____	_____
Taxes	_____	_____

Food

Groceries/Household Supplies	_____	_____
Meals Out	_____	_____

Automobile

Payment	_____	_____
Gas/Oil	_____	_____
Repairs	_____	_____
Insurance	_____	_____
Tags	_____	_____

Life Insurance (List beneficiaries)	_____	_____
_____	_____	_____
_____	_____	_____
_____	_____	_____
Health Insurance (not listed as income deduction)	_____	_____

School

Tuition	_____	_____
Supplies/Fees	_____	_____

Child Care Expenses

To allow for employment/ education	_____	_____
To allow for recreation	_____	_____
Lessons (e.g. music, dance, art)	_____	_____
Allowance	_____	_____
Clothing/Uniforms	_____	_____
Dry Cleaning/Laundry	_____	_____
Medical Expenses (Unpaid by insurance)	_____	_____
Charitable Contributions	_____	_____
Recreation	_____	_____
Vacations	_____	_____
Miscellaneous:		
_____	_____	_____
_____	_____	_____

Periodic Payments Required on Bills:

_____	_____	_____
_____	_____	_____
Total Monthly Expenses	_____	_____

*NOTE: If you are paid weekly, multiply your weekly gross wages by 4.3 to arrive at yur monthly gross wage. If you are paid every two weeks multiply your bi-weekly gross wages by 2.15 to arrive at yur monthly gross wage.

PLEASE ATTACH LATEST WAGE STATEMENTS SHOWING YOUR DEDUCTIONS

LIABILITIES

Type of Debt	To Whom Owned	Date Incurred	Total Amt. of Debt	Amt. Paid to Date	Balance Due
		Total Liabilities			

ASSETS
(List as separately or jointly owned with spouse)

SUMMARY

	Separate	Joint		Separate	Joint
Cash			Total Assets		
Automobiles			Less Total Liabilities		
Bank Accounts			Net Worth		
Bonds					
Notes					
Real Estate					
Stocks					
Personal Property					
Total Assets					

I certify that this statement indicates my current financial situation to the best of my knowledge.

Subscribed and sworn to before me this _____ day of _____, 20____

_____
(Deputy Clerk or Notary Public)

334

Master Child Support Worksheet

Case Number _____

CP _____

NCP _____

Forms Attached:
☐ ☐ ☐ ☐ ☐
M2 A B C D

Children Subject to this Agreement:

Number	Age Cides:

I. CP's Income and Adjustments

1	CP Gross Annual Income (Income from all sources before taxes)		1	
2	Prior Support Order *(date:) Annual Amount	2		
3	Base Income Disregard	3	14,500	
4	No. of Children x $2,000	4		
5	Income Offset (Line 3 plus Line 4)		5	
6	CP Annual Child Care Expense		6	
7	CP Adjusted Gross Annual Income (Line 1 minus Lines 2, 5 and 6—*enter 0 if negative*)		7	

II. NCP's Income and Adjustments

8	NCP Gross Annual Income (Income from all sources before taxes)		8	
9	Prior Support Order** (date:) Annual Amount	9		
10	Medical Insurance Premiums (from Form A)		10	
11	**NCP Adjusted Gross Annual Income** (Line 8 minus Lines 9 and 10)		11	

III. Support Calculations

12	Basic Guideline Percentage (expressed as decimal, from table on reverse side)		12	
13	Basic Guideline Annual Amount (Line 11 multiplied by Line 12)		13	
14	CP's Adjusted Income (from Line 7)	14		
15	NCP's Adjusted Income (from Line 11)	15		
16	TOTAL Incomes (Line 14 plus Line 15)	16		
17	Offset Ratio (Line 14 divided by Line 16, *to four decimal places*)	17		
18	Offset Amount (line 13 multiplied by Line 17)		18	
19	Adjusted Guideline **Annual** Amount (Line 13 minus Line 18)		19	$
20	**MONTHLY SUPPORT AMOUNT** (Line 19 divided by 12) ◆		20	$
21	3% of **NCP's** Adjusted Gross Income (Line 11 multiplied by .03)	21		
22	HIGH 3% Monthly Amount (Line 19 **plus** Line 21, divided by 12) ✚		22	$
23	LOW 3% Monthly Amount (Line 19 **minus** Line 21, divided by 12) ▬		23	$

*This is support paid by the custodian for children not living with him or her

**This is support paid by the non-custodian for children not living with him or her

Child Support Guideline Form A
Non-Custodial Parent Medical Insurance Deduction

Note: See Guideline Report pp. 22-23 for further explanation of requirements for this deduction.

1. Name(s) of NCP's Medical Insurer(s) _____

2. Present Medical Insurance: Individual   Family   None

3. If NCP currently has medical insurance, list names of:

Children Covered _____

Children Not Covered _____

4	NCP's Annual Cost for Family Medical Policy	4	
5	NCP's Annual Cost for Individual (NCP Only) Policy	5	
6	**Child-Related Premiums** (Line 4 minus Line 5)	6	
7	Total No. of Individuals Other than NCP Covered by Family Medical Policy	7	
8	Per Capita Share of Family Medical Policy Cost (Line 6 divided by Line 7)	8	
9	Number of Children Subject to this Agreement	9	
10	**Deduction for Premiums** (Line 8 multiplied by Line 9) Enter on Worksheet Line 10	10	

Child Support Guideline Form B
Multiple Families—Custodial Parent

Note: First calculate Guideline Amount using Master Worksheet, then complete following items:

1	NCP Adjusted Gross Household Income (Master Worksheet Line 11 **PLUS** Income from Other Adults)	1	
2	NCP Annual Guideline Support Amount (Master Worksheet Line 19)	2	
3	NCP Net Household Income (Line 1 minus Line 2)	3	
4	Poverty Level for NCP Household from Table on reverse of Master Worksheet	4	
5	**NCP Standard of Living** (Line 3 divided by Line 4)	5	
6	CP Gross Household Income (M. Worksheet Line 1 **PLUS** Income from Other Adults)	6	
7	CP Total Household Income (Line 6 plus Line 2)	7	
8	Poverty Level for CP Household (from Table on reverse of Master Worksheet)	8	
9	CP Standard of Living (Line 7 divided by Line 8)	9	

If Line 9 is larger than Line 5, the Guideline does not apply presumptively. The award may be adjusted to make the NCP's standard of living no lower than the CP's.

		Case Number

Child Support Guideline Form C
Multiple Families: Non-Custodial Parent

Note: First do a Master Worksheet *(using total children to get Guideline percentage).*
Then complete this form. Finally do a Worksheet for the children subject to this agreement.

Children Subject to this Agreement:	Number	Age Oldest	Other Children Living With NCP for which S/He is Responsible:	Number	Age Oldest	TOTAL:	Number	Age Oldest

1	NCP's Gross Annual Income (from **First** Master Worksheet Line 8)			1	-
2	Total Number of Children for Whom NCP is Responsible	2			
3	Annual Guideline Support Amount for total number of Children (**First** Worksheet Line 19)			3	
4	Pro Rata Share of Support for Each Child (Line 3 divided by Line 2)			4	
5	Total Deduction from Gross Income (Line 4 times no. of children in NCP's household)			5	
6	Gross Annual Income for Line 8 of **Second** Master Worksheet (Line 1 minus Line 5)	▶		6	

Child Support Guideline Form D
Shared Custody—Advisory Calculation

Note: "Shared Custody" means actual visitation which exceeds 40% of the days of the year.
A "day" is at least 18 out of 24 hours. A weekend counts as no more than two days.
First complete a Master Worksheet for **each** parent, one assuming the Mother has sole custody,
one assuming the Father has sole custody. Then complete this form (the results are advisory).

1	Mother's Percentage of Time with Children (2 decimal places)			1	
2	Father's Percentage of Time with Children (2 decimal places)			2	
3	Father's Support if Mother Had Sole Custody (Worksheet Line 19)	3			
4	Line 3 multiplied by 1.5			4	
5	Mother's Support if Father Had Sole Custody (Worksheet Line 19)	5			
6	Line 5 multiplied by 1.5			6	
7	Father's Obligation x Mother's Percentage of Time (Line 4 multiplied by Line 1)			7	
8	Mother's Obligation x Father's Percentage of Time (Line 6 multiplied by Line 2)			8	
9	**Net Transfer** via Support (Larger of Lines 7 and 8 minus the Smaller), Paid by _____	▶		9	
10	Child Care or Other Major Expense, Paid Wholly by _____	10			
11	Credit (If **F** pays, Line 10 multiplied by Line 1; if **M** pays, Line 10 multiplied by Line 2)			11	
12	Final Annual Support Amount: A) If the Line 9 payor is the **same** as the Line 10 payor, Line 9 **minus** Line 11 B) If the Line 9 payor is **different** than the Line 10 payor, Line 9 **plus** Line 11	▶		12	
13	MONTHLY SUPPORT AMOUNT (Line 12 divided by 12)	▶		13	

Overview of Child Support Guideline Procedures and Forms

I. Non-Custodian Medical Insurance Form A

Is the Non-Custodian presently paying child or family medical insurance to cover any child subject to this agreement?

❶ Complete Form A.

❷ Complete the Master Worksheet.

II. Multiple Families (Custodian) Form B

Is the Custodian legally responsible for children (who live with him or her) by a parent other than the second party in this case?

❶ Calculate the support amount using the Master Worksheet.

❷ Complete Form B.

III. Multiple Families (Non-Custodian) Form C

Is the Non-Custodian responsible for other children living with him or her (excluding any who are already the subject of a court order)?

❶ Do a Master Worksheet using the total number of children for whom the NC is responsible for purposes of the base Guideline percentage. Use the number of children subject to this agreement when determining any income offset.

❷ Use Form C to calculate a new figure for NC's gross annual income.

❸ Using this new figure, complete a second Master Worksheet to determine a final support amount.

IV. Multiple Families (Custodial and Non-Custodial Parents) Forms B and C

Are both parents responsible for other children living with them?

❶ Follow Procedure III (Form C) above.

❷ Follow Procedure II (Form B) above.

V. Shared Custody Form D

Does actual visitation with both parents exceed 40% of the days in a year?

If so, the Guideline does not apply presumptively. Calculate an advisory support amount:

❶ Complete a Master Worksheet for *each* parent, one assuming the mother has sole custody, one assuming the father has sole custody.

❷ Complete Form D

SUPERIOR COURT OF THE DISTRICT OF COLUMBIA
FAMILY DIVISION
DOMESTIC RELATIONS BRANCH

_____	)
(YOUR FULL MARRIED NAME)	)
_____	)
(STREET ADDRESS)	)
_____	)
(CITY, STATE, ZIP CODE)	)
PLAINTIFF,	)
	) CASE NO._____
V.	)
	) RELATED CASES:
	)
_____	) _____
(YOUR SPOUSE'S FULL MARRIED NAME)	)
_____	) _____
(STREET ADDRESS)	)
_____	)
(CITY, STATE, ZIP CODE)	)
DEFENDANT.	)

COMPLAINT FOR ABSOLUTE DIVORCE
(ACTION INVOLVING CHILD SUPPORT)
(Based on Six Months Mutual and
Voluntary Separation With Children)

I,_____ am the plaintiff in this case and state that:
    (YOUR NAME)

1. Jurisdiction of this court is based upon D.C. Code Section 11-1101 (1) (1989).

2. The _____ has been a bona fide resident of the District
       (PLAINTIFF/DEFENDANT)

of Columbia for more than six months immediately prior to filing this complaint for absolute

divorce.

3. My spouse, _____, and I were lawfully married on
      (YOUR SPOUSE'S FULL MARRIED NAME)

_____ in _____.
(MONTH DAY, YEAR)   (CITY, STATE)

4.   Beginning on or about _____ 20___ and continuing
                                                     (DATE OF SEPARATION)
until the present, my spouse and I mutually, voluntarily and continuously have lived separate and

apart from each other. This separation has continued without interruption or cohabitation for a

period of more than six months prior to the filing of this complaint for absolute divorce.

5.   From the time of the separation until the present, I have lived at the following

address(es):

_____

_____

_____

_____

ITEMS 6 through 10 ADDRESS CUSTODY AND CHILD SUPPORT. READ THEM CAREFULLY. IT MAY BE ADVISABLE TO SEEK THE ADVICE OF COUNSEL ABOUT CUSTODY AND SUPPORT ISSUES. YOU MAY NOT WANT TO USE THESE FORMS TO START A DIVORCE CASE UNTIL YOU HAVE CONSULTED AN ATTORNEY.

6. My spouse and I are the parents of the following _____ child(ren)

     NAME/   SOCIAL SECURITY NUMBER/   BIRTH DATE
     _____

     _____

     _____

     _____

7a.   The minor child(ren) live(s) with the _____. In the last five
                                                     (PLAINTIFF/DEFENDANT)
years, the minor child(ren) has (have) lived at:

ADDRESS   WITH WHOM

_____

_____

_____

_____

7b.   The only litigation involving the custody of the minor child(ren) is the following: (if none, state "none")

TYPE OF CASE   ORDER ISSUED?   DATE   OUTCOME

_____

_____

_____

ITEMS 8, 9, AND 10 ADDRESS CHILD SUPPORT.

8a.   There (HAS/HAS NOT) been a court order addressing child support. The

Plaintiff (DOES/DOES NOT) receive public assistance. [IF THERE HAS BEEN AN ORDER,

COMPLETE THE FOLLOWING; IF NOT GO TO ITEM 8b.]

The order was issued on _____, 20_____, by the
                        (DATE OF LAST ORDER - MO. DAY,   YR.)

_____.   The _____
(CASE NUMBER AND COURT   (PLAINTIFF/DEFENDANT)

is ordered to pay $ _____ every _____
                   (AMOUNT)   (month/week/two weeks)

for the support of the parties, minor child(ren).

[IF YOU AND YOUR SPOUSE AGREE ABOUT CHILD SUPPORT AND/OR ARE
CONTINUING THE AMOUNT OF CHILD SUPPORT ORDERED IN 8a ABOVE,
COMPLETE ITEM 8b.]

8b. The _____, who is financially able to do so, has agreed to
           (PLAINTIFF/DEFENDANT)

pay, and the _____ has agreed to accept the sum of $ _____
           (PLAINTIFF/DEFENDANT)   (AMOUNT)

every _____ for the support of their minor child(ren).
      (month/week/two weeks)

(IF YOU ARE ASKING THE COURT TO ORDER CHILD SUPPORT AND YOU
HAVE NOT AGREED WITH YOUR SPOUSE ABOUT CHILD SUPPORT OR YOU
DON'T KNOW WHETHER YOU AGREE, THEN COMPLETE ITEM 9 BELOW;
OTHERWISE, GO TO ITEM 11.]

[It may also be advisable to seek the advice of legal counsel about custody and
support issues. You may not want to use the forms to start a divorce case until
you have consulted an attorney.]

9. The Plaintiff is in need of child support to care for the parties' minor children and

(IS/IS NOT) requesting support.

10. The Defendant has the ability to contribute towards the support of the parties' minor

children.

11. My spouse and I have no property, either real or personal, and no debts that we are

asking the court to divide or distribute.

12. There is no reasonable expectation that my spouse and I will reconcile.

13. I [DO/DO NOT] request restoration of my former name,

_____. This request is not made for any illegal or
(YOUR BIRTH NAME OR PRIOR NAME)

fraudulent reason.

14. (Check one):

_____ I do not know of any other cases in the District of Columbia or any state or territory involving the same claim or subject matter as this case.

OR

_____ I know of the following related cases concerning the same claim or subject matter as this case. (List all cases, in any state, including D.C., whether, custody, divorce, intrafamily violence, child support or earlier cases that dealt with marital property; provide case numbers)

_____

_____.

WHEREFORE, I ask that:

1. The Court grant me an Absolute Divorce on the ground that my spouse and I have lived mutually and voluntarily separate and apart without cohabitation for six months next preceding the filing of this complaint.

2. The Court award the _____, permanent custody of
   (PLAINTIFF/DEFENDANT)

the parties' minor child(ren), namely,

_____

_____.

3. The Court order the _____ to pay child support
   (PLAINTIFF/DEFENDANT)

toward the support of the parties' minor child(ren).

4. The Court divide and distribute our marital property and/or debts as is equitable, just, and reasonable.

5. I (DO/DO NOT) wish to be restored to my former name,

_____.
(YOUR BIRTH NAME OR PRIOR NAME)

    6. The Court award such other relief as it deems just and proper.

Respectfully submitted,

_____

PLAINTIFF'S SIGNATURE

_____

(Address)

_____

(phone and fax number, if available)

        I, _____, solemnly swear or affirm under criminal penalties for the making of a false statement that I have read the foregoing Complaint for Absolute Divorce and that the factual statements made in it are true to the best of my personal knowledge, information and belief

_____

PLAINTIFF

GOVERNMENT OF THE DISTRICT OF COLUMBIA
DEPARTMENT OF HEALTH
CERTIFICATE OF DIVORCE,
DISSOLUTION OF MARRIAGE OR ANNULMENT

D—

108—

COURT IDENTIFICATION
(Court File Number)

FILE NUMBER

TYPE IN PERMANENT INK

PINK—COURT COPY

YELLOW—STATISTICAL COPY

WHITE—VITAL RECORDS PERMANENT FILE

HUSBAND

HUSBAND—NAME	FIRST	MIDDLE	LAST
1.			

USUAL RESIDENCE — STREET ADDRESS		CITY, TOWN OR LOCATION	
2a.		2b.	

COUNTY	STATE	DATE OF BIRTH (Mo, Day, Yr.)
2c.	3.	4.

WIFE

WIFE—NAME	FIRST	MIDDLE	LAST	MAIDEN NAME
5a.				5b.

USUAL RESIDENCE — STREET ADDRESS		CITY, TOWN OR LOCATION	
6a.		6b.	

COUNTY	STATE	DATE OF BIRTH (Mo, Day, Yr.)
6c.		8.

DATE OF THIS MARRIAGE (Mo, Day, Yr.)	CHILDREN UNDER 18 IN THIS FAMILY (Specify)	PLAINTIFF CHECK	HUSBAND	WIFE	BOTH	OTHER (Specify)
9.	10.	11.				

ATTORNEY FOR PLAINTIFF—NAME (Type or Print)	ADDRESS OF ATTORNEY—STREET OR R.F.D. NO.	CITY OR TOWN	STATE	ZIP
12.	13.			

DECREE

THIS DECREE IS GRANTED ON (MONTH DAY YEAR.) ONLY COURT RECORDS CAN INDICATE THE DATE ON WHICH A DECREE BECOMES FINAL.	TYPE OF DECREE CHECK	DIVORCE	DISSOLUTION	ANNULMENT
	15.			
14.	TITLE OF COURT SUPERIOR COURT OF THE DISTRICT OF COLUMBIA
	16.

SIGNATURE OF CERTIFYING OFFICIAL	TITLE OF OFFICIAL CLERK OF THE COURT
17.	18.

INFORMATION FOR STATISTICAL PURPOSES ONLY

HUSBAND

RACE—HUSBAND Specify (e.g., White, Black, American Indian, etc.)	NUMBER OF THIS MARRIAGE Specify (First, second, etc.)	WIFE	RACE—WIFE Specify (e.g., White, Black, American Indian, etc.)	NUMBER OF THIS MARRIAGE Specify (First, second, etc.)
19.	20.		21.	22.

DHS-1601 (7/97)

THIS CERTIFICATE IS TO BE FILED WITH THE CLERK OF THE COURT WITH THE PETITION

97-0960 PMS

(AN ORIGINAL OF THIS DOCUMENT MUST BE OBTAINED DIRECTLY FROM THE COURT.)

Superior Court of the District of Columbia
FAMILY DIVISION
DOMESTIC RELATIONS BRANCH

_____ *Plaintiff(s)*	
vs.	Case No. _____
_____ *Defendant(s)*	

MOTION TO PROCEED IN FORMA PAUPERIS

Comes now the _____ and respectfully request this honorable court to allow them to proceed without prepayment of costs for the following reason(s):

Printed name: _____   Signature: _____

Address: _____   Home phone no. _____

Business phone no. _____

CERTIFICATE OF SERVICE

I certify that a copy of the above was mailed, postage prepaid, on _____

To:

Name: _____   Name: _____

Address: _____   Address: _____

Signature

POINTS AND AUTHORITIES

(Write the reasons why the Court should grant your motion and include Court rules, laws and cases, if any, that support your reasons.)

Signature

Superior Court of the District of Columbia

FAMILY DIVISION
DOMESTIC RELATIONS BRANCH

Plaintiff

_vs._   Civil Action No.

Defendant

AFFIDAVIT IN SUPPORT OF MOTION TO PROCEED IN FORMA PAUPERIS

I further swear that the responses which I have made to questions and instructions below relating to my ability to pay the cost of proceeding in this action are true.

1. Are you presently employed? Yes O   No O
   a. If the answer is yes, state the amount of your salary or wages per month, and give the name and address of your employer.

   b. If the answer is no, state the date of last employment and the amount of the salary and wages per month which you received

2. Have you received within the past twelve months any money from any of the following sources?
   a. Business, profession or form of self-employment? Yes O   No O
   b. Rent payments, interest or dividends? Yes O   No O
   c. Pensions, annuities or life insurance payments? Yes O   No O
   d. Gifts or inheritance? Yes O   No O
   e. Any other sources? Yes O   No O

If the answer to any of the above is yes, describe each source of money and state the amount received form each during the past twelve months.

3. Do you own any cash, or do you have money in checking or savings account? Yes ○ No ○ (Include any funds in prision accounts). If the answer is yes, state the total value of the items owned.

4. Do you own any real estate, stocks, bonds, notes, automobiles, or other valuable property (excluding ordinary household furnishings and clothing)? Yes ○ No ○ If the answer is yes describe the property and state its approximate value.

5. List the persons who are dependent upon you for support, state your relationship to those persons, and indicate how much you contribute toward their support.

I have read and subscribed to the above and swear, under oath, that the information is true and correct. I understand that a false statement or answer to any question in this affidavit will subject me to penalties for perjury.

_____
(Plaintiff's signature)

being first duly sworn under oath, presents that he has read and subscribed to the above add states that the information herein is true and correct.

_____
(Plaintiff's signature)

SUBSCRIBED AND SWORN TO before me this

day of _____

IN THE SUPERIOR COURT OF THE DISTRICT OF COLUMBIA
FAMILY DIVISION
DOMESTIC RELATIONS BRANCH

Plaintiff,	))))) Civ. Action No:))))
vs.	
Defendant.	)

AFFIDAVIT OF SERVICE BY CERTIFIED MAIL

CITY OF WASHINGTON
DISTRICT OF COLUMBIA., ss:

_____ being duly sworn, deposes and says:

1. I, _____ am the Plaintiff in this action.

2. On _____ I caused a copy of the Complaint herein, as well as

a duly issued summons, to be served by certified mail, return-receipt requested, upon the

_____

3. I have received the return-receipt bearing the signature of _____ and

dated _____ (See return-receipt attached hereto).

4. The Plaintiff has reviewed this return-receipt and avers that the signature

thereon is that of the Defendant in this action, namely _____

Respectfully submitted,

_____

Subscribed and sworn to before me this ___ day of _____

_____
Notary Public

My Commission Expires:_____

SUPERIOR COURT OF THE DISTRICT OF COLUMBIA
FAMILY DIVISION
DOMESTIC RELATIONS BRANCH

_____)
Your Name)
)
_____)
Address)
)
_____)
City, State, Zip)
         Plaintiff,)
Vs.)
)
_____)
Defendant's Name)
)
_____)
Address)
)
_____)
City, State, Zip)
     Defendant_____)
	CASE NO.:_____

MOTION TO ALLOW SERVICE BY PUBLICATION

Plaintiff, _____, moves this Court to allow Plaintiff to
             (Your Name)
to accomplish service on the Defendant, _____, by publishing a notice in
                         (Defendant's Name)
two newspapers. The Plaintiff has attempted to serve the Defendant at his/her last known address

which was _____on or
        (State Last Known Address)
about _____. As grounds
        (State Date of Attempted Service)
for this Motion, Plaintiff refers this Court to the accompanying Points and Authorities and

Affidavit.

                       Respectfully submitted,

                       _____

SUPERIOR COURT OF THE DISTRICT OF COLUMBIA
FAMILY DIVISION
DOMESTIC RELATIONS BRANCH

_____)	
Your Name)	
_____)	
Address)	CASE NO.:_____
_____)	
City, State, Zip)	
Plaintiff,)	
Vs.)	
_____)	
Defendant's Name)	
_____)	
Address)	
_____)	
City, State, Zip)	
_____Defendant_____)	

AFFIDAVIT OF ATTEMPTED SERVICE & NON RESIDENCY
IN SUPPORT
OF MOTION TO ALLOW SERVICE BY PUBLICATION

DISTRICT OF COLUMBIA, *ss:*

The Plaintiff,_____, being duly sworn, states:
              (YOUR NAME)

1.   I, _____, am the Plaintiff in this action.
            (YOUR NAME)

2.   I have attempted to have the Defendant, _____,
                                        (Defendant's Name)
personally served and all attempts were unsuccessful.

3.   I have contacted:

       _____the Defendant last on or about_____

at _____

under the following circumstances:_____

_____

I have had no other direct or indirect communication since that date.

_____Defendant's last known employer who was_____
(Name of Employer)

on or about _____ and who has no further information about Defendant's

whereabouts.

_____Defendant's last known family or friend whose name(s)

is (are): _____

and who live(s) at _____

_____,

and who could not tell me where the defendant currently lives or works.

4.   I have also caused a search to be conducted for the Defendant at the following places and

organizations:

CHECK ALL THAT APPLY

_____ D.C. Department of Motor Vehicles

_____ D.C. Department of Human Services

_____ United States Military Locator Services

_____ Telephone directories for the D.C. metropolitan area,

        and/or

_____ Other: _____

_____

_____

Also see attached Evidence of all other searches

5. All inquiries have produced no information as to the whereabouts of the Defendant.

Further, Affiant sayeth not.

_____
Signature of Affiant

_____
PRINT YOUR NAME
Residing at:
(List your address)

_____
_____
_____

SUBSCRIBED AND SWORN TO before me this _____ day of _____, _____.

_____
NOTARY PUBLIC, D.C.

My Commission Expires: _____

_____ | _____
Attorney | *Address*

ORDER PUBLICATION — ABSENT DEFENDANT _____

Superior Court of the District of Columbia
FAMILY DIVISION
DOMESTIC RELATIONS BRANCH

_____
Plaintiff

vs.

Jacket No._____

_____
Defendant

The object of this suit is_____

_____

_____

_____

_____

_____

_____

On motion of the plaintiff, it is this _____ day of _____,

20___, ordered that the defendant _____

_____

_____

cause_____h_____appearance to be entered herein on or before the fortieth day, exclusive of Sundays and

legal holidays, occurring after the day of the first publication of this order; otherwise the cause will be pro-

ceeded with as in case of default. Provided, a copy of this order is published once a week for three suc-

cessive weeks in the Washington Law Reporter, and the _____.

before said day.

Attest:

_____
Judge

Clerk of the Superior Court
of the District of Columbia

By_____

Deputy Clerk

SUPERIOR COURT OF THE DISTRICT OF COLUMBIA
FAMILY DIVISION
DOMESTIC RELATIONS BRANCH

_____) Your Name) _____) Address) _____) City, State, Zip) Plaintiff,) Vs.) _____) Defendant's Name) _____) Address) _____) City, State, Zip) _____Defendant._____)	CASE NO.:_____

POINTS AND AUTHORITIES
IN SUPPORT OF MOTION TO ALLOW
SERVICE BY PUBLICATION

1.   Plaintiff has been unable to serve Defendant, _____,

despite diligent efforts.

2.   Plaintiff will not be able to continue with this case if this Motion is denied.

3.   D.C. Code § 16-4505(a) (4) (1989)

4.   D.C. Code §§ 13-336(a) (2) & 13-340 (a) (1989)

5.   SCR-Dom Rel. R. 4 (j)

6.   Bearstop Vs. Bearstop, 377 A.2d 405 (D.C. 1977)

SUPERIOR COURT OF THE DISTRICT OF COLUMBIA
FAMILY DIVISION
DOMESTIC RELATIONS BRANCH

_____)
(YOUR SPOUSE'S NAME)   )
_____)
(STREET ADDRESS)   )
_____)
(CITY, STATE, ZIP)   )
       PLAINTIFF,   )
)   CASE NO. _____
   V.   )
)   RELATED CASES:
)
_____)   _____
(YOUR NAME)   )   _____
_____)
(STREET ADDRESS)   )
_____)
(CITY, STATE, ZIP)   )
       DEFENDANT   )

ANSWER TO COMPLAINT FOR DIVORCE

I, _____, am the defendant in this case and respectfully
     (YOUR NAME)

answer the complaint for divorce as follows:

   1. Jurisdiction of this court is based upon D.C. Code Section 11-1101(l) (1989).

   2. The _____ has been a bona fide resident of the District of
     (plaintiff/defendant)

Columbia for more than six months immediately preceding the filing date of the complaint for

absolute divorce.

   3. The plaintiff and I are lawfully married to each other.

   4. I agree with the remaining allegations contained in plaintiff's complaint.

5. There is no reasonable expectation that my spouse and I will reconcile.

6. I (DO/DO NOT) request restoration of my former name,

_____. This request is not made for any illegal or
(YOUR BIRTH NAME OR PRIOR NAME)

fraudulent reason.

WHEREFORE, the defendant prays:

1. That the plaintiff be awarded an absolute divorce.

2. For such other relief as the court deems fit and proper.

3. I (DO/DO NOT) wish to be restored to my former name,

_____.
(YOUR BIRTH NAME/PREVIOUS MARRIED NAME/OTHER)

_____
DEFENDANT (Your signature)

I, _____, solemnly swear or affirm under criminal
(Your name)
penalties for the making of a false statement that I have read the foregoing Answer to Complaint
for Absolute Divorce and that the factual statements made in it are true to the best of my personal
knowledge, information and belief.

_____
DEFENDANT

CERTIFICATE OF SERVICE

I hereby certify that on the __ day of _____, 200_, a copy of the foregoing Answer was mailed, postage prepaid, to _____ at _____.

_____
(Signature)

SUPERIOR COURT OF THE DISTRICT OF COLUMBIA
FAMILY DIVISION

PRAECIPE

Jacket No.: _____   Date: _____

Social File No.: _____

_____

(Plaintiff)   *vs.*

_____

(Defendant or Respondent)

The Clerk of said Court will please enter a default and set an exparte hearing.

Attorney's Name: (Please Print)	Attorney's Name: (Please Print)
☐ Plaintiff ☐ Government	☐ Defendant ☐ Respondent
Address:	Address:
Attorney's Signature:	Attorney's Signature:
Registration No. Telephone No.	Registration No. Telephone No.

SUPERIOR COURT OF THE DISTRICT OF COLUMBIA
FAMILY DIVISION
DOMESTIC RELATIONS BRANCH

Plaintiff

vs.

Defendant

Jacket No. _____

AFFIDAVIT IN SUPPORT OF DEFAULT

DISTRICT OF COLUMBIA, ss:

_____, being first duly

sworn on oath, deposes and says that he is the attorney of record for the plaintiff in the above-

entitled cause; that the defendant was personally served with process on the _____ day of

_____, 20 ____, that no appearance has been entered by the said

defendant, no pleading has been filed and none served upon the attorney for the plaintiff; that

no extension has been given and the time for filing answer has expired; that the defendant is

neither an infant nor incompetent person.

The clerk is requested to enter a default against said defendant.

Signature of Attorney

Subscribed and sworn to before me this _____ day of _____, 20 ____

Deputy Clerk

SUPERIOR COURT OF THE DISTRICT OF COLUMBIA
FAMILY DIVISION
DOMESTIC RELATIONS BRANCH

_____ : Plaintiff

vs.

Jacket No._____

_____ : Defendant

AFFIDAVIT IN COMPLIANCE WITH
SOLDIERS AND SAILORS CIVIL RELIEF ACT OF 1940

_____, being first duly sworn, deposes and says that (he, she) is (agent for) the plaintiff, in the above entitled case, and makes this affidavit pursuant to the provisions of Section 200 of the Soldiers and Sailors Civil Relief Act of 1940; that (he she) has caused a careful investigation to be made to ascertain whether or not the above-named defendant is in the military service of the Army of the United States, the United States Navy, the Marine Corps, the Coast Guard, the Air Force or an officer of the Public Health Service detailed by proper authority for duty either with the Army or the Navy; and that as a result of said investigation affiant does hereby state that the defendant is not in any of the above-named branches of the military service and further that the defendant has not received notice of induction or notice to report for military service.

▶ _____

                                                    Signature

Subscribed and sworn to before me this_____ day of_____, 20 ____

_____

                              Deputy Clerk (or Notary Public, D.C.)

Superior Court of the District of Columbia
FAMILY DIVISION
DOMESTIC RELATIONS BRANCH

-- *Plaintiff*	
vs.	Jacket No. -------------------------------
-- *Defendant*	

DEFAULT

It appearing that the above-named defendant has failed to plead or otherwise defend this

ction though duly served with summons and copy of the complaint on the ------------------- day of

---, 20----., and an affidavit on behalf of the plaintiff having been

led, it is the----------------- day of --, 20---- declared that----------

----

----

efendant herein is in default.

Witness, the Honorable Chief Judge of the Superior Court and the seal of said Court.

Clerk of the Superior Court
of the District of Columbia

By --
Deputy Clerk

form 16

SUPERIOR COURT OF THE DISTRICT OF COLUMBIA
FAMILY COURT

Domestic Relations Office
Paternity and Support Office
Juvenile and Neglect Office
Mental Health and Retardation Office

Counsel for Child Abuse and Neglect

PRAECIPE

Jacket No. : _____   Date: _____

Social File No.: _____

_____
(Plaintiff or Petitioner)

vs.

_____
(Defendant or Respondent)

The Clerk of said Court will please note: that this matter is uncontested as to all issues; please set a hearing date as soon as possible.

Attorney's Name: (Please Print)	Attorney's Name: (Please Print)
[X] Plaintiff or Petitioner	[X] Defendant
[ ] Government	[ ] Respondent
Mailing Address:	Mailing Address:
E-Mail Address:	E-Mail Address:
Attorney's Signature:	Attorney's Signature:
Registration No. Telephone No. Fax No.	Registration No. Telephone No. Fax No.

Form FD-358/Apr.02

White – Legal Record Copy   Yellow – Copy

SUPERIOR COURT OF THE DISTRICT OF COLUMBIA

WASHINGTON, D. C.

CONSENT TO HAVE PROCEEDINGS CONDUCTED BY HEARING COMMISSIONER

_____   Case Number:
                    Plaintiff
   v.

_____
                    Defendant

Consent Granted. Pursuant to SCR-Civ. 73 and the Initial Order signed by Chief Judge Ugast, dated October 1, 1992, plaintiff(s)/ defendant(s) hereby consent to have all proceedings in the above captioned case conducted by a hearing commissioner rather than a judge. It is understood that this consent constitutes a waiver of jury trial. It is further understood that this consent may be withdrawn only upon leave of the Presiding Judge of the Civil Division, or that Judge's designee, for good cause shown.

_____   _____   _____   _____
Plaintiff/Defendant   Date   Plaintiff/Defendant   Date

_____   _____   _____   _____
Plaintiff/Defendant   Date   Plaintiff/Defendant   Date

SUPERIOR COURT OF THE DISTRICT OF COLUMBIA
FAMILY DIVISION
DOMESTIC RELATIONS BRANCH

_____ (YOUR NAME)	)
_____ (STREET ADDRESS)	)
_____ (CITY, STATE, ZIP CODE)	)
Soc. Sec. No._____	)
PLAINTIFF, VS.	) CASE NO. _____
_____ (YOUR SPOUSE'S NAME)	)
_____ (STREET ADDRESS)	)
_____ (CITY, STATE, ZIP CODE)	)
Soc. Sec. No._____	)
DEFENDANT.	)

<u>FINDINGS OF FACT, CONCLUSIONS OF LAW AND JUDGMENT OF ABSOLUTE DIVORCE</u>

This matter was heard on the _____ day of

_____, 20_____, upon the pleadings filed herein. Upon the

evidence adduced, the court makes the following:

FINDINGS OF FACT

1. The _____ is and has been a bona fide resident of the
   (PLAINTIFF/DEFENDANT)

District of Columbia for more than six (6) months next preceding the filing of the complaint herein.

2. The plaintiff and defendant were lawfully married to each other on

_____ in _____.
(MONTH DAY, YEAR)   (CITY, STATE)

3. Since _____, 20_____, the plaintiff and defendant
                (MONTH, DAY   (YEAR)

have continuously lived separate and apart from each other without cohabitation.

4. The plaintiff and the defendant together are the parents of the following _____
                                                                                (#)

child(ren) born or adopted prior to or during the marriage:

NAME   SOCIAL SECURITY NUMBER   BIRTH DATE

_____ ___/___/___

_____ ___/___/___

_____ ___/___/___

_____ ___/___/___

_____ ___/___/___

_____ ___/___/___

5. The following prior orders have been issued regarding custody, visitation, and child

support:

_____
_____
_____
_____
_____

6. The minor child(ren) are in the care and custody of the _____,
                                                            (PLAINTIFF/DEFENDANT)

who is a fit and proper person to have custody of the minor child(ren).

2

7. The _____ shall have reasonable rights of visitation with the
(PLAINTIFF/DEFENDANT)

parties' minor child(ren). The following is additional information about visitation:

_____

_____

_____

8. The _____ who is financially able to do so, will pay
(PLAINTIFF/DEFENDANT)

$_____ every _____ for the support of their minor
(amount)   (mo./wk./two weeks)

child(ren).

9. There are no property rights to be adjucicated between the plaintiff and defendant.

10. There is no reasonable prospect of reconciliation of this marriage.

11. The _____ requests restoration of his/her former name,
(PLAINTIFF/DEFENDANT)

_____. This request is not made for any illegal
(BIRTH NAME OR PRIOR NAME)
or fraudulent reason.

CONCLUSIONS OF LAW

Based upon the foregoing Findings of Fact, the court concludes as a matter of law that the

plaintiff is entitled to a Judgment of Absolute Divorce from the defendant on the ground of

mutual and voluntary separation without cohabitation for six months next preceding the

commencement of this action.

JUDGMENT

WHEREFORE, it is by the court this _____ day of _____,

20_____,

ORDERED, ADJUDGED AND DECREED:

1. That the plaintiff, _____, be and hereby
(YOUR FULL MARRIED NAME)

is awarded an Absolute Divorce from the defendant, _____
(YOUR SPOUSE'S FULL MARRIED NAME)

on the ground of separation without cohabitation for one year next preceding the commencement

of this action;

PROVIDED, HOWEVER, that this Judgment shall not become effective to dissolve

the bonds of matrimony until the time allowed for taking an appeal has expired or until the final

disposition of any appeal so taken.

2. That the _____, be and hereby is awarded
(PLAINTIFF/DEFENDANT)

permanent custody of the parties' minor child(ren), namely,

_____

_____, with reasonable

rights of visitation reserved to the _____. The following
(PLAINTIFF/DEFENDANT)

information is provided about visitation: _____

_____

_____

_____

_____

3. That the _____ be and is hereby ordered
               (PLAINTIFF/DEFENDANT)

to pay to the _____ the amount of $ _____
                 (PLAINTIFF/DEFENDANT)   (AMOUNT)

every _____ toward the support of the parties' minor children beginning
          (week/month/two weeks)

on _____, 20_____.
      (MONTH/DAY/YEAR)

All payments are to be made payable to the "Clerk, D.C. Superior Court" and must include this case number. Payments are to be made through the Financial Clerk of the Family Division, Room 4335A, 500 Indiana Avenue, N.W., Washington, D.C. 20001. The Clerk shall forward all payments to the _____.
                                                                                  (PLAINTIFF/DEFENDANT)

4. That both parties must notify the Court within ten days of any change of

employer or income. If the non-custodial parent is in arrears in an amount equal to 30 days

of support payments, the support payments shall be withheld from his/her employment income or

from any other income. Once withholding begins, all payments must be made through the Court

Registry. Any other payments shall be considered a gift and shall not offset the duty to support.

Any withholding order entered herein may be changed if any party moves for a reapportionment

of periodic arrears payments to reflect a change in the non-custodial parent's ability to pay.

5. That the _____ be and hereby is restored to the use of
               (PLAINTIFF/DEFENDANT)
his/her former name, _____.
                              (BIRTH NAME OR PRIOR NAME)

_____
JUDGE/COMMISSIONER
D.C. SUPERIOR COURT

Copies to:

_____
(YOUR NAME)

_____
(STREET ADDRESS)

_____
(CITY, STATE, ZIP)

_____
(YOUR SPOUSE'S NAME)

_____
(STREET ADDRESS)

_____
(CITY, STATE, ZIP)

SUPERIOR COURT FOR THE DISTRICT OF COLUMBIA
Domestic Relations Branch
Family Division

	:	
	:	
	:	
_____	:	
Plaintiff	:	
	:	
vs.	:	Domestic Relations No. _____
	:	
_____	:	
	:	
Defendant	:	_____

JOINT WAIVER OF APPEAL

Pursuant to DC Code 16-920, the Plaintiff, _____ and the Defendant, _____, jointly waive their rights to appeal this Court's judgment of order of absolute divorce in the above entitled matter.

_____   _____
Signature of Plaintiff   Date

_____   _____
Signature of Defendant   Date

Index